Beyond the Label

Beyond the Label

A Guide to Unlocking
a Child's Educational Potential

KAREN L. SCHILTZ, PhD

Amy M. Schonfeld, PhD & Tara Niendam, PhD

OXFORD
UNIVERSITY PRESS

OXFORD
UNIVERSITY PRESS

Oxford University Press, Inc., publishes works that further Oxford University's objective of excellence in research, scholarship, and education.

Oxford   New York
Auckland   Cape Town   Dar es Salaam   Hong Kong   Karachi
Kuala Lumpur   Madrid   Melbourne   Mexico City
Nairobi   New Delhi   Shanghai   Taipei   Toronto

With offices in
Argentina   Austria   Brazil   Chile   Czech Republic   France   Greece
Guatemala   Hungary   Italy   Japan   Poland   Portugal   Singapore
South Korea   Switzerland   Thailand   Turkey   Ukraine   Vietnam

Published by Oxford University Press, Inc.
198 Madison Avenue, New York, New York 10016

www.oup.com

Oxford is a registered trademark of Oxford University Press
Oxford University Press is a registered trademark of Oxford University Press, Inc.

Library of Congress Cataloging-in-Publication Data

Schiltz, Karen L.
  Beyond the label : a guide to unlocking a child's educational potential /
Karen L. Schiltz, Amy M. Schonfeld, Tara Niendam.
    p. cm.
Includes bibliographical references and index.
ISBN 978-0-19-974705-4 (hardcover : alk. paper)
1. Academic achievement. 2. Study skills. 3. Motivation in education.
4. Self-actualization (Psychology). I. Schonfeld, Amy M. II. Niendam, Tara A. III. Title.
LB1062.6.S34   2011
370.15'4—dc23   2011025289

1 2 3 4 5 6 7 8 9

Printed in the United States of America on acid-free paper

*In loving memory of my brother, Gary Fred Schiltz,
and mentor, Paul Satz.*

*"Life is a puzzle, Not every peice
you find fits, You have to keep
on going untill you find the
right piece that fits."*

Grace Mellor
9 years old

CONTENTS

PREFACE

This book is for parents, educators, and any person who cares for and wants to help children who are struggling in school. In my twenty-five years of practice, parents have asked the following questions:

> Does my child have a problem?
> Is the problem a big problem?
> What can I do to help my child at school?

This handbook was written to provide you with helpful pointers when you know something is "a little off" with your child. It is an uncomfortable and sometimes painful feeling when you suspect something may really be wrong. Like many parents, you may search the Internet or browse books at the local bookstore looking for information that reflects your concerns. However, you may not even be sure what to look for in the first place. The rationale for this handbook was to help you recognize the warning signs that may indicate a potential problem with your child and then guide you in how to obtain the necessary assessments to answer your concerns. The assessments will help you to better understand your child's strengths and weaknesses and supply you with recommendations for appropriate interventions and services. This handbook will also help you appreciate what an educational accommodation is and how it can serve as a bridge to learning. Every child has the right to fully access the learning environment and to show what he or she truly knows when taking tests. Suggested accommodations will be recommended that are based on the current literature. These accommodations will be discussed with respect to weaknesses that your child may have in the classroom and when taking tests. In addition, this handbook will provide you access to relevant research to help you understand the *big picture* of your child's learning and emotional needs.

I hope to provide an initial starting point for you to identify possible behaviors that are not in your child's best interests. By focusing on behaviors and not labels, you will be able to better understand the whats, whys, and hows of your child's learning and emotional challenges. Once you do, you will be able to help your child realize his or her potential, not only at school but also at home.

Karen L. Schiltz, PhD

ACKNOWLEDGMENTS

There are many people who supported me during the process of writing this book. First, I am truly grateful to Maura Mitrushina and the editorial director at Oxford University Press, Joan Bossert, who believed in this book from the very beginning. Because of you both, I was able to push forward and ultimately help children and their parents access this critical information.

I want to thank my colleagues Robert Bilder, Kyle Boone, Lou D'Elia, Karen Miller, Maura Mitrushina, and the late Paul Satz for reading the book proposal two years ago and for providing me with helpful and entertaining comments. I also appreciate the remarks from Baz and Eileen Patel at that time as well. Baz had mentioned the importance of hope and tolerance that we, as parents, all need to have on a daily basis.

The help of my reviewers, Claudia Antoine, Robin Burkholz, Robert Butler, Gwen Campbell, and Roger Light, was instrumental because of their expertise across the disciplines of education, speech-language pathology, neuropsychology, and advocacy. A special thanks to my colleagues Susan Bookheimer, Patricia Gross, and Mary Moebius for their enthusiasm and support as I worked on this book. I appreciate the assistance from Nancy Whittlesey, who reviewed the completed manuscript as a parent. Her friendship, keen insight, and humor helped steer me in the right direction when I was so enmeshed with the material.

Thank you, Amy and Tara, for your input and expertise regarding your areas of specialty. The process of writing this book was truly inspiring and it was wonderful to work with you both.

I want to thank from the bottom of my heart all of the parents and children whom I have been privileged to have helped over the years. Assessing children, teens, and young adults on a daily basis has been a joy and it has been rewarding to hear of their growth over the years. I am honored to have worked with "Diane" and her parents. Diane is truly an inspiration and role model to all students who struggle with some type of challenge on a daily basis. Her perseverance, resilience, and courage are admirable and speak to the core values that children possess when parents serve as their chief supporters.

I am fortunate to have two loving parents, Fred and Loraine Schiltz. They were my chief advocates growing up and they never hesitated in their search when *something was a little off.*

My husband, Scott Mellor, was genuinely a partner in writing this book. His comments over the past two years enhanced my thinking process and helped me "think outside of the box." I could not have written this book without his perspective as a father, husband, and critical reviewer. Last, I am truly blessed to be the mother of our beloved daughter, Grace Silc Mellor, who is now 12 years old. I want to thank my daughter for her understanding and for being so tolerant when I had to write on the weekends. Grace has taught me patience, humility, and to "keep on going until you find the right piece that fits."

KLS

INTRODUCTION

Charlie and Mother

You've just left the pediatrician's office with your son, Charlie. Your thoughts are racing as you hold his hand. You feel confused and bewildered. The pediatrician was talking too fast. You do remember he informed you that Charlie may have "ADHD" and some kind of reading problem. Charlie is now 8 years old and is struggling in school. All you remember are the labels, the diagnoses. You really can't recall much else. What do you do now?

You are not alone if you feel scared and confused. You may wonder: What do the labels *mean*? Are they serious? Will my child suffer forever? Is there anything I can do? Can it get better fast? Are they permanent? Will my child be successful? These are questions *all* parents ask themselves. What should you do now?

The idea for this book was conceived as a result of assessing children, adolescents, and young adults over the past twenty-five years. These children came to see me because of suspected problems involving weaknesses in attention and concentration, language, memory, handwriting, reading, written expression, math, and emotional challenges. Some children had no problems; but when problems were found, universally all parents wanted to *fix* the problem and help their child to function at his or her best at school.

Inevitably, the parents I saw had many questions. As discussed in the Preface, one of the questions was: Is the problem a *big* problem? I have seen parents take on an active role in advocating for their children over the years. Some failed to address a child's difficulty early on, which led to *bigger* problems, not only for the child, but also for the school. Early intervention is the key to a child's optimal functioning. Being aware of the red flags that might signify a potential problem with your child can alert you to seek appropriate evaluations to investigate the type of problem your child may have and, more important, to lay the groundwork for remediation. This process of identifying the *frequency, pervasiveness*, and *severity (intensity)* of the problem can lead to effective interventions and services within the school and home.

This handbook is not a diagnostic manual. It will not help you diagnose your child. It is important to recognize that weaknesses related to learning or thinking processes can be a result of different problems. For example, a child who has weaknesses in attention and concentration may not have a diagnosis of attention-deficit/hyperactivity disorder (ADHD). It may be that the child has problems with reading or verbal expression that cause problems with attention and concentration. On the other hand, the child may also have ADHD *and* reading difficulties *and* verbal expression problems. Additionally, not all children with a specific diagnosis of ADHD have all of the symptoms of ADHD. Furthermore, some children with ADHD have additional atypical symptoms that most children with ADHD don't have. As you can see, it is critical to have an understanding of what could actually be pointing to a potential problem before embarking on a "wild goose chase" and naively referring to the thousands of websites and technical or self-help parent guides on specific disorders.

This handbook will define problematic thinking and learning weaknesses and address how they impact a child within the classroom and home environment from different points of view. For example, a parent perceives his or her child in a different way as compared to a teacher, a neighbor, or a family member. All of these *voices* (perspectives) must be considered when evaluating the *whole* child. This handbook will provide the framework to help you understand your child from these different perspectives and provide you with the means of moving in the right direction after considering your child's strengths and weaknesses.

How Is This Handbook Organized?

The handbook is organized around thinking and emotional weaknesses that are of concern to most parents. You may be reading this handbook after your child has been diagnosed or while your child is in the process of assessment. You may be reading it upon first suspicion that something is "a little off" because of your child's challenges at school or on the home front. You may also be seeking guidance to help enhance your understanding of your child's needs.

Part One discusses the *basics* you need to know for overall school and assessment purposes. Chapter 1 explores the fundamental issues of educational law. Your child has a right to learn and it is important that you understand the legal process because it is the vehicle that you may need to use in the school system. Chapter 2 lays out the roles of accommodations and modifications for test taking and classroom instruction. Chapter 3 explores the role of assessments and the different types of evaluations to consider if your child is experiencing challenges at school.

Part Two addresses what parents should look for *beyond the label*. We advocate that you look beyond the diagnostic label when investigating your child's strengths and weaknesses. Chapters 4 through 12 provide a definition of the weaknesses. Each chapter provides examples of how the weaknesses affect a child's learning processes and behavior at school. The role of accommodations is discussed for the weaknesses presented in each chapter. These accommodations specifically target the weaknesses in order to "level the playing field" when a child is in the classroom and during test-taking situations. Accommodations are also important for larger scale examinations such as the Independent School Entrance Examination (ISEE), Scholastic Aptitude Test (SAT), and American College Test (ACT). These examinations are given significant weight in the admissions process at most schools and colleges. These "high-stakes" examinations are critical as they are considered the gateway to most colleges and higher education. They can be the basis for major decisions in a student's life. Accommodations are necessary so disabled students can show what they truly know as opposed to what their disability will allow them to show in a standardized testing environment. Clinical cases are presented that are typical in my practice to demonstrate specific issues relevant to each chapter.

Part Three explores our final thoughts as we review the *big picture* from different angles. We suggest that you consider these closing points as you embark on your journey as your child's advocate. In addition, we hear the *voice* of one student, Diane, who is now in college. Diane's determination, perseverance, and resilience to "beat the odds" will be clear when you read her story. Above all, her parents "kept on going" until they understood the *big picture*.

At the end of the book, there are four appendices. Appendices 1 and 2 list the options for classroom and test accommodations. Appendix 3 provides information on assistive technology resources. Appendix 4 lists the websites of organizations that you may want to contact for additional information.

We truly hope that this handbook will help you get started in the right direction when you know that something is "a little off." Your child may require the help of many professionals if he or she does have learning or emotional weaknesses. However, you, as a parent, will be a vital part of the team. Remember, you are your child's chief advocate. Your input as a knowledgeable parent will help shape your child's outcome by allowing full access to the laws, tools, teams, classroom and test-taking situations, and educational accommodations.

K.L.S.
A.M.S.
T.A.N.

Beyond the Label

I

THE BASICS

CHAPTER 1

The Law

A Child's Right to Learn

Educators are challenged today more than ever. They are constantly faced with students having problems with academic performance, behavior, or both. Effective school-based interventions are necessary to ensure educational success for our children. The laws that protect a child's right to learn can be confusing to parents and may seem like a foreign language. They are also often amended or changed, so it is important to stay on top of the latest developments to understand your child's educational rights.

The Individuals with Disabilities Education Improvement Act (IDEIA), which reauthorized the Individuals with Disabilities Education Act (IDEA), was signed by President Bush on December 3, 2004. The IDEA is a federal law. The purpose of the IDEA is to ensure that children with disabilities receive a free and *appropriate* public education. The federal government provides financial assistance to states and local school districts to support special education and related services for eligible children with disabilities. The school district must identify and assess children who may need special education services. What exactly is special education? Special education is instruction that is specially designed to meet the unique needs of a child with a disability and is provided at no cost to parents. A school district must provide special education services and programs for an eligible child for ages 3 through 21 years. A child is entitled to a free and appropriate public education (FAPE) when he or she qualifies for special education. The educational law No Child Left Behind (NCLB) was passed in 2001. The purpose of the NCLB Act is to increase accountability for schools, which is done by enforcing state educational standards for all students in math and reading. State testing is also required to determine whether children are meeting the benchmarks for their grade level. This law promotes the use of research-supported teaching methods and early intervention. Research-supported teaching methods are also called evidence-based interventions. Both terms refer to teaching programs, strategies, and classroom interventions that are based on objective and systematic research in determining their effectiveness.[1,2]

A Word on Disorder, Impairment, and Disability

What is a disorder? What is impairment? What is a disability? They *sound* similar. Do they mean the same thing? These concepts are frequently misunderstood, not only by parents, but also by professionals. These three terms underlie many of the decisions made by health professionals, educators within a public school district, and educational testing agencies. However, professionals typically view these terms differently depending on their role and the context in which the student is seen.[3,4]

What is a disorder? There are physical and mental disorders. Examples of physical disorders include epilepsy, migraines, severe back pain, and cerebral palsy. The task force of the American Psychiatric Association's *Diagnostic and Statistical Manual of Mental Disorders, Fourth Edition, Text Revision,* or DSM-IV-TR, reported that the term "mental disorder" has persisted because they had "not found an appropriate substitute." The task force conceptualized a mental disorder as a group of symptoms (syndrome) that occurs with distress (a painful symptom) or disability (impairment in one or more important areas of functioning). The syndrome can also occur with a significantly increased risk of suffering, death, or pain or an important loss of freedom. In addition, they indicated the group of symptoms could not be attributed to another cause, event, or situation that would result in the same symptoms. For example, sadness is a response to the death of a loved one, but this is a typical response to a death and would not be classified as a mental disorder.[5]

A disorder can also be thought of as a group of behaviors or symptoms that *significantly* interfere with a child's ability to function at school or at home. The behaviors should be severe enough over time to be problematic in a child's life. It is the *frequency, pervasiveness,* and *severity* of the behaviors that are of interest to health professionals. Disorders are typically diagnosed by health professionals. While educators can describe problematic behaviors within the school setting that might point to a disorder, they usually are not qualified to make clinical diagnoses. These behaviors may *substantially limit* the child's functioning within the school. The behaviors may represent a *need* that will then require related services and/or accommodations within a school district. Related services are supports that public schools are required to provide under the IDEA for the disabled student who needs them in order to learn. Examples of related services are physical therapy, speech therapy, psychological services, and occupational therapy.

What is impairment? According to the World Health Organization, impairment refers to a loss or abnormality of structure or function that can involve a tissue or organ.[6] This loss or abnormality can lead to disability. The legal regulatory definition lists the types of conditions that constitute impairment. These conditions involve any physiological, mental, or psychological disorder.

For example, a physiological disorder can involve the loss of senses such as hearing, sight, or speech. A mental or psychological condition refers to disorders such as mental retardation, emotional or mental illness, and specific learning disabilities.

It is important to understand the role of impairment in the context of the legal definition of disability. The Americans with Disabilities Act Amendments Act of 2008 (ADAAA) was signed into law on September 25, 2008, and became effective on January 1, 2009. The law made significant changes to the definition of the term "disability."[7]

What is a disability? Section 902 of the 2008 ADAAA documents a disability as being a physical or mental impairment that substantially limits one or more *major life activities*. The ADAAA also classifies an impairment that is episodic or in remission as a disability if it substantially limits a major life activity when active. Remember, impairments refer to physiological, mental, or psychological disorders. Impairments may or may not affect an individual's life. For example, health conditions may or may not represent impairment from a legal perspective. Your child may wear glasses for a vision condition. The glasses help your child to see and your child's everyday activities are not limited. Your child's condition would not be classified as an impairment. The impairment has to affect a student's ability to function compared with *most* students.

What is a "major life activity"? Major life activities include, but are not limited to, caring for oneself, performing manual tasks, seeing, hearing, eating, sleeping, walking, standing, lifting, bending, speaking, breathing, learning, reading, concentrating, thinking, communicating, and working. A disability will significantly affect a student in many ways, and not just at school. A student may suffer from a disorder with documented impairments but may not be disabled. It is the *degree* of disability that is considered from a legal perspective. For example, your child may be markedly anxious when taking a test and when giving oral presentations in class. This anxiety has been occurring for many years. However, your child's nervousness remains in check when he or she uses relaxation exercises during tests and oral presentations. This "performance anxiety" would not be legally classified as a disability since it does not *substantially* limit your child's ability to perform during the test or oral presentation in class. The nature of the disability needs to be severe enough to warrant specific help within the school environment or test-taking situation. Disabilities that are minor are not covered by the Americans with Disabilities Act of 1990.[8]

As we will describe in this handbook, there are a variety of disabilities that can affect a child's ability to perform in school. For example, as described in Chapter 11, a student with severe mood instability experiences significant impairment and is unable to cope with the everyday demands of school and home. Similarly, a student with a reading disorder is unable to read test questions quickly and would be classified as disabled in the test-taking situation (see Chapter 10). Both of these students would meet the criteria for disability because they have an impairment that substantially limits a major life activity, such as taking tests, compared with *most* peers their age. As you can see, there is ambiguity in the meaning and proper usage of these terms that can create confusion among parents and educators.

Evidence-Based Intervention

In the past educators and clinicians used "whatever worked" for the child with special needs. However, this approach was not effective. The NCLB Act requires all schools to use scientifically validated practices in order to bring all students to proficiency by 2017. This brings us to the term "evidence-based intervention." The NCLB Act refers to evidence-based intervention but does not offer a specific definition of it. Some people think of evidence-based intervention as validated by scientifically based research. What is evidence-based intervention and how does it affect your child? Evidence-based interventions are those that are shown by rigorous and objective research to be effective. This research uses systematic and empirically based methods that are reviewed by qualified colleagues or a panel of experts. Simply stated, it is intervention that works based on research findings. As a result, many teachers are now incorporating evidence-based interventions within their daily curriculum. However, educators must still determine if the suggested intervention works for a particular student based on the nature of the child's individual strengths and weaknesses.

Response to Intervention

The response to intervention (RTI) model is a recent approach to the early identification of students within public school districts who are having academic or behavioral difficulties, as soon as they begin to struggle. This model was developed in response to the 2004 revision of the IDEA. This is in contrast to the traditional system that identified students as possible candidates for special education only after they consistently failed to perform as well as their classmates. RTI was developed to help students who are having difficulty keeping up with their peers academically early in the educational process. In the RTI model, students receive evidence-based instructional practices and interventions that are based on a school's assessment of their abilities. The level of instruction and intervention is matched to their level of need. Students are monitored frequently in order to determine their response.[9]

RTI is a controversial topic for educators and health professionals. Some people think this approach will eliminate failure because of the early identification process. However, others have noted that RTI approaches only identify students with academic, as opposed to behavioral, challenges. The use of RTI is questionable for those students who have problems outside of reading or for those students beyond the early elementary grades. It is also not known to what extent the teachers will be supported and trained in this model. James McDougal and his colleagues have argued that the RTI model is dependent on a school implementing the right type of evidence-based intervention and then successfully carrying out and monitoring the intervention with the student. As a result of these issues, the effectiveness of RTI is currently under investigation.[10-12]

RTI can be thought of as one important part of the assessment process. It is our opinion that RTI can be integrated into other evaluation procedures such as neuropsychological assessment. Many issues can affect a student's learning process at school and during homework, including anxiety, depression, attention problems, medical disorders, poor sleep patterns, and other co-occurring disorders. Obtaining additional information from teachers, parents, and significant others and reviewing medical and educational records will help us understand the child from many perspectives. This information, along with a comprehensive neuropsychological assessment, will give us a better understanding of the child's strengths as well as weaknesses. Comprehensive testing can also play a role in investigating why certain students may not be responding to RTI.[11]

Individualized Education Program

The Individualized Education Program (IEP) is a document that provides a detailed description of a student's individualized educational needs and a plan to help the child achieve educational goals. A parent or even a teacher can request an IEP. There is a formal process that a parent must go through in order to set the IEP in motion. There will be an initial meeting at school that determines whether your child is eligible for special education services under the IDEA 2004. As mentioned earlier, special education services refer to instruction that is specifically designed to meet the unique needs of a child with a disability. There are 13 eligibility categories for special education:

- Autism
- Deaf-blindness
- Deafness
- Emotional disturbance
- Hearing impairment
- Mental retardation

- Multiple disabilities
- Orthopedic impairment
- Other health impairment
- Specific learning disability
- Speech or language impairment
- Traumatic brain injury
- Visual impairment including blindness

The IDEA designates that a student is eligible for a free and appropriate education if he or she needs special education services. Special education services are based on the student's *need* and not necessarily on a medical diagnosis. The IEP will provide a written description of your child's educational program. The written description should cover the specific programs or classes for your child, specific services, and supports such as accommodations and modifications. A discussion and examples of accommodations and modifications are presented in Chapter 2.

It can be uncomfortable for you to focus solely on your child's weaknesses, but the IEP is a "deficit"-driven process. It is designed to address your child's deficits, not what your child *can* do. Services are based on the goals within the IEP plan, and the goals are tied to a child's deficits. The IEP will address your child's present level of performance and then identify goals and objectives tailored to your child's needs. The focus of the IEP will be on your child's weaknesses within the educational environment and not within the home setting. Accommodations, modifications, services, and classroom placement options are also addressed by the IEP. Note that the individualized program does not have to be the "best" program for your child. Rather, it has to provide an "appropriate" educational experience that is reasonable given your child's weaknesses. Think of the IEP process as a type of transportation. You may want a sports car, but the school is only required to provide a bus as long as it will get you where you need to go. As parents, we are like the US Army; we want our children to "Be All They Can Be." The IEP process, however, is not designed to bring out the optimum in a child, but rather to stop failure.

Section 504

Section 504 of the Rehabilitation Act of 1973 is a broad civil rights law. This law protects children and adults with disabilities and ensures they have equal access to education compared with their nondisabled peers. Section 504 protects a child from discrimination and is not a service. Section 504 requires all agencies that receive federal assistance to provide "access" to individuals with disabilities. It is designed to "level the playing field" for individuals with disabilities. A disabled student may not need special education. Section 504 is ideal for the student who is not in special education but requires accommodations for a documented disability.[13] Some of the conditions under Section 504 include the following:

- Acquired immune deficiency syndrome (AIDS)
- Allergies
- Asthma
- Attention-deficit disorder (ADD)
- Attention-deficit/hyperactivity disorder (ADHD)
- Brain tumor
- Cancer
- Diabetes
- Disorders of written expression
- Dyslexia
- Fetal alcohol spectrum disorder
- Hearing impairment
- Orthopedic/mobility impairment
- Prior special education student
- Psychiatric disability
- Short-term injury
- Tourette's syndrome
- Traumatic brain injury

The school will determine whether your child has a physical and/or mental impairment; whether the impairment *substantially* limits his or her "major life activities," including learning; and what types of accommodations he or she needs to receive a free, appropriate public education. Section 504 addresses equal access to learning and the ability to take tests using accommodations or modifications in the regular education classroom. The 504 plan is tailored to a child's areas of need so that he or she receives the help required to succeed in school.

CHAPTER 2

The Tools

Although you may have others helping you to look out for your child, *you* need to be a strong advocate for your child. In 2009, Torkel Klingberg, professor of cognitive neuroscience at the Karolinska Institute in Stockholm, Sweden, wrote a book entitled *The Overflowing Brain*.[1] For those challenged by attention problems, he suggested that implementing "external structures" is key to reducing distraction and "lightening the load" caused by maintaining large amounts of information in one's mind. You may find your child needs *tools* to overcome challenges at school. Perhaps Dr. Klingberg was talking about accommodations as those "external structures" to help lighten the load. Think of school-based accommodations as a *toolbox of strategies*. These tools help a child access classroom instruction and demonstrate their *true* knowledge of a subject in test-taking situations.

Accommodations

Accommodations are used by students and implemented by educators. Accommodations are necessary to provide access to learning for students with special needs. In 2009, Noël Gregg, psychologist and leading accommodations researcher, noted that accommodations used by adolescents and adults with learning disabilities provide equal access to, and demonstration of, knowledge.[2] By recognizing a student's individual differences, accommodations can be tailored to "level the playing field" for the student who has marked learning difficulties. It is important to note that these accommodations do not create an unfair advantage in favor of the student. In other words, *reasonable* and *appropriate* accommodations provide *access* to learning and the ability to demonstrate knowledge of the subject material in classroom and test-taking settings. In the day-to-day classroom environment, the material taught is identical to that taught to the other students, but the method of delivery might be different, such as allowing a student to preview lecture notes from a teacher before the class starts. A test accommodation, such as extended time for a student with a learning disability, does not change the nature of the test but gives the student the ability to show what he or she knows. In addition, extended time does not significantly benefit those students who are nondisabled. These findings provide evidence for the rationale of giving students who are learning disabled extended time on reading, mathematics, and writing tests. Accommodations do not change the substance of the materials learned, nor do they reduce the requirements for expressing knowledge when taking a test.[3-6] Consider a wheelchair ramp providing access to a restaurant. The patron receives the exact menu and service as all other patrons at the restaurant; they just arrive at the table by another route.

There are many types of accommodations used as a bridge to learning in the classroom and during test taking. Their goal is to enable students with learning disabilities to show what they truly know. For example, accommodations can provide access to the material through the use of read-alouds (electronic or human reader) or even a facilitator to help the student understand test instructions. Use of a scribe can aid the student who has trouble with writing. The scribe will exactly transcribe what the student dictates. Extra time or frequent breaks during a lengthy examination may be accommodations given to students who experience fatigue because of a medical disorder. Accommodations may also permit a student to take a test in a private room or a small group setting to decrease any distractions. These accommodations should be specifically tailored to the student's deficits and the functional impact of the disability. Frequently requested accommodations for classroom purposes are listed in Appendix 1. In addition, common accommodations requested for test taking are listed in Appendix 2. We discuss classroom and test accommodations that are appropriate for various challenges in Part Two.

A Word on Accommodations for High-Stakes Testing

Sam is 16 years old. He was identified as having a learning disability in the areas of reading and written expression when he was in third grade. Reading was a struggle for Sam because he could not sound out unfamiliar words. The process of reading was effortful and sometimes he substituted words and skipped words when reading a passage. As a result, Sam's reading comprehension suffered and it took him a lot longer to read material compared to his classmates. His writing suffered too. Sam always had trouble with spelling words that he could not memorize. His essays were so short that Sam's teachers called him "the minimizer." A neuropsychological assessment identified Sam's learning disabilities. The school initiated a 504 plan and Sam was granted the accommodation of 50 percent extended time for tests at school and was allowed to use AlphaSmart, a keyboarding system, for all written assignments. These accommodations allowed Sam to show what he knew on all tests and writing assignments.

Sam knew the SAT (Scholastic Aptitude Test) would be challenging. He was also aware that obtaining extended time for the SAT was not a foregone conclusion. He heard from his classmates that you had to prove your disorder and disability all over again, even though he had been assessed twice in the past. It seemed so ridiculous. Sam dreaded those tests and felt "stupid" when taking them. However, he knew the evaluator would understand his disabilities and also that he was really trying to do his best. Sam was relieved the ETS (Educational Testing Service) had stopped "flagging" students who were granted accommodations on the SAT.[7] He did not want to be labeled as a "dummy."

Your child may be experiencing a similar scenario. Many students must take these so-called "high-stakes" examinations such as the SAT, ACT (American College Testing), and ISEE (Independent School Entrance Examination). These tests are thought of as the gateways to success, and they can bring out the best and worst in students. Many students experience test anxiety, stress, lack of sleep, and emotional "blocks." However, test anxiety is a common reaction for many students when faced with a test. Such reactions are considered normal and not reflective of disabilities. Because Sam has a history of learning disorders and resulting disabilities, the school district has provided him with accommodations based on his needs via a 504 plan. However, a student with a diagnosed learning disability may not necessarily be considered as having a *legally* recognized disability. Similarly, a student who has a 504 plan or an IEP may not be recognized as being legally disabled because educational interventions, educational services, and school-based educational testing are not *medically* diagnostic. We discuss the role of disability and the role of substantial limitations in Chapter 1. These terms play a critical role when applying for test-taking accommodations for the SAT and other high-stakes examinations. For example, your child may be medically diagnosed with an attention disorder and receiving average to above-average grades in school. In this scenario your child probably would not be considered as *substantially limited* compared to most other students. The criteria for a legal disability would not be met for the purposes of extended time on the SAT because your child is receiving the grades *most* students do.[8-10]

Qualifying for accommodations for high-stakes testing requires a thoughtful analysis of a child's *current* functioning as well as previous functioning in school, home, and other contexts. A professional evaluator will have to incorporate all aspects of a student's functioning into a report. It is critical for the assessor to identify a child's current disorders and disabilities. A key factor that should be incorporated in the evaluator's report is the discussion of so-called *substantial limitations* and how they impact learning and test-taking conditions. Factors such as the *frequency, pervasiveness,* and *severity* of the behaviors under investigation can be determined by rating scales completed by the parents, teachers, and student; test scores; previous examinations; educational and medical background; previous documented accommodations;

additional information provided by the teachers; and behavioral observations. Simply put, the evaluator has the burden of gathering information from many sources to render an honest and thorough report of the student. *Reasonable* accommodations should be tailored to the report findings in order to "level the playing field." A student or parent might have his or her own idea of what is needed in terms of accommodations, but this may not be supported by the evaluation results. This can be confusing and disappointing if your child has been granted accommodations in school and is now denied those accommodations for high-stakes examinations. We will discuss the role of accommodations for school tests and high-stakes testing purposes in Part Two.

Modifications

Modifications reflect *changes* to instruction and testing. These changes alter the standards of the materials and content to be learned. For example, Jonathan is a young boy who has significant difficulties with calculation. He cannot learn at the same rate as his peers. Jonathan is given a different (modified) set of addition and subtraction problems than his classmates. These problems are set at his lower ability level compared to his classmates. You can also think of this as a restaurant offering a different menu to a senior customer at the "early bird" seating. This different menu is adjusted toward the needs of the senior person and is not the same menu that the other customers receive. Modifications can be implemented during classroom instruction and test taking. Examples of test modifications include reduced problem sets in math and spelling words.

Modifications and High-Stakes Testing

Modifications alter the nature of a test. Modifications are also referred to as "nonallowable accommodations" or "nonstandard accommodations." Each testing program or state determines what accommodations and modifications are allowed. For example, most states recognize spell-checking software as a modification for tests assessing writing. In contrast, the majority of states consider the scheduling of a test over multiple testing days as a test accommodation. However, one state (Minnesota) identifies multiple testing days as a modification.[11]

It is important for you to understand the "tools" we have discussed as you continue your journey. There are many issues to grasp, and access can be provided in many ways. This access can "open the door" toward enhancing your child's performance within the classroom and during test taking. Understanding your child's unique strengths and weaknesses is critical for your child's overall development, not only academically, but also socially and personally.

CHAPTER 3

The Team

Assembling the right team is crucial for understanding your child's strengths and weaknesses and then remediating them. We refer to the assessment of your child's functions as a *roadmap*. Evaluators and intervention specialists from various professions bring different perspectives to the evaluation process and will contribute to the overall roadmap. Each child is an individual, and understanding your child's profile of needs is critical. The roadmap serves as a guide so interventions and services can be tailored specifically to your child's needs. This will allow your child *access* to appropriate learning environments and the ability to demonstrate knowledge of the subject matter in the classroom and in test-taking situations. The following types of evaluations may be required in your child's care:

- Educational evaluations: These evaluations can be performed by professional private educational therapists who evaluate and remediate the learning disabilities or problems of children, adolescents, and adults. These problems can include dyslexia, attention-deficit disorders, and learning disabilities. Educational therapists also combine educational and therapeutic approaches for remediation purposes. In addition, they assist with case management and advocacy needs.[1]
- Functional/behavioral assessments: These are done by behavioral specialists to address behavioral management issues. For example, the assessment will identify the behaviors leading up to a child's explosive tantrums and mood fluctuations. This information can be integrated into the process of developing, reviewing, and modifying a student's IEP. Behavioral approaches, such as applied behavioral analysis (ABA), are used to help children on the autistic spectrum decrease inappropriate behaviors and increase desirable behaviors. For example, a therapist may remind or "cue" a child to initiate eye contact with a peer when entering a classroom and then praise him or her for following through. Cognitive-behavioral approaches may also be applied. These behaviorists address errors in thinking that might be causing distress. Specifically, the therapist may help a

student understand the impact of a sarcastic comment from the point of view of his or her peers. The emphasis is on understanding how the student's peers may think and feel in a similar situation.

- Genetic evaluations: Genetic evaluations are done by a physician to determine the presence of inherited diseases. The physician will also counsel the parents and treat the child who has a genetic disorder or syndrome.

- Medical checkup from the pediatrician: A pediatrician is a medical doctor who specializes in the treatment of children. Pediatricians can prescribe medication. The medical evaluation is necessary to see if other medical conditions may be causing the difficulties for your child. For example, your child may be exhibiting significant attention and concentration difficulties in many situations. If these difficulties are due to a medical disorder, the disorder can then be treated and monitored over time. For instance, your pediatrician may discover that your child has a correctable condition such as a vision or hearing problem that is affecting attention. The medical checkup is a good starting point before other evaluations are sought.

- Neurology evaluations: A neurologist is a medical doctor who specializes in the evaluation and management of nervous system disorders such as tumors, head injury, or seizures. Neurologists can prescribe medication. A neurological examination assesses basic motor and sensory abilities. Medical diagnostic procedures such as magnetic resonance imaging (MRI), computerized axial tomography (CAT), and an electroencephalogram (EEG) may be used.

- Neuropsychological evaluations: Pediatric neuropsychological evaluations are done by clinical psychologists who are specifically trained in developmental neuropsychological assessment. The neuropsychological assessment creates an integrated blueprint for intervention. It can also prioritize the order in which interventions or treatments should be done.[2] The assessment will measure attention and concentration skills, language skills, motor skills, the learning and recall of verbal and visual information, planning and organizational skills, abstract reasoning skills, verbal and visual reasoning skills, working memory skills, speed of processing, and achievement, as well as the interplay of social-emotional functions, social communication, and daily living skills. Neuropsychologists explore additional factors by systematically rating attention, concentration, and social-emotional behaviors such as depression or anxiety as observed by parents and teachers within the home and school. The pediatric neuropsychological evaluation typically incorporates a *multidimensional* view of the child. This model demands an integrative approach as advocated by researcher Nöel Gregg.[3] It also leads to a roadmap for effective intervention and helps in planning goals and objectives.[4]

- Occupational therapy evaluations: An occupational therapist specializes in the evaluation and management of problems with daily living skills.

The primary focus of occupational therapy (OT) is to identify and treat problems involving fine motor and perceptual skills that can interfere with a child's functioning at school, home, and play. For example, students who have specific difficulty using a pen and pencil when writing will benefit from this therapy. A child's self-care functioning is also addressed.

- Physical therapy evaluations: A physical therapist addresses problems having to do with motor development and mobility. Physical therapists will identify and treat children with delayed or impaired motor development such as issues with the ability to walk and run.

- Psychiatric evaluations: These evaluations are done by a medical doctor who can diagnose emotional disorders and prescribe medications. An assessment of emotional status is accomplished by taking a history and performing a clinical interview and mental status examination. As mentioned previously, children will frequently exhibit more than one significant problem. This is a good starting point when evaluating the possibility of psychiatric conditions. Many psychiatrists also receive training in psychotherapy that they may use as part of their treatment.

- Psychological/educational (also known as psychoeducational) evaluations: These evaluations are typically done by either a psychologist working within a school district for special educational purposes or by a clinical psychologist on a private basis. Special education evaluations are used to determine a child's eligibility for, and progress in, special education. They also determine which special education services will be helpful for a child. These evaluations are based on observations, tests, and educational performance. The tests provide information regarding a child's cognitive, academic, social, and emotional status. Evaluations by a school psychologist should not be confused with school assessments. Assessments conducted by public school districts are mandated statewide tests that evaluate the yearly academic progress of all students toward meeting state standards under the IDEA. The assessment system serves as a vehicle for public reporting and for school and district accountability purposes. Psychological/educational evaluations are also performed by clinical psychologists working on a private basis or in a clinic. Clinical psychologists have a PhD and are licensed by the state in which they work. These evaluations can be requested by pediatricians, psychiatrists, psychologists, educational therapists, and other professionals who treat children. These evaluations not only identify a child's strengths and weaknesses on tests assessing psychological and academic functioning but also delineate clinical diagnoses and specific interventions and suggestions for school use. Clinical psychologists are also trained to provide a variety of evidence-based psychotherapeutic interventions aimed at alleviating emotional distress and improving mental health functioning.

Clinical psychologists often work in multidisciplinary teams with other professionals such as psychiatrists, occupational therapists, and social workers to bring a multifaceted approach to the treatment of emotional problems.

- Speech and language evaluations: A speech-language therapist will typically do an assessment of speech and language skills. These assessments also measure a child's social communication skills—for example, your child's ability to understand facial expressions and emotions. A referral to a speech-language therapist is also indicated when there are problems with oral-motor coordination affecting speech. Goals and objectives for intervention should be documented in the report.

As you can see, each type of assessment serves a different purpose depending on the background and training of the professional administering it, as well as the specific needs of the child. Parents often think that one evaluator can "do it all." The reality is that you may need to see several of these professionals in order to obtain an accurate roadmap of your child's strengths and weaknesses. Additionally, each professional will document diagnoses or descriptions of a child's behaviors consistent with his or her specialty guidelines. You may notice that health professionals typically diagnose a child with medical "labels." For example, a child may manifest behaviors consistent with ADHD, predominantly inattentive type. On the other hand, educators within a public school system will not use medical terminology. They will use classification systems such as "other health impairment" because this is the terminology used within the school system under the IDEA, as mentioned in Chapter 1.[5] The "other health impairment" category encompasses diagnoses such as ADHD. The label ADHD is an example of a chronic health condition that can adversely affect a child's educational performance. This means that different definitions of a child's condition can be used and this depends on *who* is evaluating the child.

What use are these labels? Educators and intervention specialists cannot *treat* a label. The label says virtually nothing about the child as an individual. Children can have many strengths and weaknesses, and the weaknesses can negatively affect the learning process. Professionals, collaborating as a team, can truly help by understanding a child's unique strengths and weaknesses and working to remediate those problematic behaviors and weaknesses.

In contrast, a label is *essential* when applying for accommodations for high-stakes testing or for obtaining insurance benefits for a specific treatment. Ensuring the best possible match between the student, the accommodation(s), the task, and the context is vital. Each evaluator must tailor the assessment to the current and reasonably foreseeable needs of the child.[6]

PART

BEYOND THE LABEL

Recognizing, Assessing, and Accommodating
Your Child's Challenges

CHAPTER 4

Attention and Concentration

WHEN YOU JUST CAN'T PAY ATTENTION LONG ENOUGH NO MATTER HOW HARD YOU TRY

At Home

Claire is 10 years old. It is 6:30 on Monday morning. Claire can't get up from bed. Her mother tells her to get up but then has to go downstairs to make breakfast. Ten minutes later, she looks at the clock. Claire is not up yet. She runs upstairs and calls her daughter again. This time, she puts her hand on Claire's head demanding that she get up. Claire yells, "Mom, you are so mean!" Mother feels upset but can't deal with it because the bus is coming in thirty minutes. Claire comes down the stairs wrapped in her blanket and she collapses in a heap on the floor. Her mother once again says, "Come on, Claire. This is no time to fool around. You gotta eat and we have to go." Claire drags herself to the kitchen table and immediately starts whining. She demands that her mother cook her oatmeal instead of the waffle that is already on the table. In exasperation Mother says, "It's not a restaurant; you get what I've made!" Claire argues that she does not want a waffle, she wants oatmeal. Mother knows full well that she should not get sucked into THIS argument again, but her temper is fraying and she shouts, "Just eat what I give you! I don't have time to make you another breakfast. YOU HAVE TO GET READY TO CATCH THE BUS!" Her mother walks up the stairs again to Claire's room and gets her clothes out for school. She sees Claire's backpack on the floor, homework strewn about. "Oh no!" she thinks. Claire forgot to put her homework in her backpack again. The clock ticks. "Claire!" she snaps, impatiently, "you have to come up now and get ready. I'm not kidding. OR ELSE!" She decides to pack up Claire's backpack. "I'd better do it myself or we'll never get out of the house," she thinks. The bus ends up waiting for Claire yet again.

It turns out that Claire never did complete the homework assignment from last night; Mother gets a call from the teacher later on that day.

Claire's Mother

Claire's mother is stressed and feels bad. Nothing ever goes right. She feels angry most of the time, is tired of repeating herself, and wonders why she can't figure out how to stop the daily tension-ridden fire drill. She feels like she must be lacking as a parent or maybe is just a terrible mother. Claire's father feels the same way but doesn't know what to do either. Both parents feel isolated. None of their friends at work seem to be going through this. This is not fair!

Grade Four Teacher

Mrs. Bushmill knows that Claire is bright, is very creative, and has a wonderful vocabulary. She recently scored in the eightieth percentile on the Iowa Achievement Test. Claire is well liked by others. In fact, she makes other kids in the classroom laugh with her jokes. But, she muses, Claire does have some trouble focusing. She talks to her girlfriends when she should be working. Claire also seems to be thinking of things other than her work during study time. It seems that she needs continual reminders. Other than that, Claire is a great kid. However, Mrs. Bushmill is concerned because it seems that Claire's attention skills are not what they should be. Her attention problems are affecting her grades. It is time to call a conference with her parents.

Claire's parents are not completely surprised when they are called to meet with the teacher at school. Since the first grade, teachers have consistently reported that Claire had problems with attention and concentration. However, nothing was done because Claire's grades were so good. Now, they are really concerned. What should they do? It is one thing for Claire not to pay attention at home, but it's another thing at school. How can their daughter be struggling so much? *They* never had any problems like this growing up. Well, sort of. Claire's father remembers that he had problems with attention at school when he was Claire's age but, in those days, nothing was done about it. He works as a game warden and his problems with focusing do not seem to be an issue anymore. His wife is NOT in agreement with him on that statement. Exhausted, Claire's mother thinks, "What do we do now?"

Claire

Claire feels lousy when she overhears her teacher call her parents during break. Claire thinks that she is doing well in school and she likes school. She has many friends. However, lately, Claire has begun to feel a bit anxious and "off." She just can't seem to get it together after school. There is so much to remember.

Her assignment notebook needs to be in her backpack as well as the extra enrich-ment assignments. Claire remembers that she has a project due on the Chumash Indians but can't recall when it is due. Now what is she going to do? It seems that all of her friends are "getting it." On top of that, Claire is sick and tired of her mother nagging her at night. Claire feels tired after the school day and just wants to rest and watch cartoons. She does not understand why her mother gets angry since she is doing so well on tests. Claire wonders, "Doesn't that count?" However, Claire knows that she sometimes zones off in class and is not clear how to make it better. She wants help but doesn't understand how to ask for it from her teachers or parents. Claire feels lost.

Does this sound familiar? Claire cannot organize her work during homework time. She has trouble focusing on homework, and then does not complete it. She also forgets to put her homework in her backpack the night before no matter how many times her mother tells her. She *constantly* has difficulties getting out of the house on time for the bus.

Claire's parents love their child and want to help but are not sure how to move forward. They do not understand how Claire can be so smart but also be distracted and unaware of things going on around her. It seems that Claire's focusing problems have worsened as she has gotten older. Their daughter is clearly not "growing out of it." How many times have you heard *that* one? The trouble is that Claire has always done well on tests but can't seem to get it together when it comes to completing homework assignments or projects. It is clear to Claire's mother and father that they need to take control of the situation. Their love for their daughter just isn't enough to solve the problem.

What Is Attention and Concentration?

"My husband thinks that the 'real' problem is me and I'm too protective as a mother. He says I should 'get over it.'"

"My son's pediatrician told me that he is just a boy. Boys are like that. He will grow out of it."

"My friends tell me that it's all the school's fault. They let the classroom run wild. It's not structured enough."

"Emily's teacher says she is lazy. She's just not interested and she needs more structure and support at home."

"You're mean, mommy. I'm really trying. It's not fair."

"It wasn't my fault. Mary was talking to me."

"I just forgot. I was on my way to the library. I'll get the assignment done in the morning."

"My daughter is so smart and her mind goes so fast. She's just bored in class."

Do these comments strike a chord? How many times have you heard one or more of the previous statements? Do you feel guilty, as if you are doing something wrong? You love your child and, despite your repeated efforts to help, you are getting nowhere. Your insurance company won't pay for intervention because the pediatrician feels that your child's behavior is an "age" thing.

Far too often, these children and teens "slip through the cracks." They look and act "normally," can get good grades, and may even do well on tests, as we see with Claire. Some students may fail tests and do well on homework. Others may do fairly well in school but get in trouble with their peers because of things they say. These children may look surprised when parents give them a time-out or when their teacher reprimands or redirects them. Sometimes they will even lose friends. This is certainly a no-win situation for everybody.

Attention and concentration are very important for your child's current and future success. Everything depends on attention. You need attention for learning new concepts in the classroom, managing homework duties, and engaging in conversations. Attention is also required when getting ready for school in the morning or when driving a car. Students with attention problems are often misinterpreted and are frequently "labeled" incorrectly. For example, these children may be told repeatedly that they are "lazy" or "unmotivated." The reason for this is that children will have good days and bad days. Claire will usually turn in her assignments on time during the beginning of the school week; however, she may not turn in other assignments later in the week. She just can't seem to get it together. This pattern of behavior confuses parents, teachers, and even the children themselves. The importance of attention and concentration grows as children age. These areas become increasingly taxed as children get older. They are expected to become more independent, rely on themselves to pay attention in school, manage their work at home, and cultivate friendships.

When Is the Problem a *Big* Problem?

Part of the problem may be that you believe your child's behaviors are caused by some situational or family stressor. You may also be wrestling with guilt and are unsure how to proceed. You feel responsible but confused. The behaviors that your child shows combined with your overall gut feelings as a parent will alert you as to when to seek help. When are lapses in attention and concentration a *big* problem? When are they not a problem? When should you really become concerned and get help? Your child may be completely "normal" despite your thinking that something is terribly wrong. Most of us suffer from attention problems in one situation or another. Attention and concentration can be affected by hunger, poor nutrition, lack of sleep, boredom, anger, depression, nervousness, familial discord, and the age of the child. We would not say Claire has a *big* problem if her behavior only seemed to be recent or was related to some change in her life. However, the fact that she has a history of focusing problems, which have gotten worse and more frequent over the years at school and at home, gives cause for concern. The key here is the *frequency, pervasiveness,* and *severity* of the attention problems that clearly impact Claire's behavior in school, home, and social situations.

In 1998, Russell Barkley, psychologist and leading researcher on attention disorders, wrote that a child's behavior could be pictured as falling somewhere on a continuum. The behaviors underlying attention and concentration are not seen as fixed points of reference, but rather as a continuous scale or spectrum of behavior. Dr. Barkley suggested that this continuum could range from normal to abnormal.[1] Claire's mother decided to plot her daughter's current problematic behaviors on a line. She wrote the numbers 1 to 10 on the line. She chose the number "10" as indicating maximum difficulty (severe) and "1" as signifying minimum struggles. She realized that certain behaviors could be unclear at times because many different things can affect attention and concentration. For example, problems with blurting out in a classroom can be completely normal for a child's age or completely abnormal. The *frequency, pervasiveness* (the number of situations in which the behavior occurs), and *severity* (intensity) of your child's challenges are important to consider. The following questions and comments may help Claire's mother sort it out:

- Are these behaviors occurring more often than not?
- Are many of the behaviors close to severe?
- Are the behaviors occurring in more than one situation such as school, homework, and chore time?
- Have these behaviors been a problem over time for you and for other individuals such as teachers and peers?
- Are these behaviors impacting your child's ability to learn in the classroom?
- Are these behaviors affecting your child's ability to follow through on tasks at home and school?
- Are these behaviors causing unbearable stress at home?
- Are you finding out that you are "going back to school" because you are completing your child's homework and calling other parents and teachers to help your child?
- Are you finding that your child needs frequent reminders?
- Are the behaviors affecting your child's peer relationships in a negative way? For example, does your child have problems resolving conflicts and keeping friends?

If you have answered yes to many of these questions, your child's behaviors are significant enough to get help. You may seek professional help if you feel that your child's behavior has been "out of control" for some time. You may also seek help if you feel frustrated on a daily basis and nothing that you do seems to work. The good news is, you should be able to help your child at home and at school once you understand what the *real* difficulties are.

Claire's Mother

Claire's mother's heart begins to pound when she receives yet another call from the teacher. "Oh no," she thinks. There have been several conferences with the homeroom teacher and Claire's behavior is getting worse. She has difficulty remembering to bring her homework binder home and can't seem to get organized enough to complete the homework at night. Claire is having difficulty turning in her homework on time and sometimes even forgets where she put it in her locker. She needs frequent prompting and reminders from the teacher. Her grades are declining even though she still does well on tests. These problems really seem to have gotten worse in the fourth grade.

Perhaps you or the teacher is noticing the following behaviors in your child:

- Spaces out in class and misses parts of a lecture
- Makes careless errors on tests and homework
- Rushes through tests and assignments
- Blurts out and interrupts others in class
- Requires frequent teacher prompting
- Shows difficulty keeping attention on work
- Has a glazed look when a teacher is lecturing
- Fails to follow through on tasks when given multiple instructions
- Appears fidgety and restless
- Forgets books and assignments at home and at school
- Is highly distractible by noises and by his or her thoughts
- Loses and misplaces things required for a project
- Runs around the classroom and has trouble sitting still
- Appears impatient with others and talks quickly
- Is easily frustrated and quick to anger
- Is oblivious to the time it takes to complete homework and projects
- Has trouble waiting in line
- Has to have everything "now"
- Makes comments that are hurtful to others

These behaviors may or may not occur on a daily basis. Some may not be evident at home but are observed at school. It is the consistency of the inconsistency that is driving you crazy. As a parent, you probably feel angry and frustrated because you think that your child *should* be doing things independently by now.

Claire's mother takes an honest look at her daughter's behaviors. She realizes that she must be her daughter's advocate. Claire has pervasive problems with inattention, restlessness, and impulsivity. These behaviors are frequent, occur in multiple situations, and are severe on a daily basis. The behaviors affect Claire in every way, from following through on social gatherings, to getting ready in the morning, to remembering to hand in long-term projects in school. Preparing for tests is another challenge for her daughter. Inattention is clearly a problem. Claire's mother realizes that her daughter:

- Makes careless mistakes repeatedly on tests such as skipping questions or even making "stupid" mathematical errors.
- Is unable to sustain her concentration long enough to read one page of a book. She rereads the page several times.
- Does not seem to listen when her mother speaks to her directly.
- Does not follow through on instructions given by the teacher or one of her parents at home.
- Does not finish a project although motivated to do so.
- Has difficulty organizing projects, her backpack, and her closet at home.
- Avoids any "work" task that requires sustained effort. However, Claire has no problems playing video games or watching her favorite shows on television.
- Loses things for projects constantly or forgets to bring the school assignments home.
- Is easily distracted by noises around her or even her own thoughts.
- Is forgetful in remembering what her homework is and must call her classmates every night to verify homework.
- Forgets the time of social gatherings even though she is excited to be involved.
- Has problems resolving conflict with her friends and is frequently impatient with them.

Claire's mother also sees that her daughter is frequently restless. Some doctors call it "hyperactive-impulsive" behavior. She recalls that Claire, throughout her schooling, would:

- Keep talking throughout a conversation even though her girlfriends would give her cues to stop.
- Jiggle her feet slightly when doing homework.

- Describe herself as "restless" and not likely to sit through any reading or writing project that took time.
- Not like to do any activities by herself.
- Interrupt her friends and teachers even though the "moment" was not right.

Many health professionals and educators believe that a child's difficulty with attention and concentration can affect learning and behavior. The label "ADHD" is a medical diagnostic term used by many professionals when the behaviors negatively affect a child's ability to function at school, at home, or even socially.[2] This term can be misleading to parents and educators. Claire's mother thought that her daughter did not have any problems with attention because she could play a video game for hours. Researchers Hallowell and Ratey propose that the word *deficit* is a misnomer. Instead, they suggest that it is the *inconsistency* and *variability* of attention that is important.[3] Claire's mother noted, "*My daughter can focus hours on end when she is on a video game or playing a game on her cell phone. But, when it comes to doing her homework, it is another story. She just can't pay attention for long. And, that is what school is all about.*"

Here are some questions that mental health professionals may ask you:

- Does your child make careless errors in schoolwork?
- Does your child zone out when you speak to him or her directly?
- Does your child fail to finish homework and chores?
- Does your child need constant prompting to complete schoolwork?
- Does your child have difficulty following through on directions that have more than one step?
- Does your child have difficulty planning and organizing tasks or chores?
- Does your child resist work-related tasks such as homework and school-work that require focusing for long periods of time?
- Does your child forget to bring home books and assignment sheets that are necessary for tasks or activities?
- Does your child forget what he or she is doing?
- Does your child underestimate the time it takes to finish tasks?
- Is your child easily distracted by sounds around him or her or by his or her thoughts?
- Does your child fiddle with his or her hands or feet when expected to sit quietly?
- Does your child leave his or her seat in the classroom or in other situations such as the dinner table in which remaining seated is expected?
- Is your child restless and always moving?
- Does your child consider consequences before acting?
- Does your child talk nonstop and in situations in which it is inappropriate?

- Does your child interrupt others when talking?
- Is your child impatient?
- Is your child easily frustrated?
- Does your child seem to have no difficulty focusing when the task is interesting?
- Do your child's focusing difficulties occur at home *and* at school? Or, do they occur just at home *or* at school?
- Have other people commented on your child's lack of focus, impulsivity, inattention, and/or restlessness during any part of elementary or middle school?
- Do these difficulties occur in other settings such as social gatherings?
- Are the difficulties with attention and concentration worsening as your child ages?
- Are the problems with attention and concentration affecting your child's grades and social relationships?

Difficulties in many of these areas could indicate that your child may have *significant* problems with attention and concentration. However, attention and concentration problems rarely exist all alone. *Psychological disorders* such as depression, anxiety, and obsessive-compulsive disorders can affect attention and concentration. *Learning problems* such as reading, math, and writing difficulties can also throw children a "curveball" when attending to a task. Some children who encounter problems with language have challenges with attention and concentration. Additionally, *medical disorders* such as traumatic brain injury, cerebral palsy, epilepsy, cancer, Tourette's syndrome, allergies, and sleep apnea can impact focusing ability. Problems with attention and over-activity can also occur with other *developmental* conditions such as mental retardation and autism spectrum disorders.

Looking Ahead

WHAT DO YOU DO NOW?

Many parents view their child as "perfect." Claire's mother did. She felt very upset when she first realized that Claire had difficulties with attention and concentration. She found out that attention problems could be caused by many factors. She asked herself, "Was Claire depressed?" "Did she have a learning disability?" "Was it our parenting skills?" "Were we too stressed as a family?" "Did Claire have some medical disorder?" "Was Claire just normal and I was overreacting?" She also wondered if her daughter had any other problems along with attention and concentration.

Many students have more than one area of difficulty when they have problems focusing, such as in being able to organize. As mentioned in Chapter 6, children with attention and concentration weaknesses frequently show associated deficits such as a poor sense of time, impaired planning ability, inefficient expression of ideas, delayed motor coordination, greater problems with frustration tolerance, and poor persistence of effort.[4]

Children with attention problems may also have difficulties with social skills as discussed in Chapter 12. Claire has a pattern of being bossy and controlling with her friends at times. In addition, she appears to gravitate toward friends who have ADHD. Claire seems insensitive to the needs of her friends and misreads social cues. However, her mother is also aware that Claire is sensitive and deeply cares about her friends. In fact, her daughter feels sorry for the way she acts in a conflict without understanding why she acts that way. Claire's mother sees that it is her daughter's impulsivity that seems to get in the way of friendships at times. Her daughter has problems managing her anger, gets easily frustrated, and overreacts to minor problems on a daily basis. Claire's impatience takes a toll when there is a conflict with her peers. Claire always seems to be in a hurry to get things over with. Her friends, because of this, feel like she doesn't listen to them. Dr. Barkley suggests that this "emotional impulsiveness" is a part of ADHD and can negatively affect social interactions. This was important information for Claire's mother to understand.[4–7]

Claire's mother knew that her daughter had a *real* attention problem and that she was not just overreacting. She saw that Claire's attention problems had not affected her grades early on because there were not as many demands on Claire, such as homework and projects. Teachers always reported that Claire was a pleasure to teach. However, Claire's mother noticed that her daughter's problems became more evident in the fourth grade. Deadlines were not met and Claire kept getting further behind on daily work despite her mother's constant reminders at home. Claire also became frustrated at home. That is when her mother took action. Claire's mother realized it was not just Claire's unique way of handling things. The problem was *real* and Claire needed specific direction from her school and specialists. But it took a while for Claire's mother to admit her daughter had attention difficulties and that it was a *problem*.

THE ROADMAP

Claire's mother decided to track her concerns and kept precise documentation. This was important because the health professionals and educators asked questions about Claire's developmental milestones, her grades, her social skills, and what teachers had said about her academic progress. She created a file of all report cards and reports from the health professionals. At the same time, Claire's mother tried not to panic. Shame and guilt haunted her, but she realized these emotions were only holding her back. She was okay and Claire was okay. She needed to move forward in a proactive way to help her daughter.

Getting the right roadmap is crucial for understanding a child's strengths and weaknesses. As discussed in Chapter 3, Claire's mother discovered that evaluators from various professions brought different perspectives to the evaluation process. She also noticed that each type of assessment served a different purpose depending on the background and training of the professional. Claire's mother initially thought one evaluator could "do it all," but this was not the case. In addition, each professional documented diagnoses or descriptions of her daughter's behaviors differently, consistent with *their* specialty guidelines. Claire's mother noticed the *health* professionals were diagnosing her child with medical "labels." On the other hand, the *educators* did not use such medical terminology but instead used the words "other health impairment" under the IDEA. The "other health impairment" category encompasses diagnoses such as ADHD.[8] Claire's mother learned ADHD was an example of a chronic health condition that adversely affected her child's educational performance. Different definitions of her daughter's condition were used depending on *who* was evaluating her.

What was clear was that a *label* was meaningless. The label said nothing about Claire as an individual. Claire had specific problems that were affecting her learning. Educators and intervention specialists could not treat a *label*. However, they could help her daughter by understanding her *strengths* and *weaknesses*.

Claire's mother decided to seek advice from Claire's pediatrician as the first step. This was a good place to start for many reasons. The physical examination could determine whether her daughter had any underlying medical issues that were possibly affecting her ability to concentrate. Claire's mother found out her daughter was healthy. Vision and hearing tests revealed no problems. The pediatrician then suggested a neuropsychological assessment to further investigate Claire's intellectual, cognitive, achievement, and social-emotional strengths and weaknesses. The neuropsychologist found Claire had frequent, pervasive, and severe problems with attention and concentration that were significantly impacting her learning processes and her performance during tests. Claire's mother was also told that her daughter was not depressed or anxious. She was a healthy and well-adjusted child. However, there were indicators of some test-taking anxiety. Claire's mother could now see why her daughter was nervous before tests, since she was so distracted by noises in the classroom. The neuropsychologist also found Claire had problems with time management, planning, and organizational skills. This made sense, too, because Claire always had problems with turning in her assignments on time. In addition, Claire had difficulty completing tests. Claire reported she had trouble moving on when she encountered a difficult question. Time just seemed to slip by too fast. Last, the neuropsychologist indicated Claire had a writing disorder. Claire tended to write very little on essays because she was quite distractible during any task that required sustained attention and concentration. She also struggled to use a pencil or pen. In fact, it hurt to write. This slowed her down even more! Claire's mother felt sad but relieved. Now they were on the right track to success and getting the help that they needed.

The Accommodation Plan

WHAT TYPES OF ACCOMMODATIONS WOULD BE HELPFUL AT SCHOOL?

Based on the evaluations from the pediatrician and neuropsychologist, Claire's mother found out her daughter had an attention disorder and problems with fine motor skills. Her planning, organizational, and time management skills were problematic as well. Producing neat written work was extremely difficult and effortful for Claire, and this only added to her difficulties with attention. How could Claire be helped to pay attention and concentrate so her learning would not be affected? How would Claire show what she truly knew on tests? Now that they had a "roadmap" of the problem and needs, Claire's mother realized they needed "tools" to help Claire as soon as possible. She did not want Claire to get even further behind.

As discussed in Chapter 2, accommodations are necessary to provide a student *access* to learning. Accommodations are meant to "level the playing field," not to tilt it. They are meant to be neutral tools to ensure an individual with a disability can compete fairly with others and is allowed equal access to classroom instruction and tests. Recall that accommodations do not alter a task, but make the task accessible to the student with a disability. Accommodations may be offered by teachers when students struggle or they may need to be mandated. Students with documented attention difficulties have a legal right to accommodations to "level the playing field."

Many of the specific accommodations recommended for students with attention difficulties also apply to other disabilities. Disabilities do not exist all alone. They often are interwoven with other weaknesses (comorbidity). Claire's mother became aware of this when she noticed that many of the accommodations suggested for Claire's attention disorder were also recommended for her writing difficulties and her problems with planning, organization, and time management.

Claire's mother wondered what would happen in the classroom outside of a test situation. How would her daughter keep her attention on the teacher and not talk with her friends or daydream constantly? How would Claire learn the new information in the classroom? What types of interventions would help in the classroom?

Claire's mother discovered that the IDEA permits local education agencies to focus on consultation and intervention services in order to identify a student's needs and to monitor his or her progress over time. As discussed in Chapter 2, the IDEA also targets those students in kindergarten through grade three who require additional academic support and who have not received special education. In addition, the latest version of the law requires that the services listed in the IEP be based on peer-reviewed research when possible.[8,9]

With this in mind, school-based accommodations should *enrich* a student's academic and social experience and not just target behaviors that are not acceptable within the classroom. The best course of action is to minimize the demands within the classroom when a student has attention and concentration weaknesses. Memory aids and cues have also been useful in enhancing learning outcomes.[10]

Grade Eleven Teacher

Claire is now in the eleventh grade. Mr. Levit has always liked Claire as a student. He knows Claire needs to sit in the front of his class and use a computer to take notes. He asks Claire questions frequently and confirms she has understood all homework assignments. Mr. Levit also allows Claire extra time on classroom assignments. In addition, Mr. Levit has made arrangements for Claire to receive any homework assignments in writing.

The following list targets those classroom accommodations that are frequently considered by evaluators when assessing students with attention and concentration weaknesses:

- Advance warning on projects/tests
- Assignment sheets and schedules (daily, weekly, monthly)
- Assistance with focusing on tasks from teacher
- Audiotaped lectures
- Books on tape
- Breaks (additional, extended, frequent)
- Checklists (self-monitoring forms) requiring student to evaluate his or her performance and completion times on specific academic tasks
- Clear and consistent instructions
- Copies of homework assignments, lecture material, and notes
- Educational facilitator to encourage proofreading and remaining on task
- Extended time on homework, in-class work, and projects
- Extra set of books at home
- Eye contact established and maintained with student
- Graph paper for students with large, sloppy handwriting
- Large assignments broken into smaller assignments
- Minimal distractions
- Note taker
- Outline of instruction prior to class instruction
- Peer assistance for in-class assignments

- Preferential seating
- Routines and rules displayed visually
- Speech-to-text software
- Study guides for quizzes/tests
- Text-to-speech software
- Videotaped class sessions
- Visual tools (outline/PowerPoint) used in combination with oral instruction
- Word processor for assignments including written expression

WHAT TYPES OF ACCOMMODATIONS WOULD BE HELPFUL FOR TESTS?

Claire

"It's a difficult process because of my attention. Since taking tests is challenging, I know it is important I don't get distracted, and my concentration has to be there if I want to be able to retrieve facts. The fact is I do get distracted. It's very hard to take tests because I have to 'fight with myself' to concentrate and remain focused. This battle to stay focused becomes harder as the test progresses because I start to get really tired. I think of this as brain fatigue or brain fog. As I get more mentally tired, I remember less and begin to make even more stupid mistakes. I can get really frustrated as a result. This is why I really need extended time for tests and breaks. I don't feel pressured when I know I have extra time. I need the breaks to regroup and refocus as well."

Grade Eleven Teacher

Mr. Levit and other teachers allow Claire extended time for tests. He is very pleased with Claire's progress. Claire is a dedicated student. Mr. Levit understands Claire and knows she is able to produce what she knows on paper only when she receives extra time. Claire is allowed 50 percent extended time for all tests, and uses the extended time fully. Mr. Levit realizes some teachers do not understand the definition of an accommodation. They complain the accommodations give Claire an advantage over her nondisabled peers. Mr. Levit knows this is not true, and he thinks it is unfortunate they are not familiar with the studies on this topic. After all, they are educators!

As discussed in Chapter 2, there are many different types of test accommodations. The categories of accommodations granted by professionals are as follows: the presentation of the test material, the scheduling of the examination, the setting where the examination occurs, and the format of response.[11,12] Most students will typically use more than one accommodation. For example, Claire is allowed 50 percent extended time on tests and is also permitted to use a word processor for tests that require essay writing.

What are reasonable test accommodations for the student with attention deficits? The most frequently studied accommodation for students with attention difficulties is extended time. However, extended time may or may not help the student with attention weaknesses. Some students work so quickly that they make careless errors and, even though they know the material, they "bomb" the exam. Other students can fail because they have some other problem that is affecting their ability to process the test question. For these students, extended time would not be productive. Still other disabled students do benefit from extended time when they are applying their newly learned tools (such as a word processor) when answering a test question, or when their focus waxes and wanes during a test. Claire does benefit from extended time on tests because in order to maintain her focus, she has to make notes on the side of the page. Writing her thoughts down on the page keeps her actively involved with the test question. The accommodation of extended time also gives Claire the opportunity to write legibly since she struggles with handwriting. However, many students who are allowed extended time still have difficulty *managing* their time during a test. Therefore, teaching the student how to manage his or her time during a test-taking situation is beneficial. The National Institute of Literacy documents that teaching a student *how* and *when* to use an accommodation is essential for test-taking purposes. *Explicit* and *consistent* strategies are necessary to help a student learn how to structure, manage, and organize time.[12] This type of remediation can be learned with the help of an educational therapist.

It is vital that the evaluator *matches* the specific accommodation to the identified weaknesses within the student's overall profile of strengths, weaknesses, and intervention history. In other words, a specific accommodation does not "fit" all students with a particular weakness.

A word about extended time as an accommodation: Extended time allows *access* to the content of the test or classroom instruction. It also permits a student to demonstrate knowledge of that content. It does not *alter* a test, nor does it give preference. There are a number of studies that support this accommodation for students with different disabilities (see Chapter 10). The National Institute for Literacy, a federal agency, recently published peer-reviewed findings on the topic of extended time. Researcher Noël Gregg concluded that extra time during test taking has proven to be an effective accommodation. Several researchers have also indicated that students with learning disabilities who are given extra time will show greater gains in test scores compared to their nondisabled peers. This means that a disability significantly depresses test scores and that extra time "levels the playing field." The research is clear: such an accommodation does not give preference, but rather "bridges" a student's ability to access the test and show what he or she knows. In other words, an accommodation provides *access* to test material.[11-13]

Evaluators typically consider the following test accommodations for students with attention disorders:

- Breaks (additional, extended, frequent)
- Calculator

- Extended time (with amount of time specified)
- Graph paper for the student with large, sloppy handwriting
- Monitoring by teacher
- Multiple-choice format
- Multiple-day testing sessions
- One examination per day
- Oral examination
- Orientation aids
- Recording of responses in test booklet
- Scribe
- Speech-to-text software
- Test setting (private, semiprivate, small group)
- Text-to-speech software
- Word processor

A Word on Access to High-Stakes Examinations

CLAIRE: GRADE ELEVEN

"Extended time is the key to my academic success. The way I process the material during tests is time consuming. My whole life I have always had trouble completing tests in the time required. At a young age, I remember taking language arts and history tests and failing to complete them in time. Luckily, teachers gave me extra time informally. Back then, I had not been diagnosed with an attention disorder. I remember feeling not smart enough. I would sit and take tests and get frustrated because it was almost as if I couldn't take the test, even though I knew the information. Taking tests was a traumatic experience for me. I became a different person when I was allowed extra time. The team at school decided 50 percent additional time would be best because I fully used that amount of time and was able to complete tests. I did not need any more time. I hope to apply for extended time for the SAT and the ACT. I know I need the time to show what I know. I get nervous just thinking about taking the test without extra time!"

Claire mentioned to her mother that she could be a candidate for the accommodation of extended time on the "big" tests. She was scheduled to take the SAT and the ACT examinations in the spring. Claire is worried her attention problems will prevent her from finishing the examinations in the standard amount of time allowed. Claire knows she has disorders in attention and writing as well as associated problems with time management, planning, and organizational skills. Claire understands that these associated problems are part of executive functioning (see Chapter 6). She still has difficulty with these areas despite educational therapy and the medication that she now takes. These disorders *substantially* affect her ability to compete with her peers in test-taking conditions when she is not allowed extended time. Claire was allowed 50 percent more time on her tests in school because she had documentation of her pervasive and frequent weaknesses, and they were severe enough to warrant the time extension for tests. They were implemented formally as a result of her IEP. Without the accommodations, Claire would function below the level of "most" people because of her substantial limitations. Although she has documentation identifying her disorders and disabilities since the fourth grade, Claire was told that she needed to be reevaluated because of the College Board guidelines. This was necessary because her documentation needs to reflect the *current* status of her functional limitations and explain why she needs testing accommodations. Even though Claire knows that her learning challenges have been affecting her since she was very young, she requires further documentation to reflect the impact of these challenges on her *today*. What does this reevaluation entail? Claire found that the following "talking" points had to be addressed in the report:

- Current level of functioning
- An update of any changes in her performance at school since the last evaluation(s)
- Statement of presenting problem(s)
- History of presenting attention and writing problems and evidence of ongoing attention problems that have resulted in impairment
- Interviews with her parent(s)
- Developmental history
- Family history
- Relevant medical and medication history
- Relevant psychosocial history and interventions implemented
- Academic history since the elementary school period
- Review of prior psychoeducational reports and standardized test results
- Review of school transcripts, report cards, teacher comments, and tutoring evaluations
- Review of medical reports, rehabilitation reports, and previous intervention(s)
- Written documentation from teachers of approved prior and current accommodations and rationale for current test/classroom accommodations
- Employment history if relevant
- Behavioral observations of student, including effort during the evaluation
- Description of comprehensive testing techniques per specific board requirements
- Description of current functional limitations pertaining to the educational setting that are a direct result of problems with attention
- Discussion of disorders, descriptions of behaviors, and the relationship of the disorder and functional impairment observed at school and home

- Discussion of other possible explanations for the student's difficulties
- Identification of the specific accommodation(s) tailored to the student's weaknesses and the rationale for the current request

Claire knew she was not necessarily guaranteed the accommodation of extended time for the "big" tests even though she was allowed the time extension during tests at school. She, along with her parents and teachers, had to *prove* her attention difficulties were *frequent, pervasive,* and *severe* enough to impair her ability to finish tests compared to "most" of her peers.

Claire did some more research. She found that the following test accommodations could be requested when applying because of her significant problems with attention and concentration:

- Breaks (additional, extended, frequent)
- Extended time (with amount of time specified)
- Multiple-day testing sessions
- Recording of responses in test booklet
- Test setting (private, semiprivate, small group)
- Word processor

Claire understood these accommodations could be considered by the evaluator, but she also knew the accommodations needed to be supported by the test findings, her history of difficulties, and the current need to "level the playing field" because of her documented evidence of a disorder and disability. Claire only requested extended time at 50 percent since she had fully used this amount for tests in the past. This was granted to her as a result of her reevaluation and comprehensive documentation. Claire did not request additional accommodations because her experience showed she did not need them. For example, she no longer needed a private test setting or extra breaks because the medication had really helped her attention problem.

Beyond High School

CLAIRE

Claire is now 19 years old. It is 6:30 on a Monday morning and she is in college. She wakes up from bed. It feels like a good day. Claire is motivated to get up and get ready for her first class. She picks up her personal digital assistant (PDA) and reviews her "list" of morning duties. Claire knows that the list is important and plans on checking off each task that she entered the night before. College is much more demanding than high school. Her parents are not around to remind her to get up in the morning, prepare for projects, and turn papers in. Prompted by her list, Claire remembers her organic chemistry assignments and places them in her backpack. Check. That one is done. Claire runs downstairs from her dormitory room and has breakfast. Her peers are laughing in the cafeteria. Claire would love to stay and chat with her new friends but realizes she has to leave for her first class of the day. It will be a long day. Claire understands she must stick to her schedule. She is not a "crammer." That never worked for her and she accepts it. Claire also meets with a facilitator at the college's learning center who helps her prepare for upcoming tests. She feels good about herself. Everything is going to be all right!

CLAIRE'S MOTHER

"My husband and I had to be trained. It was not just Claire. We realized we were not very good at following through with consequences when she was younger. We were just too tired. I guess we were all tired. Part of it had to do with our frustration. No one gets a manual on how to raise a kid when he or she is born! My husband and I had to learn how to parent. It seemed simple but it wasn't. Claire was getting pretty oppositional as she got older. Parent training helped us understand that her problems weren't our fault. We learned a lot of truths about her problems and found we had some misconceptions. We also discovered how stressed out we were as a family. It had snowballed over time. We learned to use praise, follow through on what we said, and put Claire on what's called a 'behavioral' program. Most of all, we learned we had to be consistent and predictable. When Claire got older, we learned about problem-solving techniques and the therapist helped us communicate better with each other. Claire also benefited from social skills intervention and we participated in that as well. So, all of this did not happen overnight. We had to change as we all got older."

Claire's mother said it all. It really is up to us to be our child's advocate. We need to move ahead with the help of health professionals and educators. It is up to us to give the necessary "tools" to our children so they can access all learning and social situations and show what they truly know.

CHAPTER 5

Memory

WHEN YOUNG MINDS FORGET

At Home

Derrick is 8 years old and in the third grade. Derrick and his mother are reviewing the solar system and both are clearly frustrated. She asks him to repeat the names of the planets. "Earth, Mars, Jupiter. . . I forgot." Derrick looks ashamed when he can't do it. He gets angry and throws the papers off the table. "Mom, I can't do this! It's too hard!" Derrick feels bad because he is really trying to do his best. He is aware he has trouble with remembering things. On top of that, he feels stupid and wants to quit studying for his test. Learning is just too hard.

Derrick's Mother

Derrick's mother does not understand why everything she asks Derrick goes in one ear and out the other. She feels tired because nothing is working at this point. It has been such a struggle for Derrick to learn the nine planets. She can't tell if Derrick is just lazy or really forgetful. However, her "gut feeling" is he is working very hard.

Derrick was born to an alcoholic mother who drank wine during her pregnancy. His maternal aunt, now his mother, adopted him when he was 1 year old. Derrick has always been active. He also has had many emotional ups and downs. When the pediatrician heard about Derrick's difficulties in preschool, she suggested an evaluation by a clinical genetics specialist because of Derrick's history of prenatal alcohol exposure. This specialist diagnosed Derrick with fetal alcohol spectrum disorder (FASD) after reviewing the prenatal history, conducting a detailed physical examination, and reviewing genetic testing to consider other explanations. A pediatric psychiatrist then evaluated Derrick when he was in first grade. The psychiatrist told the mother that Derrick's attention problems were likely related to the FASD. Derrick's mother has also noticed that he is forgetful even when he seems focused. This forgetfulness occurs both with schoolwork and during outings with his friends.

She notices that Derrick forgets to do his chores and even has trouble remembering where he put his homework at home. Derrick's mother thought addressing the attention problem was going to fix her son's difficulties in school, but it just doesn't seem like it has.

Grade Three Teacher

Mrs. Fields adores Derrick and appreciates how hard he tries. On tests, Derrick often has incomplete or missing answers. He does better on multiple-choice tests. Derrick's attention has improved but it is not clear why he has trouble with memory. Is he daydreaming when he looks like he's paying attention? Is that why Derrick isn't remembering what he's learning? Why can he successfully repeat what she has said, but then forgets it soon after?

What Are Memory Problems?

"Everything Lilly learns goes in one ear and out the other."

"Gabby seems to remember what she has read, but can't remember information she is told verbally."

"Daniel can remember information if he's given a hint, but he can't come up with it all on his own."

"My son is supposed to begin driving soon, but I'm worried because he can't remember how to get from point A to point B. He's terrible with remembering locations."

"Byron can never remember where he put his belongings; backpack, cell phone. . . you name it."

"My daughter can repeat information back to me, but she doesn't remember that information 15 minutes later."

"Harrison can remember every detail from a television show he watched, but can't remember details of the book for his book report. Why is that? They are both stories."

These are all examples of how memory problems can appear in children. We all know what it's like to be forgetful, particularly as a parent with many things to remember. However, it can be very frustrating when you have told your child something (even multiple times) and he or she often forgets what you have said or quickly forgets what you have told him or her to do. You may also feel helpless when your child forgets what he or she was told in school because you cannot be there to help your child learn and remember the information. Memory is complicated! There is a vast amount of research in the area of memory. We will separate memory into different components so you can get a clear picture of different memory functions and their impact on your child.

What Are the Different Components of Memory?

- Working memory: Working memory is critical for learning and academic success. It holds information in your mind and "works with" or manipulates that information for processing. Processing information involves thinking about it at a deep enough level to understand it and eventually file it away. Working memory is used when you are calculating math problems in your head, rehearsing a phone number over and over until you are able to dial it or write it down, or recalling the five things you need to do before leaving the house. Your child may have trouble with working memory if he or she forgets to bring books or assignments home or forgets what he or she was about to say when speaking. Working memory is also involved when a student takes notes in the classroom because he or she needs to remember what the teacher is saying while writing the information down. In addition, working memory is used in social interactions. For example, problems with working memory are seen in children with ADHD.[1,2] These children may find it difficult to "hold on" to different parts of a conversation, and that can cause problems with resolving a conflict or even understanding a friend's point of view. What happens to information in working memory can lead to either successfully learning the information or forgetting the information. Working memory is like the RAM (random access memory) in your personal computer. As long as the information can be temporarily stored and retrieved quickly for processing, or archived permanently on the hard drive, everything runs smoothly.
- Encoding: This is the process by which we learn information. It enables us to get the information or material into storage. Encoding is a product of working memory. That is, it must go through working memory to be learned. If information is not learned or *encoded*, then clearly it is not there to remember later. Your child will not encode information if he or she has trouble with focusing. This is one of the big reasons that children with attention issues do poorly in school. If a child *only* has an encoding problem, it will typically appear as forgetfulness.
- Short-term memory: This is the part of memory that holds information *temporarily*. You *do not* work with this information as you do with working memory. It is a holding place for information and is used in the present. You take in information by any of your senses and it rests in short-term memory. To remember the information, it needs to move into working

memory and then become encoded. This last part is where the processing or thinking about the information occurs.

- Long-term memory: Long-term memory is the storage place from which we retrieve or pull out needed information. Long-term memory consists of memory for past events, for factual knowledge, and for physical actions like riding a bike. People may have good memory for some aspects of long-term memory but have difficulties with others.[3] In other words, problems in this type of memory are not "all or nothing." Working memory also draws on information stored in long-term memory to work out problems in the present. For example, this occurs when your child has to pull out a memorized math fact in order to calculate something. In addition, some information may transfer from short-term to long-term memory without effortful encoding. Think about when you witness a traumatic event, like a traffic accident. This does not need to be processed at a deep level in order to be remembered. It is automatically recorded in your mind. You can think of long-term memory as the hard-drive storage on your personal computer.

It is also important to note that we may have an easier time learning and remembering information depending on whether it is presented verbally or visually to us. You may have heard people say that they are "visual learners" or "verbal learners." On the other hand, individuals can be both visual and verbal learners.

- Verbal memory: This is memory for information that is verbally told to you or material that you read. For example, your child may experience verbal memory problems when he or she forgets the details of a chapter when taking a test. Following three-step commands also may be difficult for a child with verbal memory weaknesses. For instance, your child may exhibit problems when told to brush his or her teeth, organize his or her backpack, and feed the cat. Often, children with language impairments (see Chapter 7) or reading disorders (see Chapter 10) struggle with verbal memory.
- Visual memory: This is memory for information that is presented visually to your child. Your child may have difficulties remembering where he or she placed his or her backpack or recalling a math formula when taking a test. Strengths with visual memory, on the other hand, can help children who have difficulty recalling information that they hear. Children with language impairments (see Chapter 7) will need to learn information visually in addition to verbally whenever possible since their language problems interfere with verbal learning.[4,5]

There are several components to memory. These components work together. Any breakdown in memory will negatively impact a child in the classroom. For example, problems with encoding and working memory affect fundamental academic skills because they are necessary for reading, written expression, and arithmetic operations. In addition, if your child is not using strategies to help him- or herself learn or remember information, then he or she will probably struggle with retrieval or pulling information from memory. In Derrick's case, he can sometimes learn information and repeat it back to his mother later that day, but when taking a test the next day he has significant difficulty remembering it because he did not process or think about the information at a deep enough level to learn and remember it. Strategies, or ways of remembering information, are critical for a student to encode information efficiently and retrieve it effortlessly at a later time. Information may be temporarily held in short-term memory, but only efficient encoding within working memory will transfer it successfully to long-term memory for storage and subsequent retrieval. Improving one area of memory can therefore have a positive impact on other memory functions.[3,4,6]

It is possible for a child to have poor encoding skills but still be able to retain information in memory. This means the child is actually able to remember only *some* of the information that he or she successfully learned at an earlier time. Poor encoding coupled with the ability to remember the little amount of verbal material that "gets in" has been reported for different populations of children with various developmental disorders such as FASD, dyslexia, and autism spectrum disorders.[7-9]

When Is the Problem a *Big* Problem?

Attention problems often affect memory. Stress, lack of sleep, poor nutrition, pain, and lack of motivation can also influence a child's ability to learn and remember information. Like the other challenges presented in this book, an evaluation by a professional is warranted if your child's memory problems are *frequent, pervasive* (occurring in several situations), and *severe*. However, not all memory difficulties are problematic. For example, memory is probably not a concern if your child is forgetful occasionally. This may occur if your child is forgetful at home, such as following through on assigned chores, but not at all forgetful at school when handing in work and completing projects.

Weaknesses in memory functions can occur with medical disorders and developmental conditions such as traumatic brain injury, epilepsy, autism spectrum disorders, language disorders, overall cognitive impairments, learning disabilities, FASD, and ADHD.[4,10] Amnesia, or loss of memory for large periods of time, is a condition that rarely occurs in childhood. When it does occur, it is typically caused by a traumatic brain injury or a reduction in oxygen (such as from birth complications or following severe carbon monoxide poisoning) to brain areas responsible for memory.[11-13] Your child should see a physician if he or she experiences sudden difficulties with memory that co-occur with a change in overall behavior, because this could reflect a medical condition or injury. Typically, such a change in functioning will be very apparent to you and others.

A thorough assessment will be able to identify your child's strengths and weaknesses across different memory functions. These assessments can guide your child's team to the most helpful strategies for your child. For most children, the ability to use memory aids or "tricks" (called mnemonics) to remember information comes naturally or is learned and implemented easily. For children with memory problems, this process is not natural. In fact, even when they have been taught these tools, they need to be reminded on a daily basis to use these strategies to help with remembering. Therefore, the child with memory weaknesses needs to be educated about his or her memory difficulties, taught strategies to encode the information, and then prompted regularly to use the strategies.[4]

Looking Ahead

WHAT DO YOU DO NOW?

Derrick's mother had him evaluated by a pediatric psychiatrist in the first grade when his attention problems and activity level became a problem at home and school. He was diagnosed as having ADHD consistent with FASD and was regularly monitored thereafter by the psychiatrist. Many children with attention problems suffer from poor encoding and working memory; Derrick's difficulties continued even though his attention issues were being addressed. Difficulties with executive functions, attention, emotional control, and memory are frequently seen in children like Derrick with FASD.[8] Derrick's mother sought out a comprehensive cognitive and academic assessment from a pediatric neuropsychologist because of her son's continuing challenges at school in grade three. While Derrick's factual knowledge base and basic academic skills were on track for his age and grade, she found he had weaknesses in executive functions such as problem solving, reasoning, working memory, and organizational skills. These areas impact his attention and concentration. The testing also found that Derrick had trouble encoding and retrieving information. Because of these cognitive weaknesses, Derrick's school performance suffered. The results of the assessment led Derrick's mother to request an IEP in the school. He was also tested by a psychologist at the school district. The school psychologist agreed with the neuropsychologist's findings. Both assessments were considered for IEP purposes. The IEP provided Derrick with speech-language services to help him learn and recall information that he hears and reads. He was granted several accommodations for the classroom and test taking. Derrick is allowed to preview the teacher's notes prior to class and is given preferential seating. In addition, he is allowed 50 percent extended time for all tests.

This extra time is necessary so that he can successfully apply the strategies the speech-language therapist taught him when taking a test.

THE ROADMAP

To whom do you turn for help with your child's memory weaknesses? Oftentimes, children with memory troubles have difficulties in other areas as well, such as overall cognitive ability, attention, executive functioning, and language, or in learning abilities for reading, written expression, or math. As with Derrick, the first step is to have a complete assessment of your child's particular strengths and weaknesses. In Derrick's case, his mother sought out a neuropsychological assessment. She thought this assessment was necessary because she was concerned about Derrick's problems with attention, emotional ups and downs, problem solving, organization, memory, and academics. Derrick's mother also wanted to know if these problems were related to the FASD. Speech and language services were offered by the school district because of the neuropsychological test results, as documented in his IEP. This intervention helped him by giving him strategies to improve learning skills and access information from memory. Derrick's psychiatrist was given the results of the neuropsychological assessment. Because of these findings, he was able to "fine-tune" and enhance Derrick's course of treatment.

The Accommodation Plan

WHAT TYPES OF ACCOMMODATIONS WOULD BE HELPFUL AT SCHOOL?

The following list includes classroom accommodations evaluators may consider for students with memory weaknesses. Recall that accommodations must be chosen to match the needs of the child based on the results of a thorough assessment and a review of the student's academic and behavioral functioning within the classroom.

- Additional time to answer questions
- Additional time to process information
- Assistance with focusing from teacher
- Audiotaped lectures
- Books on tape
- Breaks (additional, extended, frequent)
- Clear and consistent instructions
- Copies of homework assignments, lecture material, and notes
- Extended time on homework, in-class work, and projects

- Minimal distractions
- Note taker
- Oral and written instructions regarding announcements/assignments
- Outline of instruction prior to class instruction
- Preferential seating
- Scheduling of more demanding academic tasks in the morning hours to prevent fatigue
- Speech-to-text software
- Study guides for quizzes/tests
- Text-to-speech software
- Videotaped class sessions
- Word processor
- Written directions

WHAT TYPES OF ACCOMMODATIONS WOULD BE HELPFUL FOR TESTS?

As discussed previously, memory impairment in children may occur along with a primary disorder such as a head injury, carbon monoxide poisoning, general cognitive delay, or ADHD. Students who exhibit memory weakness require accommodations when taking tests in school. The following options are typically considered by evaluators when assessing the student with memory challenges:

- Breaks (additional, extended, frequent)
- Extended time (with amount of time specified)
- Orientation aids
- Scratch paper to work out math problems
- Scribe
- Test setting (private, semiprivate, small group)
- Word processor

DERRICK: THREE MONTHS LATER

"The speech and language therapist is awesome! Mrs. Nelson taught me how to remember information. I told her how I couldn't remember the planets. She taught me tricks to help me remember things that are hard to learn. Mrs. Nelson said that the first letter for each word in the sentence 'My Very Excellent Mother Just Sent Us Nine Pizzas' is also the first letter for each planet in their order from the sun. After only one session, I was able to learn and remember the planets and where they are in the solar system: Mercury, Venus, Earth, Mars, Jupiter, Saturn, Uranus, Neptune, Pluto!

Mrs. Nelson also told my mom that showing me a solar system model could help my learning because I would be learning with my eyes and ears.

I used to hate studying and I'd quit all the time. It was so frustrating. By the time I had to take my tests, I felt like my mind was empty. I felt stupid because I only could write like two or three things down since I couldn't remember everything. I still don't really like studying, but now it's totally better. I can do it. Mrs. Nelson gives me the best ideas to help me remember my homework. My grades are better now and it feels good to be able to remember what I need to on quizzes and tests."

DERRICK'S MOTHER

Derrick's mother is finding that, with the appropriate support for Derrick's challenges, she is feeling happier and more confident about his ability to handle school. He is much less frustrated and emotional now when they do schoolwork. When she reminds him of the strategies, it can turn homework time into something fun. Several breaks are always necessary, but with their "tools" in hand, they find the after-school routine is much smoother. Derrick's mother knows they will need to refine the strategies and tools as Derrick ages, but she is confident that her son is making good progress.

A Word on Access to High-Stakes Examinations

The College Board does not recognize memory weaknesses as a disability category. However, we know memory difficulties typically occur along with psychiatric disorders, medical conditions, learning disabilities, and potentially even physical disabilities (like chronic pain), which *are* recognized as eligible by the College Board. These conditions may qualify for testing accommodations. Adolescents with memory weaknesses will require accommodations to "level the playing field" relative to their peers on high-stakes tests such as the SAT and ACT. For example, imagine how difficulties with working memory can impact a student's ability to follow and recall what they read in the critical reading passages of the SAT. They will have trouble answering questions in a timely fashion. When a student like Derrick takes these examinations, he will be at a disadvantage relative to his peers due to his cognitive challenges. With the appropriate documentation of memory deficits and disability, the following test accommodations may be considered for the high-stakes examinations:

- Breaks (additional, extended, frequent)
- Extended time (with amount of time specified)
- Read-alouds (electronic/human)
- Recoding of responses in test booklet

- Screens to block out distractions
- Scribe
- Test setting (private, semiprivate, small group)
- Word processor

Beyond High School

Derrick is now 19 years old. He is in trade school to obtain a certification in auto mechanics. His goal is to work his way up to a certified master technician at a dealership, and then to open his own independent shop. Derrick loves to fix cars and found out from neuropsychological and school psychological evaluations that he was a "visual" learner. This actually helps him as a technician, because he can look at mechanical things and figure out how they operate. Derrick still uses the strategies he learned in speech-language therapy on a daily basis and is more than able to compete with his peers. He received 50 percent extended time on the ACT and also was granted a semiprivate room and additional breaks when taking the examination. Derrick did well and was proud of his performance on the examination. As a result of his dedication and hard work, he was accepted in several trade schools. Yesterday, Derrick's head instructor told him that he had been offered an apprenticeship at a large car dealership. Derrick feels elated that his plan is really falling into place.

CHAPTER 6

Executive Functioning

CONDUCTING THE ORCHESTRA

At School

Bayley is 12 years old and in the seventh grade. She closes her locker and trudges down the hall to her math class. She can't believe the book report for language arts is due tomorrow. She knows she wrote it down somewhere but swears they were told another due date. Bayley wishes she could fake being sick so she could go home before lunch and get started on it right away. The wait to go home seems endless and as soon as she spots her mom parked outside of school, she can't get to the car fast enough. She feels herself about to cry and starts to run before anyone can see her. Bayley feverishly hopes her mother can help her fix this.

As soon as Bayley closes the door, her mother says, "What's the matter?" Tears begin to trickle down her face. "My book report is due tomorrow! I thought I had more time!" Bayley sobs. "Okay, change of plans. Let's head home," mother states as she drives off. Bayley calms down a bit in the car and says, "I didn't know that the book report was due this week. The teacher sprung it on us!" Mother does not respond to this, but instead asks her daughter about the book. They begin discussing the assignment so Bayley can start to write as soon as they get home. Mother is relieved that Bayley loves to read and knows the book well enough to get through this. In fact, she is always impressed at how her daughter is able to verbally summarize and interpret what she's read. However, she knows the real work will be when Bayley begins to write, since she always falls apart then. "It's gonna be a long night! I'd better get takeout for dinner," mother says as she replans the evening schedule in her head. Mother can't believe that she's spending her evening doing homework with her daughter AGAIN. Why didn't Bayley start this report a week ago? Amazingly, halfway home, Bayley asks about figure skating practice. Mother gives her "that look" and Bayley knows not to say another word.

Bayley's Mother

Bayley's mother is at school at 3:00 o'clock to take her to figure skating practice. She sees Bayley is distraught as she walks and then runs toward the car. As Bayley opens the door her mother can see the tears welling up in her eyes. When Bayley says her teacher has sprung the deadline on the class, Mother knows too well that this is not the case. She tries to hide her frustration and begins to plan the project with Bayley in the car.

She is aware Bayley's troubles have become worse since beginning middle school and now her grades are starting to suffer. Bayley is always late, disorganized, and forgetful. Today's problem seems like another "dropped ball," and this has become typical for Bayley in recent months. Bayley's mother is so confused. She feels guilty for being irritable when she has to micromanage Bayley, because Bayley is a sweetheart and truly does care about doing well. She wonders why her daughter can't track her school schedule and assignments on her own. Bayley's friends seem to do these things independently. She worries Bayley has become overly dependent on her to manage her responsibilities. Bayley's father thinks the figure skating is interfering with school. Her mother has begun to wonder if Bayley has some sort of attention or memory problem. She doesn't know whether Bayley needs some kind of help or if they just need to be stricter with her.

Grade Seven Teacher

Ms. Segal thinks that Bayley has abilities that she is not demonstrating in school. Bayley is a great reader and appears to have a deep understanding of the material, but her written work just doesn't reflect what she is able to express during class discussions. It's also hard to understand why Bayley is surprised and anxious after the class is reminded of their report deadlines. After all, she's known about them for weeks. Bayley appears scattered and arrives late to class most days of the week. Ms. Segal is frustrated because Bayley is a good kid who obviously wants to do well, yet she keeps repeating the same troublesome behaviors.

Bayley's parents recently asked her if their daughter pays attention in class. Ms. Segal watched her closely for several days and concluded that, while Bayley could pay attention during lectures, she seemed to lose focus when taking notes. She also noticed she is giving Bayley more reminders than most of her other students. Ms. Segal knows Bayley's parents are trying their best to help Bayley, but she now thinks outside help is needed.

Bayley

Bayley wants to do well in school, but it seems like there is never enough time in the day to get her assignments done. How do her friends manage so easily while she has to work so hard? She doesn't even think that anything good comes from all of her effort. People just keep telling her that she's not trying hard enough. Bayley feels exhausted and can't understand how she could "try" any harder.

There are many issues going on with Bayley. How can it be that this hard-working student is having so much trouble? Bayley is a bright girl, but she began to have noticeable difficulties in late elementary school. These problems became more pronounced as she progressed through middle school. Throughout her schooling, Bayley's mother has consistently helped to keep her organized and on schedule. Bayley is challenged in several areas: organization, managing time, planning tasks, remembering day-to-day responsibilities and assignments, and producing written work that matches her knowledge.

Bayley's case is complicated because there are so many inconsistencies. She used to get good grades, but now she does not. She can speak very intelligently, but her schoolwork does not show this. She is totally "on it" with everything regarding her figure skating, but she's scattered and forgetful with her other responsibilities. Like Claire in Chapter 4, it is the consistency of inconsistencies that confuses Bayley's parents. Many things about Bayley are positive and going well. This makes her parents think her difficulties are temporary or a result of their parenting style. Typically many of these parents are conflicted, frustrated, and disappointed because their child can't "get it together." They feel guilty because they love their child and do not want to see her struggle so much. It's time to seek outside support.

What Is Executive Functioning?

"Dwayne has a huge report coming up, which he's known about for three weeks, and he hasn't even begun to work on it."

"Jennifer is always surprised when a deadline comes up. She becomes anxious and stressed as she works on her project at the last minute."

"My son does not know how to take a test. According to his teacher, he gets caught up on a problem, spends way too much time on one question, and forgets that he has to finish all the other questions in a certain amount of time! He often ends up with incomplete answers, careless mistakes, and very sloppy work."

"The inside of Jaime's backpack is an absolute mess; he can't find his assignments because they are put in his notebook randomly. He gets overwhelmed and frustrated when he can't find things."

"My daughter is in tears over her homework because she says she can't get through her book report despite having read and understood the material. She keeps saying she's confused."

These are some examples of how trouble with executive functioning affects school-aged children. You may have heard this term if you've had a formal assessment of your child. Perhaps you have heard it from your child's educators. Executive functions are the skills that allow us to finish all the steps of a task, from beginning to completion, in order to reach a goal. You can think of it as "the process of doing." Good executive functioning involves the ability to reach goals in an efficient way. When working on a task, your ability to monitor your progress, including behavior, accuracy, and time management, is critical for success.[1,2]

What Are the Different Executive Functions?

Executive functions "manage" our complex thought processes, which is why the term "executive" is used. In other words, these functions are our brain's own managers, similar to an orchestra's conductor. Researchers have listed various abilities as executive functions. We present how they are applicable in home and school settings here:[3-5]

- Initiation: The ability to begin a task. Children who have trouble with initiation may know they have a task that needs to get done but are not able to get started unless given assistance. Examples of difficulties include:
    - Trouble starting long-term school assignments like book reports or science projects
    - Inability to begin something because they get overwhelmed when presented with a complex task or a lengthy one
    - "Shutting down" when overwhelmed and under pressure
    - Difficulty starting chores even though they have been reminded several times
    - May be accused of being lazy or procrastinating
- Planning and organization: The skills that allow us to take steps and move toward a goal in an ordered manner. This involves thinking about a task in advance, outlining the necessary steps, and effectively working toward the goal. Being able to plan and manage time is critical in successful planning and organization. Examples of difficulties include:
    - Not planning ahead for long-term projects and assignments
    - Trouble organizing and planning the necessary steps to complete assignments
    - Difficulty keeping track of assignments and tests for school
    - Trouble finding assignments in backpack or locker
    - Written work not organized
    - Schoolwork often filed in notebook in a random manner

- Self-monitoring: The ability to take stock of your thinking and behavior in a situation and the ability to change actions as the situation changes. One aspect of this skill is called "metacognition." This is how you reflect on, or think about, your own thought processes and approaches to problem solving. Researchers Peg Dawson and Richard Guare describe this as the ability to "take a bird's-eye view of oneself in a situation."[5] Another aspect of self-monitoring involves managing your emotions. Trouble with self-monitoring can cause social difficulties for the child with executive functioning problems (see Chapters 4 and 12). Examples of difficulties include:
  - Often saying inappropriate things to others without thinking first (it is *not* done with poor intentions)
  - Making careless errors
  - Talking too loudly
  - Not checking work effectively
  - Not recognizing or correcting self when something is said or done incorrectly or in error
- Working memory: As discussed in Chapter 5, this is information you need to keep in your memory for a short amount of time. Think about solving a math problem in your head. The information is in there temporarily, but you need to remember it (short-term memory) and then you need to *do* something or *work* with the information. Multitasking also involves working memory. Examples of difficulties include:
  - Trouble solving math problems in their head without the use of pencil and paper
  - Quickly "forgetting" what they've been told to do, like household chores, when they were clearly listening
  - Forgetting what they have just written about and difficulty organizing their thoughts as they continue to write
  - Forgetting the next point they were going to make in a conversation
  - Short attention span
- Flexibility: This is the ability to be adaptable in your behavior when plans change. Poor flexibility also impacts social skills functioning. Examples of problems include:
  - Trouble adapting and making a new plan when circumstances change
  - Becoming frustrated or "stressed out" when a habit or regular schedule is altered
  - Having temper outbursts, sulking, or being irritable around people other than their parents when they do not get their way or things don't go according to *their* plan
  - Believing that their way is the only way of seeing things or solving a problem
  - Getting "stuck" on an activity or problem, leading to frustration

- Not wanting to compromise with friends, leading to social difficulties
- Time management: The ability to figure out how much time is needed to get a task done and follow that timeline effectively. It requires good planning skills. Many children with time management problems struggle when they need to complete tasks quickly. Examples of problems include:
  - Inability to pace themselves on tests in school
  - Not finishing a test in the allotted time
  - Taking too long to answer individual test questions
  - Not knowing how much time is required to get each portion of their long-term project done
  - Late getting ready to leave the house, not arriving home on time, or late getting to appointments or obligations

Executive functions are very important because these abilities enable us to grow into independent and responsible adults who function well in society. Executive functions begin to show up in infancy and develop well into our twenties. This is consistent with brain maturation that continues in our twenties.[3,6] For example, the 9-month-old begins to use working memory when he or she looks for a block that has been hidden in a box. When mom and dad move that block to a new location, the baby has to ignore the desire to look in the first hiding place. The 20-year-old is in early adulthood and should be able to live almost independently, albeit with some guidance and advice from mother and father. However, when a very intelligent teenager or young adult makes poor decisions, seemingly "without thinking," it is because his or her executive functions are still under construction! Do not be alarmed because your 6-year-old is not exhibiting great executive functioning; we don't expect them to have these abilities at that age. However, some aspects of their executive functioning will be observable. It is difficult to observe impairments in executive functioning until about age 7 or 8 or possibly even later. Problems with executive functions usually appear around the third grade, when the demands of school increase. This is the time you should expect a child to *begin* independently managing his or her schoolwork, homework, and daily responsibilities. Executive functioning is progressively challenged by increasing responsibilities during the critical school transitions of first grade, third grade, middle school, and high school.

When Is the Problem a *Big* Problem?

You might become concerned when you see the following behaviors: your child seems to be "high maintenance" while other children of the same age get things done after being told only once or twice. Parents of other children do not seem to be doing so many things for their children, like reminding them to get dressed or spending so much time working on homework with them. Other children seem to know how to behave appropriately in different social situations. Perhaps you have convinced yourself you're too lenient or you have created the behavior by "babying" your child or that he or she will "grow out of it." You may worry your child was just born with a needy disposition. Maybe you think this is something you and your child must just live with.

How do you decide if your child has a real problem in this area? Typically, when teachers confirm the difficulties you are seeing at home, your child's behaviors are cause for concern. Although some of us show these behaviors every once in a while, you must decide if your child is frequently having trouble in one or more areas that are disturbing life at home, in school, and in social settings. That is, relationships, grades, self-esteem, and the ability to carry out daily activities are effortful or a struggle for your child and are being negatively impacted. Do you think you are nagging or arguing with your child more often than not? Do troubles in your relationship with your child revolve around these specific problems?

Deficits in executive functioning do not indicate a diagnosis, but are usually symptoms of a disorder. Typically, these difficulties are seen in those with ADHD, learning disabilities, autistic spectrum disorders, harmful exposures during pregnancy from heavy alcohol use or drugs, or a direct injury to the brain as a result of an accident, to name a few. Executive functions are considered a cognitive deficit that is "secondary" and co-occurs with these diagnoses. Executive functioning problems can also exist as isolated weaknesses in a child with no other cause or explanation. In Chapter 12, we will discuss deficits in executive functioning that have also been linked to difficulty with social functioning. In addition, researchers have found that children with ADHD and those having autistic-like features share common problems with executive functioning.[3,7,8]

Your child may be of average to above-average intelligence but have executive functioning problems. Basic skills such as reading, writing, and arithmetic may be fine (at least until the demands of the task or situation increase, as mentioned earlier). Your child may also be able to verbalize complex information or explain what is asked of him or her but then be unable to write what he or she knows for a book report, science project, or history paper. Your child may not be able to follow through on performing chores or other responsibilities. Impairment in executive functioning does not mean that one is unintelligent or lazy. On the contrary, these deficits become very confusing and frustrating for children and their parents *because* one can be smart and also have executive functioning deficiencies. It is possible for one or more areas of executive functioning to be a challenge for your child. For a child with impairments in intelligence or academic skills, executive functioning abilities are usually also deficient.

If these behaviors sound familiar to you, your child probably needs support for executive functioning challenges. Once you see that there are programs and interventions to improve executive functioning in your child, you may be able to breathe a sigh of relief. This support will make things easier. You will be able to tell your child, "This is not your fault. We did not realize this was something that really is a challenge for you. We know now this has been very stressful for you. We are going to help you get through this. We are going to come up with a plan." Now it is time to draw the roadmap as we mentioned in Chapter 3.

Looking Ahead

WHAT DO YOU DO NOW?

In elementary school, Bayley had some attention and organization problems that were managed easily by her teachers. A few accommodations, such as extra time for her work and frequent breaks, were implemented after a few parent-teacher conferences. In addition, Bayley's mother assisted her daughter at home with organization, planning, and time management by prompting her on a daily basis. She also reviewed her daughter's work for accuracy. As a result, Bayley's difficulties did not seriously impact her schoolwork because of her mother's daily support.

When Bayley's struggles worsened in middle school, her parents began searching for answers. They wondered about the effect of two past concussions caused by figure skating accidents. The first fall occurred in the fourth grade and the second occurred in sixth grade. On both occasions she lost consciousness. The emergency room doctor said she should recover without any problems. However, after hearing about Bayley's current difficulties, the pediatrician suggested an evaluation by a neurologist and a neuropsychologist.

As discussed previously, executive functioning difficulties are usually symptomatic of specific disorders. Bayley had some attention and executive functioning difficulties before her concussions. Following the concussions, her problems worsened. Multiple head traumas can put children at risk for what is called *persistent postconcussive syndrome.* These problems may show up later in the child's life when daily demands and school responsibilities increase. It is possible that concussions like Bayley's may make existing weaknesses more pronounced. In these instances, evaluations by a neurologist and neuropsychologist are often recommended. It is important to obtain a profile of a child's strengths and weaknesses so everyone working with the child can focus on the specific areas requiring assistance.[9,10]

Bayley's family provided the results of the neuropsychological evaluation to the school and requested a 504 plan so she could receive the recommended accommodation of extended time for tests (see Chapter 1). The neuropsychologist also recommended Bayley see a speech-language pathologist to help her learn strategies to enhance her executive functions and an educational therapist to show her ways to improve her planning and organizational skills in the classroom and at home. Bayley learned how to use an electronic planner and to prioritize homework duties at night. She worked intensively with the educational therapist for 6 months. She has "booster sessions" whenever she needs additional support from the educational therapist. Bayley is almost fully independent in using the techniques she has been taught and her parents are amazed at her accomplishments so far. She no longer needs constant prompting. Bayley has learned ways to monitor her homework load and deadlines during the week. Finally, her academic performance is more closely matching her abilities.

Bayley: One Year Later

It was very hard for Bayley to stop figure skating. Her doctor told her that the risk of more injuries was too great. Also, everyone thought she needed to focus on getting her areas of difficulty under control before having an after-school activity. Bayley likes the therapist that she's been working with to help her with strategies in school. Whenever she feels "stuck" she knows that she can go in for a session to help her get back on track. She has a great new mobile phone and she loves using the calendar and memo pad to track her assignments. Bayley's therapist also showed her how to set the alarm to remind her of project start times and for warnings before due dates. Bayley enjoyed going to the office supply store to set up her home office with colorful organizers and large calendars as another method of tracking her due dates and assignments. Bayley feels great about doing things by herself now. Schoolwork is much less stressful and she knows she can actually get her long-term projects done with only a little support from mother. Bayley is also completely excited because her parents have allowed her to enroll in dance classes. Now that she has her supports in place and an established method for dealing with her challenges, she is going to begin dancing soon.

As we have seen, Bayley required accommodations and intervention strategies for her weaknesses in executive functioning. These deficits put her at a disadvantage relative to other children in her grade. She needed accommodations in the school to give her equal access to the information being presented. The accommodations that Bayley required included those for daily classroom work, homework, and test-taking situations. In Bayley's case, in addition to school services, support was sought from professionals outside of the school.

Bayley's Mother

Mother had a hard time emotionally after seeing the specialists. Bayley took a long time to get over the loss of figure skating, and mom was sad about the loss of the one thing Bayley really loved to do. However, she slowly came to accept that the doctors, therapists, and school were working to make things easier for her. Bayley's mother is happy to see a positive change in her daughter now. They are no longer riding the emotional rollercoaster on a regular basis. She is also glad to be in the role of "mom" again instead of homework coach and nag. Bayley's pride in being able to do things on her own now also gives mother satisfaction. She can finally see the happy girl from a few years back reappearing. Whenever any of those old issues begin to become a challenge, Bayley's mother feels secure in the knowledge that they can revisit their list of strategies or see the therapist to find a way to work through it.

THE ROADMAP

What are the options for children with weaknesses in executive functioning, and who should you see to help your child? As we saw in Bayley's case, many students have executive functioning problems alongside other challenges. Bayley also has difficulties with attention and written expression. It's difficult to say which weaknesses were present before her head injuries because the demands of school hadn't challenged her yet. Nevertheless, parents are often addressing two or more problem areas at once. Bayley's parents consulted with the pediatrician, a neurologist, and then a neuropsychologist. Following these meetings, Bayley attended speech-language and educational therapies for help with interventions at school and at home. A 504 plan was put in place to formalize her accommodation of extended time.

Once you have a plan, you will need to be a strong advocate for your child. Consistency at home and school is critical. You will need to work with your child's school and other professionals as a team to provide your child with optimal access to services to overcome his or her weaknesses. Think of yourself as the "general contractor" in this relationship, because you will be coordinating communication among your child's team and ensuring the interventions and accommodations are being carried out consistently. You will also need to provide the appropriate interventions at home. This will be crucial in helping your child to eventually become independent.

The Accommodation Plan

WHAT TYPES OF ACCOMMODATIONS WOULD BE HELPFUL AT SCHOOL?

It is possible you have been providing intervention for your child's executive functioning challenges up to this point. Parents and educators often act as the child's "stand-in" executive functioning system. This occurs when you continue to remind your child of things he or she needs to do, such as homework or getting ready for school. You may also find that you are spending a lot of time helping your child through class assignments that other children are doing on their own. You may be going through your child's backpack and notebooks on a regular basis to help organize his or her belongings so assignments and school papers can be found. In fact, there is probably a lot of "doing for" your child as opposed to your child doing it him- or herself. Thoughtfully planned home and school interventions will make this work easier for you and your child. You will be able to wean your child from your support as he or she gains independence. In addition, you will have a system of "checking in" with one another. Professionals can teach you how to implement these interventions so there is less stress on you and your child.

Interventions can reduce the impact of your child's weaknesses. However, strategies must be taught *explicitly* and *systematically* so your child can learn, remember, and apply the strategies to classroom and home settings. You can think of a strategy as a plan of action to reach a goal. Research has shown that children with ADHD and executive functioning deficits may be able to accurately describe an effective strategy when doing cognitive activities but still fail to *use* the strategy.[11] Therefore, strategies need to be taught to children explicitly and implemented on a *consistent* basis to achieve success. These strategies need to become as ingrained as brushing your teeth.

Researchers have outlined specific interventions and strategies that can be implemented in classroom and home environments. For example, Torkel Klingberg and his colleagues showed that working memory (and some other associated executive functions) is enhanced in children with ADHD following cognitive-based intervention. Peg Dawson and Richard Guare as well as Lynn Meltzer also outlined several intervention and instructional strategies. In addition, teaching a student to think about the *process* of thinking and learning is critical.[1,2,5,12]

The following are frequently suggested classroom accommodations for students with executive functioning:

ADVANCE WARNING ON PROJECTS/TESTS

- Assistance with focusing from teacher
- Audiotaped lectures
- Concept or knowledge maps
- Digitized or electronic text (e-text)
- Extended time on homework, in-class work, and projects
- Note taker
- Preferential seating
- Study guides
- Videotaped class sessions
- Visual tools (outline/PowerPoint)
- Voice notepad

WHAT TYPES OF ACCOMMODATIONS WOULD BE HELPFUL FOR TESTS?

Bayley has significant difficulty with test taking for several reasons. She has trouble with sustaining her attention, time management, organization, shifting flexibly from task to task (as described earlier), planning, and checking her work. Her written expression is also affected, making writing tasks more effortful and time consuming than for the average student. Bayley needs accommodations for test taking to "level the playing field" and to give her full access to the test material so she can demonstrate what she truly knows. The following list identifies common test accommodations that are frequently suggested for students with weaknesses in executive functioning:

- Advance warning on tests
- Breaks (additional, extended, frequent)
- Extended time (with amount of time specified)
- Oral examination
- Preferential seating
- Recording on responses in test booklet
- Test setting (private, semiprivate, small group)

A Word on Access to High-Stakes Examinations

BAYLEY: FOUR YEARS LATER

"I'm really worried about the SAT. I know it will determine if I get into college or not. How will I finish this test without extended time?"

Fortunately, there are accommodations for students with limitations when taking college entrance examinations such as the SAT. As discussed in Chapter 2, Bayley and her parents will have to document her need for accommodations on these "high-stakes" examinations. Bayley has a diagnosis of ADHD, has problems with written expression, and has suffered two head injuries. Since problems with executive functioning are not a diagnosis but can coexist with other cognitive deficits, these deficits need to be explicitly documented. In addition, the evaluator must show how these problems are substantially limiting Bayley's functioning during tests compared to *most* of her peers. Bayley's evaluator may consider the following test accommodations for high-stakes examinations:

- Breaks (additional, extended, frequent)
- Extended time (with amount of time specified)
- Read-alouds (electronic/human)

- Recording of responses in test booklet
- Test setting (private, semiprivate, small group)

Beyond High School

BAYLEY'S MOTHER

"This process was very difficult for all of us. Now that we can see the results, I realize all the hard work was worth it. We had no idea Bayley's problems were such struggles for her until we were educated about her conditions. We often thought that she was just lazy. Our relationship with our daughter has gotten so much better since we sought help for her and she finally seems happy again. We are confident that Bayley will be able to achieve the things she is passionate about."

ONE YEAR LATER

Bayley decided to take a year off after high school. She did well in high school with 50 percent additional time on her school-based tests. As a result of the second neuro-psychological assessment, Bayley was allowed 50 percent extended time for the SAT examination. She did not request any other test accommodations. Bayley needed the additional time to use the strategies she had learned. She is now applying to several liberal arts colleges. Bayley is looking forward to the experience of being on her own. In addition, Bayley is no longer frustrated because she knows that she must apply her strategies on a daily basis.

CHAPTER 7

Language

WHEN THE WORDS JUST DON'T COME OUT RIGHT

At Home

Deeksha was singing to her mother. It was easier to sing her needs and wants than to talk. Deeksha always sang when she wanted something. She is 3 years old.

Deeksha's Mother

Deeksha's mother hears her daughter sing. Her mother notices her daughter really "belts it out" when she wants something. Deeksha has difficulty communicating. Her mother knew something was "a little off" when her daughter was 24 months old. She took Deeksha to the pediatrician and told him that she was a "late talker." The pediatrician determined that Deeksha knew fewer than fifty words and could not combine words into brief phrases, which he said was not typical compared to other children of her age. The physician referred them to a speech-language therapist to help Deeksha with verbal expression. Deeksha is now 3 years old. Her mother knows that her daughter is not "putting the pieces together in her brain." She observes that Deeksha approaches other children during recess but has trouble expressing herself. As a result, Deeksha becomes clearly frustrated and withdraws from the group. Her mother thinks that it is more stressful for her daughter to talk with several children compared to conversing one on one. The teachers brought up the possibility of an autistic spectrum disorder because Deeksha has trouble interacting with others when in a group. However, her mother has seen Deeksha enjoying herself when playing with neighborhood friends and she asks for playdates all the time.

Deeksha's Father

Deeksha is now 6 years old. Deeksha's father notices that his daughter still has a hard time communicating. She has trouble expressing her feelings. He is concerned that

Deeksha repeats herself when she gets frustrated. This seems to occur when she has trouble finding the correct word when talking with others. She'll say, "Remember that thing? Remember that brown fluffy thing I sleep with?" He thinks, "She knows what she wants to say. She just can't put it together." Deeksha's father notices that she plays well when playing with one friend at home. However, the teachers have told him that his daughter can't process information if there are too many children around her, such as during recess or lunch. They observe that Deeksha tends to leave the group in these situations. Deeksha's father notes, "It's too much for her and she walks away. Playing one on one is not a problem, but she shuts down when there are more than two kids in a group."

What Is a Specific Language Impairment?

"Yolanda has a 'blank' look as if she's forgotten what she just said."
"Kieran has a hard time expressing himself and I think it may be affecting him socially."
"Lily takes forever to get her point across and can take several attempts to explain what she means."
"Alejandro doesn't seem to 'pick things up' as fast as other kids his age."
"My granddaughter Malaika doesn't have many playdates. I notice that she only gets invited to birthday parties because the whole class is invited."
"My daughter says she gets all tongue tied when she can't find the word to express herself."
"Jayden mispronounces words at times, but I can usually figure it out."

These are all examples of how language problems can affect children. Impairments in language can affect social development, academic development, employment, and ultimately the quality of life. Primary or specific language impairment (SLI) is diagnosed in children who have significant weaknesses in their development of spoken language in the absence of sensory or neurodevelopmental disorders. Many children may also acquire disorders of language because of medical conditions such as head injury, stroke, brain tumors, and carbon monoxide poisoning. In addition, language disorders are found in children who have failed to develop normal language skills because of mental retardation, autism, hearing impairment, or other disorders of early brain development. SLI affects between 2 and 8 percent of children during the preschool and early school years. Boys are more affected than girls. A parental history of speech, language, and learning problems as well as limited parental education have been found to be related to elevated rates of SLI.[1-4]

For our purposes, you can think of children with SLI as having difficulty with either producing and expressing language or understanding and being receptive to language. Expressive language is illustrated by Deeksha's difficulty in thinking of the correct word when needed and in organizing her thoughts when talking. In addition, she has problems using a word in the right context. For example, when asked why she needed a babysitter, Deeksha replied, "because they won't be lonely." Her parents could often figure out what she was intending to express by the context of the comment. These children have a limited vocabulary with shortened sentences. Children with receptive language weaknesses have problems understanding what people say to them. These children typically exhibit difficulties with expressive language and have trouble understanding words, sentences, or specific words that have a meaning that is different from the literal interpretation (figurative language).

Language is complex. Difficulties with language can also affect reading and writing. Spoken and written language is linked. It has been proposed that approximately two thirds of children with oral language difficulties also have problems in the areas of reading and writing. For example, a child who has difficulties pronouncing words will typically have trouble with spelling words. In addition, a student who has problems comprehending the meaning of words and sentences will have problems with reading and written expression. Language is the "anchor" for all learning processes.[5]

What Are the Different Components of Language?

- Morphemes: This term refers to the smallest part of words that carries meaning.[6] For example, the "s" in "trees" is a morpheme. It conveys meaning because the "s" indicates more than one tree. The "s" is a very small component but changes our image of the speaker's message (tree versus trees) radically. Young children learn about morphemes by using prefixes and suffixes when they are learning to speak, read, and spell. "Pre" means *before* and "fix" means to *attach*. A prefix is attached to the beginning of a root (or base word). For example, the prefix "aud" means *sound*. Knowing this enables your child to discern the meaning of many new words immediately such as *auditorium*, *audible*, and *audiotape*. A suffix is simply an ending that is attached to a base word to form a new word. "Suf" means *under* or *below*. For example, the suffix "ing" when added to the base word *interest* makes the new word *interesting*. The suffix "let," meaning a smaller version, when added to the root word *drop* makes the word *droplet*. Children use this knowledge to build words as well as to take them apart. A child will be at a considerable disadvantage when deciphering the meaning of a word if he or she does not understand the roots of a word. Understanding the root of a word provides a direct route to speaking, reading, and writing. Children with SLI show a limited use of morphology beginning in preschool.

- Syntax: This term refers to sentence structure. You can think of syntax as the building of sentences through the use of nouns and verbs. The noun and verb are central to the organization of a simple sentence. The subject (a noun) and predicate (a verb) in the sentence tells the reader who is doing the action. Conjunctions such as *and* or *but* create more complex sentences. You may be surprised to know that understanding syntax begins relatively early in a child's life. By the age of approximately 2 years, many children start to combine words and phrases to form main clauses. A main clause is a group of words that contains a subject and a verb and expresses a complete thought. An example of a clause would be, "Mommy loves pizza," which is also a simple sentence. Throughout the preschool and primary grades of elementary school, children listen to and tell stories. During the elementary school years, children are expected to read and write.[7] Children also combine clauses into complex sentences by the middle of elementary school. It is at this time that a child's writing mirrors his or her speaking abilities because he or she is able to write sentences that are as complex and grammatically correct as those he or she speaks.[8] You can see that greater demands are placed on a child's use of syntax as the child gets older, particularly when he or she reaches school age. Understanding complex syntax is important because it is one of the basic building blocks for success within the classroom and social contexts.
- Semantics: Semantics refers to comprehension of meaning. Children who have difficulty with semantics have trouble understanding the meaning of words in sentences and text. They may also experience trouble understanding conversations. The first sign of SLI is late onset of first words, and these children typically begin to link meaning with words at a much later time than do children without SLI. It has been hypothesized that children who have problems with understanding words, such as word order and the roots of words, will experience additional trouble with understanding the meaning of sentences.[9] Some children may have difficulties with attaching meaning to what they read even though they have no problems with decoding skills (see Chapter 10). Semantic deficits can also affect oral language. Children with semantic deficits may confuse the listener because they do not know the meaning of words in conversational speech. For example, children with hyperlexia have no difficulties reading words. In fact, hyperlexic children read single words very early as a toddler or preschooler. They are fascinated by letters and numbers. However, hyperlexic children do not *understand* what they are reading. They have very poor reading comprehension and verbal language. These deficits also impact their ability to form and maintain relationships with peers and adults.
- Pragmatics: Pragmatics is defined as using language in a socially sensible way. Many parents think language difficulties have to do with articulation

problems or even the mispronunciation of words. However, pragmatics serves a vital role in initiating and maintaining communication. Pragmatics is a part of social communication (see Chapter 12). It is the nonverbal aspect of language that is so important to master. Pragmatics involves some of the following components:

- Knowledge of social norms, such as knowing what *not* to talk about in a certain setting. Some researchers think of this as the "hidden curriculum."[10]
- Knowing the purpose (intent) of the communication
- Knowing when to start, maintain, and terminate a conversation appropriately
- Making appropriate comments and asking related questions to a specific topic
- Determining what visual cues, such as gestures, and language are appropriate for certain situations
- Using appropriate sentence structure with others
- Understanding the "rules" for politeness
- Understanding how to "repair" an inappropriate comment and how to introduce other alternatives
- Knowing when to take turns when talking with others
- Providing a smooth flow of conversation and not being too repetitive or verbose when conversing with others

Let's go back to Deeksha. She not only has trouble pronouncing words but also confuses the meaning of words when conversing with others. Her peer group at school has difficulty understanding what she is trying to express to them, which increases Deeksha's frustration during social interactions. She then walks away from the group. Deeksha's problems with building words, using correct sentence structure, and understanding word meaning affect her ability to communicate with others. Deeksha may have a problem with pragmatics. However, her problems with syntax and semantics affect her overall language structure and vocabulary so much that it is difficult for her to maintain a conversation with others. Her deficits with language impact her ability to communicate with peers in a group setting. But other children, such as those on the autistic spectrum, may not have problems with syntax or semantics and yet still experience significant difficulty with the structure of social communication (pragmatics).

- Reading and writing: As mentioned previously, problems with oral language generally affect reading and written language as well. Children with SLI are usually first identified between the ages of 3 and 5 during preschool. These children have trouble with vocabulary, morphology, syntax, and pragmatics, despite other intact areas of development.

Students with SLI may also show characteristics of dyslexia (see Chapter 10). The child with SLI may not show any trouble with reading words but may experience problems interpreting the meaning of the text when asked questions about the material.

Language is a complex function because it involves several processes. Language difficulties typically coexist with other weaknesses. For example, children with language impairments more often than not have problems with executive functions, such as working memory (see Chapter 6). Working memory is critical for processing language. Children with poor working memory have difficulty "linking" words together when building sentences (syntax) and engaging in social discourse (pragmatics). You need to remember what you have said before expanding a thought in a conversation. These children may have a blank look on their faces because they forget what was just said during a conversation. In addition, weaknesses in working memory can impact reading and written expression. Children with SLI may appear slow in processing (taking in) information (see Chapter 9). Some researchers think that processing speed and attention may be critical for language development.[11] As mentioned in Chapter 4, attention and concentration are the "anchors" for all aspects of thinking.

When Is the Problem a *Big* Problem?

DEEKSHA'S MOTHER

Deeksha's mother noticed that her child had problems combining words at 24 months. She wondered whether this was a delay or her daughter was just a "late bloomer" compared to the other girls in their "Mommy and Me" group.

Parents often begin to realize that something is "a little off" when their child's first words emerge late. The general course and speed of language development in children with SLI are delayed compared to typically developing children (TDC). The first sign of SLI is the late onset of first words along with delays in understanding vocabulary. A child's delay in speaking will give you the first clue that something is "a little off." Children typically will say their first words around 12 months of age and phrases (two- or three-word combinations) by 18 to 24 months. As mentioned previously, delay in speaking tends to be genetic. If your child is late in talking there probably is another family member with the same pattern.[4]

Another sign of a potential problem with language is difficulties with pronunciation. Words may get tangled up, and it can appear that your child has a problem with articulation. Sounds may be omitted in a word or new sounds may even be added. There are three main types of articulation errors: omission of a sound, sound substitutions, and distortion of a sound. The most common articulation error seems to be sound substitutions. Articulation errors often occur in the presence of SLI because of the associated auditory and phonological processing problems. Pronouncing unfamiliar words will be difficult. As mentioned in the reading section in Chapter 10, these children will have difficulty repeating words and understanding the components of a sound/word. Getting their words out and pronouncing long and complicated words will be arduous for the child with phonological difficulties because he or she cannot access the sound structure of the word. These errors can impact speech intelligibility and hinder a child's ability to communicate.

In contrast to other issues outlined in this book, the difficulties that your child may have with language will be readily apparent to you and to others, such as teachers, neighbors, and co-workers. These difficulties usually appear prior to elementary school. In addition, the demands placed on a child's linguistic (syntax) system will exponentially increase as he or she ages.

The nature and severity of language weaknesses will vary from child to child. As mentioned previously, language disorders can occur in children with mental retardation of genetic causes, such as Down syndrome (DS) and Williams syndrome (WS), as well as children diagnosed with autistic spectrum disorders, hearing impairment, and unexpected difficulties in reading (dyslexia). Other related cognitive and social problems can result from poor communication. Children with SLI typically have been reported to experience marked difficulties in social and emotional development. This is thought to result from low frustration tolerance, lack of confidence when speaking, and peer rejection. A study by Gina Conti-Ramsden and Nicola Botting shows that social and behavioral difficulties are not short-term problems for those children with SLI and that additional problems can surface because weak pragmatic skills can impact socialization. The research also indicated that weak expressive language skills can lead to victimization. These researchers suggest that poor language skills make children with SLI vulnerable to teasing and isolation.[12] Early intervention is crucial in order to prevent additional behavioral and social difficulties as children get older.

If your child is experiencing problems with language, you may have noticed the following signs:

- Late onset of words
- Late onset of word combinations (phrases)
- Possibly their own sign language
- Mispronounced words
- Problems learning the alphabet
- Trouble learning nursery rhymes
- Confusion with the sounds of letters
- Difficulty remembering letters and numbers

- Avoidance of reading
- Avoidance of speaking
- Short phrases or sentences without much elaboration
- Trouble understanding what you are saying
- Problems finding the right word to say
- Difficulty with articulation
- Blank looks when talking to others
- Slow processing of information
- Problems following two- to three-word commands in a row without repetition
- Problems focusing because of difficulty understanding what you are saying
- Problems engaging in to-and-fro conversation in a group
- Too much or too little talk when conversing with others
- Difficulty organizing thoughts
- Apparent insensitivity to others' needs and interests
- Too loud or too soft speech
- Mental shutdown when overwhelmed
- Inability to ask for help when confused
- Trouble giving a presentation orally due to word retrieval weaknesses
- Difficulty completing tests
- Problems with reading comprehension
- Difficulty with writing sentences, paragraphs, and essays
- Lack of interaction with same-age peers although having the desire to engage
- Interruption of others on a frequent basis
- Physically aggressive acts used to handle disagreements

Looking Ahead

WHAT DO YOU DO NOW?

Deeksha's parents had her evaluated initially by the pediatrician, Dr. Pablo Satts, when she was 24 months old. Dr. Satts thought that there was indeed something going on but could not tell whether Deeksha's language difficulties were due to a primary language weakness, a motor problem, or her possibly being on the autistic spectrum. A physical examination indicated no problems. Deeksha's hearing and vision were also checked and the results were fine. Deeksha's father was relieved that his daughter's hearing was normal. He thought initially that Deeksha had a hearing problem and that was causing the language problems. Dr. Satts referred Deeksha to a speech-language therapist. The speech-language therapist, Mr. Borel, thought that Deeksha's overbite was interfering with articulation. However, he also noticed that she did not follow any simple commands that were directed to her and that Deeksha communicated only by single words such as "woof," "bye," "doggy," and "got." Mr. Borel estimated that her vocabulary was only about twenty words and that Deeksha was not using two-word phrases. The speech-language therapist concluded that Deeksha had problems with expressive and receptive language. He suggested therapy in order to improve speech-language delays in the areas of articulation, receptive-expressive language, and pragmatics.

Early intervention is critical for the child with SLI. Deeksha's parents had her continue speech-language intervention on a weekly basis. However, in preschool they discovered that their daughter had additional problems with fine motor control as she had trouble using scissors and holding a pencil correctly. Deeksha's writing was also illegible, which led to hand fatigue. Language problems typically exist with other problems and it is important to have these areas evaluated as well.

Deeksha's parents took her to an occupational therapist when she was 5 years old. They sought this consultation because of their daughter's weak fine motor skills. The therapist noted that the little girl could not copy shapes and extended her thumb while placing all of her fingers on the pencil. Deeksha used a disorganized approach when instructed to lace a card. The occupational therapist also told Deeksha's mother that her daughter required multiple prompts when activities required more than one or two steps. Occupational therapy sessions were scheduled once a week as a result of her evaluation.

Deeksha: One Year Later

In addition to receiving speech-language therapy and occupational therapy for the next year, her parents also thought that Deeksha would benefit from participating in gymnastics and karate to improve her motor skills. The interventions were productive. Deeksha is now in kindergarten and her reading and writing skills are rapidly improving. Deeksha's vocabulary is also growing and she readily engages with her peers. However, Deeksha still shuts down when overwhelmed. Deeksha's mother thinks it is interesting that her daughter is artistic and loves to sing. She "tinkers" on the piano and makes up her own songs.

The parents return to Dr. Satts when Deeksha is 6 years old. He recommends a neuropsychological evaluation because it appears that Deeksha still has some weaknesses with language and fine motor skills. Dr. Satts tells the parents that the comprehensive assessment is necessary to identify Deeksha's strengths and weaknesses in order to help her in school and to provide a roadmap for the speech and occupational therapists.

As you can see, children with SLI can present with thinking and social problems. Deeksha was performing below her age level in school and also had some difficulty interacting with her peers when in a group situation. In Deeksha's case, additional support was sought from professionals as well as from the school.

THE ROADMAP

As mentioned previously, it is crucial to obtain a roadmap. Deeksha's parents realized that their daughter required additional services and support from private therapists and the school. The therapists told them that Deeksha had weaknesses with language and fine motor skills. Her writing ability was fairly limited. In fact, Deeksha's parents noticed that she could only write the words, "i love you dad" and never wrote anything else on her own. Through seeking help for their daughter, they realized that there was a family pattern of language problems. Her mother also knew that she herself always avoided reading but was confident with math. In her job as an accountant, she did not need to rely on her weak reading ability.

Based on Dr. Satts's recommendation, Deeksha's parents decided to seek out the services of a neuropsychologist in order to identify their daughter's strengths and weaknesses and also to create the roadmap for possible participation in school-related services. The neuropsychologist's report documented continuing expressive and receptive language deficits along with associated weaknesses in syntax, semantics, and pragmatics. However, the neuropsychologist concluded that Deeksha was not on the autistic spectrum. Deeksha desired friendships, but her significant language delays prevented her from getting actively involved in social interactions at school. Deeksha said that the "girls are too fast" (their speech was fast) and that her ability to respond in a group was "too slow." The neuropsychologist also noted that Deeksha had problems with attention and concentration that were independent of the language impairments. These problems were exacerbating her difficulties with social skills. Deeksha's pediatrician and parents now had a comprehensive roadmap and a menu of specific goals and objectives. It was time to request services from additional specialists and the school district.

Deeksha's Father

"We followed the plan as outlined by the neuropsychologist. We decided to continue the speech-language and occupational services on a private basis. However, we opted to seek out a consultation with a psychologist to give us parenting strategies to decrease our daughter's frustration when interacting with others. My wife and I were slowly becoming more impatient with Deeksha and each other. I guess we just needed the support because it was not appropriate to burden our friends with our problems. We also decided to ask for an IEP [see Chapter 1] in the middle of our daughter's kindergarten year. She was 6 years old. Deeksha had another evaluation by the speech-language therapist at the school district. The speech-language therapists, occupational therapist, and IEP team met with my wife and me. We were told that Deeksha met the eligibility for 'speech-language impairment.' The IEP document indicated that our daughter had a disorder and a disability. The IEP document also described our

daughter's disability as follows: 'Deeksha's speech and language delays affect her social interactions with peers and adults and may make her speech difficult to understand at times.' The IEP recommended speech and language therapy for 200 minutes a month in a small group setting and participation in RTI [see Chapter 1]. Accommodations were identified in the IEP, such as extended time for all tests and for work in the classroom. In addition, we were told that Deeksha would be reevaluated in 3 years. I expect that the combination of private and school-based therapy will really help Deeksha come out of her shell."

The Accommodation Plan

WHAT TYPES OF ACCOMMODATIONS WOULD BE HELPFUL AT SCHOOL?

The following list identifies the types of classroom accommodations considered by evaluators when they assess children with language challenges with morphology, syntax, and semantics. Educational accommodations should match the needs of your child based on the results of a thorough assessment, review of records, and rating scales obtained from the teacher(s) and parents.

- Audiotaped lectures
- Check for understanding of information
- Clear and consistent instructions
- Copies of homework assignments, lecture material, and notes
- Extended time on in-class work, projects, and homework
- Full/partial waiver of a foreign language class (consider substituting subject with another alternative, such as studying the culture of another non-English-speaking country)
- Note taker
- Oral presentations prepared before class
- Paraphrased information
- Preferential seating
- Repetition of oral instructions (repetition of letters, numbers, and spelling patterns)
- Scribe
- Tape recorder for dictation
- Teacher engagement (checking for understanding; multisensory approach such as hearing and seeing a word, saying the word, tracing the word through touch and muscle movement, and writing the word; supported learning involving the presentation of initial sound, syllable, rhyme, and category cues immediately after new words are presented)[13]
- Typist for dictation

- Word processor
- Written directions

Classroom accommodations for children with pragmatic delays are controversial. Certain children do not seek out social interaction. As a result, it may be ineffective to teach them to be active in conversation if they do not desire the exchange. For example, some children on the autistic spectrum do not want to interact with others and prefer to play by themselves. In Deeksha's case, she is motivated to pursue relationships. She *wants* friends. However, another child with pragmatic weaknesses may have little appreciation of what a relationship is all about and lack the understanding that interacting with others can be pleasurable. Still other children may have been teased and ridiculed for many years. These children may not want to have a relationship with other peers and may, in fact, want to escape because of anxiety over social interactions (see Chapter 11). Therefore, discovering if a child actually *wants* social interactions is important before recommending interventions. Notably, social skills interventions outside of school have been shown to improve social abilities for children on the autistic spectrum.[14–16] Classroom strategies can provide a *bridge* for a student with pragmatic weaknesses. These strategies can reinforce a socially motivated child's understanding of social communication behaviors. The following list identifies strategies that could be suggested as school accommodations, which may be beneficial for helping a motivated child's use of pragmatics:

- Be aware of possible victimization (teasing and bullying). Seek consultation with the school/director when necessary.
- Do not assume that the child is able to read your intentions by your behavior. Interpret your actions for the child.
- Do not assume that the child understands interactions if he or she shows advanced language abilities. Check for the child's understanding at all times.
- Encourage the student to volunteer to talk at appropriate times.
- Establish and encourage eye-to-eye contact.
- Explicitly outline and identify behaviors to help the child greet peers, take turns, respond, and interact with peers.
- Guide peers in how to interact with the student.
- Help the child be aware of a listener's needs.
- Help the child to begin and end a conversation.
- Help the child to correct a breakdown in communication.
- Help the child with turn-taking skills and changing topics smoothly.
- Interpret situations for the student.
- Practice role-playing. Have the child consider other points of view such as from a friend, teacher, parent, and stranger.

- Social skills need to be taught systematically and explicitly by a supportive assistant/teacher or a private social skills training program outside of the school.

WHAT TYPES OF ACCOMMODATIONS WOULD BE HELPFUL FOR TESTS?

As discussed earlier, SLI is not caused by hearing problems, medical difficulties, or general developmental delay. However, language difficulties can co-occur with medical conditions. Language challenges require accommodations when taking tests in school if the weaknesses are *frequent, pervasive,* and *severe* compared to *most* children of the student's age. The accommodations are necessary in order to allow equal access to the test material and so that the student can show what he or she truly knows on a test. Many of the accommodations recommended for those students with language impairments apply to students with achievement challenges, such as reading, written expression, and mathematic disorders (see Chapter 10). An evaluator may consider the following test accommodations for the student with language disorders:

- Breaks (additional, extended, frequent)
- Extended time (with amount of time specified)
- Multiple-day testing sessions
- Oral examination
- Orientation aids
- Scratch paper
- Scribe
- Test setting (private, semiprivate, small group setting)
- Word processor

A Word on Access to High-Stakes Examinations

DEEKSHA

Deeksha is now 17 years old. Deeksha's mother is concerned about her daughter's ability to read and write quickly on tests that are timed. Deeksha has been allowed 50 percent extended time on all tests and quizzes at school. A private room is allowed, if Deeksha thinks it is necessary, for tests as well. The IEP has been in place every year since kindergarten. Her daughter has been a "B" student in all of her classes but still needs some help in the resource room. However, she is mainstreamed in music and the arts and clearly excels in these areas. Deeksha is a "visual" learner and these subjects do not involve much reading or writing. In fact, her daughter wants to pursue voice and piano at a liberal arts college. Deeksha was told that she has high cognitive abilities (HCAs) when she was in kindergarten and music comes very easily to her. Her mother understands HCAs as describing those students who are talented and advanced learners.[17] Speed is not an issue in "reading" music. Deeksha's mother asked the pediatric neuropsychologist if he thought her daughter would be an acceptable candidate for extended time for the SAT and ACT examinations. The neuropsychologist informed her Deeksha would need to be reassessed with the recommended tests that are required by the College Board and that he would complete the report after a thorough review of the educational records, IEPs, and interviews with teachers and parents. The evaluator was especially interested in Deeksha's performance on standard timed versus extended-time tests in the areas of reading and written expression.

As discussed in Chapter 2, the College Board allows reasonable testing accommodations for those students who have a *disorder* and a *disability*. Deeksha clearly needed 50 percent extended time on all of her tests, as she had documentation of decoding and fluency difficulties since the first grade. These two difficulties in combination made reading more effortful, which increased the time it took for Deeksha to complete the tests.[6] Deeksha thinks that testing in a private room is not necessary. She has rarely used this accommodation over the years and does not need or want it for the SAT and ACT examinations.

Many of the accommodations for language impairments are discussed in Chapter 10. As discussed in Chapter 2, not all students will be granted accommodations for high-stakes testing even if they have had accommodations documented on 504 plans and IEPs. The College Board is specifically interested in a student's *current* performance on tests under standard timed and extended-time conditions. In addition, the weaknesses must impact and markedly affect a student's performance on a test compared to *most* students. The disability must clearly be "blocking" a student's true performance.

Beyond High School

DEEKSHA: TWO YEARS LATER

Deeksha is now in college studying music. Because of her advanced abilities in voice, she was accepted at a music conservatory. She was allowed 50 percent extended time on any test requiring reading and written expression skills. Deeksha had been afraid that she would be the only student with a test accommodation. However, to her surprise, there are many students who also receive accommodations during tests and in class. As Deeksha learned more about her disabilities, she also found that she had many talents. She realized that composing music is easy for her as she can almost see it in her mind's eye and understands emotionally what the musical piece is all about. In addition, Deeksha does not have to rely on her memory as much, although it does still require extensive practice for her to learn and remember music for a recital. She also loves to write lyrics because it is another way to express her feelings. Deeksha takes pride in her creativity and feels at home at the conservatory. She decided to mentor children who have difficulties with reading and writing on the weekends. Talking with younger students and helping them understand their strengths is just as important as working with their weaknesses. Deeksha is honored to be in their world.

CHAPTER 8

Visual Perceptual Ability

DO YOU SEE WHAT I SEE?

Imani

Imani is 15 years old. She is staring at the page and trying to make sense of the shapes created by the various lines. Her head aches and she still does not understand how to find the oblique angles. Geometry is so frustrating! The lines do not make sense, no matter how hard she tries to see the way to the right answer. Imani slams the textbook closed and rests her forehead on the kitchen table. How will she finish her geometry questions in time for class tomorrow? Writing was always troublesome for her, but things have become worse. Now, writing her answers takes forever and her homework is always so messy because it's hard to keep her answers neat and organized. Imani feels embarrassed every time she turns her work in to Mrs. Chandler. She is struggling to keep her head above water.

Imani's Mother

Hearing the sound of the textbook slam shut, Imani's mother knows her daughter has reached her limit for the evening. She is not surprised. Math has become so tedious for Imani since the surgery to remove the brain tumor last year. Her daughter was bright and enjoyed school in the past, but now it seems as if Imani struggles each day just to keep up in ninth grade. She knows the math concepts, but it's so hard to keep the information organized on the page. Imani forgets to include numbers when she is writing her answer to a problem and she often misreads information in a graph or chart. Math is becoming more of a struggle now and Imani's mother wonders what she can do to help her daughter enjoy school again.

What Are Problems in Visual Perceptual Ability?

"Curtis has trouble drawing familiar objects, because he forgets to include something as simple as the door in the front of the house or eyes on a face."

"Tamra's writing speed is slow and she has trouble writing letters on the line. Her spacing is also uneven."

"John will omit numbers or confuse the signs on his math worksheets. When I point out the mistake, he doesn't see what I'm talking about."

"Samantha hates math. She says it takes her forever to 'show her work' and her answers are a jumbled mess on the page."

"Alex wants to play sports, but he is so clumsy! It's as if his feet and arms don't know which way to go."

Processing what we see and the physical space around us is essential for us to understand the world. As we take in information through our eyes, we actively and attentively look around our environment for the information we want, recognize the items we want to focus on (figure-ground discrimination), and combine details to recognize whole objects (visual integration). In addition, we identify the items that are familiar or new (visual discrimination) even if we cannot see the whole object (visual closure). We then accurately organize these items into appropriate categories in relation to one another (spatial relationships), such as plants versus animals. We also must remember this visual experience in order to make sense of the visual details of our world (visual memory). Impairments in visual perceptual ability can occur from a breakdown at any step of this process, and these difficulties can cause problems in a child's everyday life.[1] Children with visual perceptual problems have trouble with aspects of daily living, from writing and learning math to understanding concepts related to time and space. Furthermore, our ability to process visual information relies on other cognitive skills, such as the ability to pay attention to the relevant information in our environment, organize that information and solve problems, and remember important visual information so we can recall it later.

As mentioned earlier, we receive information from our surroundings through our eyes, and this information receives an initial level of processing before it is integrated with other information in the brain. A number of steps are required to make sense of the information we see around us, as follows:

- Spatial relationships: Processing spatial relationships allows us to understand how objects are positioned in space, including left-right orientation and rotation. Imagine a computer image that can rotate an object back and forth or left and right or turn around. Good spatial relationship skills allow you to do this in your mind's eye. Difficulties with spatial relationships can lead a child to confuse symbols like "+" and "×" or "=" and "≤" or "≥." Problems with spatial relationships may also lead to difficulties maneuvering in physical space because the child has trouble understanding the relationship between his or her body or a reference point and other points in space. Such children may have trouble navigating a maze on paper or get lost easily in stores when required to get around on their own. Poor spatial relationships can contribute to difficulty in recognizing objects if the object is presented in an unfamiliar position. For example, a child may recognize a picture of an elephant when it is presented in a forward-facing view but not recognize the same animal when it is depicted from behind.

- Visual discrimination: Visual discrimination is our ability to recognize objects based on familiar characteristics and distinguish objects from one another, even if they are presented in a busy scene. This skill allows children to recognize common shapes, learn numbers, and recognize the different math symbols. It also helps us to learn the difference between a dog and a cat and permits recognition of them whether they are presented as a line drawing or a photograph. Visual discrimination also allows us to make sense out of visual representations of numerical information, such as graphs or charts, where we must interpret the underlying meaning behind the heights of different bars.

- Figure-ground discrimination: This is the ability to focus on visual details with distractions in the background, and it is an important aspect of visual discrimination. Figure-ground discrimination allows us to identify objects in a busy picture, such as finding the cow in a farm scene, or identify letters that have been written on a chalkboard. Children with this deficit would have trouble identifying the missing objects in a "What's Wrong?" or "I Spy" puzzle.

- Visual integration: The ability to integrate the various parts of an object or scene into a meaningful whole, or *visual integration,* is a key component to visual discrimination. Some children may only perceive parts or details of an item and miss the bigger picture, while other children are only able to see the whole and miss the important details. The inability to see both the forest *and* the trees can lead many children to have problems in school. For example, a child may only focus on one step in a complex algebra problem and miss the illustration of the problem that was presented on the lower half of the page. These difficulties can make it hard for a child to stay organized in his or her approach to schoolwork or presentation of work, and can certainly impact his or her ability to learn and remember complex information.

- Visual closure: Visual discrimination also includes our ability to recognize familiar objects even when they are not presented as a whole object or fully visible. Problems with *visual closure,* or the ability to accurately analyze an incomplete visual object, can lead to problems with visual discrimination. Children with impaired visual closure skills may not recognize a face if the nose is missing or may not identify a cat if only half of its image is visible. Such limitations can make it difficult for a child to see where he or she has omitted letters in words or sections of information on a poster.

- Visual memory: The ability to accurately remember visual information is essential. We need to remember how to find our house, recognize the faces of familiar people, and remember words or symbols that we use to communicate. As discussed in Chapter 5, visual memory relies upon good attention, visual perceptual ability, executive functions, and memory skills, because you must accurately attend to, process, and organize visual information before you can remember it correctly. School instructional practices often rely on visual presentation of information while the teacher verbally explains the concept to the class. By presenting the information in two forms—visual and verbal—it is hoped that the children will process the information on a deeper level and therefore retain the information better. However, this method assumes that all children are able to adequately process and integrate visual information, which is not the case for children with visual perceptual difficulties. In addition, impairments in visual perceptual skills can impede a child's ability to remember important visual information, such as math symbols or formulas, which can impact his or her ability to recall and utilize this knowledge later.

• Visual motor integration: As mentioned before, visual perceptual skills also interact with other cognitive areas to help us lead effective lives. One key area is the integration of visual and motor information. We use visual information to guide our movements and understand where our body stands in space. Difficulties in *visual motor integration* often cause children to seem "clumsy" or uncoordinated because they bump into or drop things. These difficulties can interfere with all areas of academic or daily functioning, as problems with fine motor coordination affect a child's handwriting or ability to use a computer. Fine motor skills consist of small muscle movements that act in a coordinated manner with the eyes. Small muscle movements can involve the hands, feet, and head. Examples of fine motor activities include writing, sewing, beading, drawing, pronouncing words, and blowing bubbles. Children who have weaknesses with fine motor skills may struggle to write or type quickly and become fatigued easily. Teachers may become frustrated with these students because they are slow or their work is sloppy. These children may have trouble tying their shoes or getting dressed in the morning. Impairments in gross motor coordination can impair their ability to participate in gym class or cause them to drop their books in the hallway, leading to teasing by peers. Gross motor skills involve the large muscles of the body and are required for such activities as walking, running, hopping, lifting, and throwing a ball. Just imagine how you would feel if you were always the last one to be chosen for a team!

• Visual perceptual ability: The relationships between visual perceptual skills and attention skills or executive functions (see Chapters 4 and 6) are also key areas that can affect a child's academic functioning. Children who struggle with visual perceptual ability and attention may not see errors on their worksheets or notice that their book report is covered in food stains. Difficulties in visual perceptual skills and executive functions can cause problems in visual organization, leading to disorganized backpacks, messy bedrooms, and haphazard projects for class. Many of these children also have trouble understanding time and space, which makes it hard for them to move quickly through a large school to their next class or complete projects within a specific time.

When Is the Problem a *Big* Problem?

IMANI'S MOTHER

Imani's mother spoke with Dr. Patel, Imani's neurologist, about her daughter's increased struggles in math. She also reported that Imani is clumsier compared to her peers and she is often sad about being chosen last during team sports in gym. Imani's mother is worried that these problems are having a big impact on friendships and the self-esteem of her 15-year-old daughter. Dr. Patel told Imani's mother that difficulties in visual perceptual skills and motor integration are common for children like Imani, who had been diagnosed with neurofibromatosis type 1 (NF1). As a result of this genetic disorder, Imani developed a brain tumor in her right frontal lobe and the neurosurgeon successfully removed the tumor over one year ago. While many of Imani's weaknesses in visual perceptual and visual motor integration existed before the tumor, Dr. Patel noted that the surgery may have made things worse. Dr. Patel referred Imani to a pediatric neuropsychologist to investigate what her weaknesses and strengths are cognitively, as well as emotionally, and to further delineate how the weaknesses are impacting her ability to learn. He also recommended an ophthalmology exam to determine if Imani has any difficulties with her vision and a CT scan to ensure that no new tumors have developed. Imani's mother feels relieved to have a plan to help her daughter and hopes that these evaluations will help Imani to get on the right track.

Impaired visual perceptual skills are associated with many causes and can be related to weaknesses in other domains, such as attention and executive functioning. Poor visual perceptual skills may result from other sources, including genetic disorders such as NF1 or Williams syndrome; prenatal issues such as low birth weight, stroke, or cerebral palsy; childhood lead poisoning; infections such as childhood lupus; and autism.[2-11] In her book *The Way I See It*, Temple Grandin describes how visual processing affects individuals with autism, making it difficult to take in information from the environment or interact appropriately in social situations.[12] However, in her book *Thinking in Pictures*, Grandin says she would never give up her way of processing information as pictures because it enabled her to achieve astonishing breakthroughs in her work as an equipment designer in the livestock industry.[13]

NF1 is a genetic disorder that affects cell growth in the organs and nervous system, contributing to a wide range of cognitive impairments that include deficits in visual spatial abilities, executive functions, and motor skills. Learning difficulties are very common in individuals with NF1, as 30 to 60 percent of these individuals experience trouble with learning and academics. While NF1 lesions can affect optic nerves in some individuals, these lesions do not completely explain the visual perceptual weaknesses observed in most children with NF1. Thirty percent of children with NF1 have comorbid impairments in both visual spatial and language abilities. As a result, many of these children experience difficulties in reading, spelling, and mathematics.[2,14–18]

No matter the source of the difficulties, you may have noticed the following behaviors or signs if your child has trouble with visual perceptual skills:

- Has trouble discriminating right from left or up from down
- Confuses similar numbers or symbols, such as "6" and "9" or "+" and "×"
- Is easily lost or has trouble following spatial directions
- Has trouble completing mazes or puzzles
- Cannot read a map
- Has trouble maintaining even spacing and staying on the line while writing
- Is clumsy and often bumps into objects or people
- Has trouble learning or remembering common objects or symbols
- Cannot find a certain object in a complex picture of multiple items, such as in the game "I Spy"
- Cannot recognize objects when they are partially hidden or incomplete
- Has trouble staying organized when showing his or her work on long math problems
- Omits key items from a picture when drawing, such as forgetting to include the windows on a house
- Has trouble tracking moving objects, such as items on a computer screen or a ball rolling toward him or her
- Has difficulty copying items from the board in class

Looking Ahead

WHAT DO YOU DO NOW?

If you have been concerned about similar behaviors in your child, an evaluation may be warranted to determine if these difficulties are *frequent, pervasive,* and *severe* enough to affect your child's ability to perform academic and daily living skills. Imani's mother noticed how much her daughter was struggling in school as a result of her challenges. Asking her child's neurologist for help was the first step in determining whether a formal evaluation was necessary. Input from your child and his or her teacher can also be helpful in moving forward.

Grade Nine Teacher
Mrs. Chandler is concerned about Imani's increasing difficulties in school. Imani often asks to stay in the classroom during lunch in order to keep working on math problems.

While Mrs. Chandler appreciates Imani's dedication to her studies, she also worries that Imani is pushing herself too hard—and missing out on important time to social- ize with her friends. During one lunch hour, Mrs. Chandler sat down with Imani to see if she could determine where the problem was. She asked Imani to complete some math problems that were incorrect on last night's math homework. Imani had trouble finding the right information on the graph of sales figures for three pet stores and couldn't keep her numbers lined up correctly when completing a long division problem. As she worked, Mrs. Chandler noticed that Imani knew the right steps, but her diffi- culties understanding visual information and keeping her work organized did not allow her to show her knowledge. She is aware of Imani's recent surgery and can now see that her student is struggling and needs help in order to stay on grade level.

THE ROADMAP

In order to understand your child's difficulties related to processing visual perceptual information, it is important to obtain the necessary evaluations, as outlined in Chapter 3. This will provide the "roadmap" of your child's strengths and weaknesses. Because difficulties with visual perceptual skills can impact many areas of academic and daily functioning, it is essential to understand the specific areas in which your child is struggling. It is also important to know whether your child's weakness in visual perceptual skills is contributing to other problems, such as poor memory, impaired motor coordination, perfor- mance anxiety, or social isolation.

As noted previously, visual perceptual ability can be impacted by weak- nesses in other areas, such as attention or executive functioning (see Chapters 4 and 6). Difficulties in attention can contribute to increased problems focus- ing on visual information. Poor organization skills can further impair our ability to analyze visual information or present information in an organized manner. A comprehensive evaluation—in addition to a vision examination— will determine which factors are contributing to, or are being affected by, your child's poor visual perceptual skills.

Evaluation by an occupational therapist would also be warranted for chil- dren like Imani. Occupational therapy focuses on treating problems with fine motor and perceptual development that interfere with play, school perfor- mance, and a child's ability to take care of daily activities, such as dressing and eating. Imani worked with an occupational therapist immediately after her surgery and her mother knows the therapist made a big difference in helping Imani's motor weakness. Imani's mother decided to get her daughter evaluated by an occupational therapist as soon as possible because she had been told that early intervention is ideal. The "wait and see" approach may not be in the best interest of the child and the family who must cope with their child's frustration on a daily basis. Imani's mother decided that she would not hesitate to ask for a second opinion about her child's care. Parents should ask for a second opinion if their child's pediatrician or other treatment provider does not suggest a referral for further evaluation or is not able to respond to questions and concerns. You need to be proactive about advocating for your child.

The Accommodation Plan

WHAT TYPES OF ACCOMMODATIONS WOULD BE HELPFUL AT SCHOOL?

Each child will have a specific pattern of visual perceptual strengths and weaknesses. For example, one child may only have trouble with spatial organization, while another may struggle with visual motor integration. Each intervention should be tailored to the child's set of specific needs.

It is important to note that many strategies for weaknesses in other areas, such as attention or memory, encourage the use of visual cues or visualization to improve comprehension or retention of information. Such visualization techniques may not be effective for children with visual perceptual difficulties. In contrast, many strategies for visual perceptual weakness focus on the use of verbalization to improve learning. With a solid understanding of your child's strengths and weaknesses, you will be able to choose accommodations that best suit his or her learning profile.

The following list provides classroom accommodations an evaluator might consider when assessing a child with visual perceptual difficulties:

- Abbreviation expander to reduce fatigue when taking notes (a software program that allows a child to type an abbreviation for commonly used words and phrases with the program completing the word or phrase)
- Calculator
- Color cues to reduce confusion between easily reversed numbers and symbols
- Copies of homework assignments, lecture material, and notes
- Educational facilitator (to ensure that the child is not lost in the halls or tardy to class)
- Examples of what is expected (showing an example of work on a long division problem, so the student can refer back to it when necessary)
- Extended time on homework, in-class work, and projects
- Graph paper (to improve linear organization of responses to math problems or enhance organization of writing by allowing the child to put one letter per block)
- Increased amount of space between items on a worksheet to reduce the amount of extra information on the page

- Note taker
- Oral presentations
- Orientation aids (allow the child to use a guide, such as a "window" cut into a blank piece of paper or a ruler, which allows him or her to focus on one line of text or set of numbers at a time while blocking out extraneous information)
- Outline of instruction prior to class instruction
- Paper divided into distinct sections to help maintain focus on an item
- Preferential seating
- Proofreading assistance (allow child to proofread first for legibility, second for spelling, third for punctuation, and last for content)
- Recorder (digital/tape)
- Scribe
- Speech-to-text software
- Talking calculator
- Tape recorder for dictation
- Typist for dictation
- Wide-lined paper or paper with raised lines
- Word processor
- Writing preference flexibility (allow the student to write in either print or cursive, whichever is fastest and most comfortable for him or her)
- Writing tool flexibility (allow the student to choose his or her writing tool, such as a pencil or pen)
- Written directions

As noted previously, many children with visual perceptual weaknesses also have trouble with attention (see Chapter 4), executive functioning (see Chapter 6), and memory (see Chapter 5). You are encouraged to read these chapters as well to determine if additional accommodations could be helpful for your child.

WHAT TYPES OF ACCOMMODATIONS WOULD BE HELPFUL FOR TESTS?

For Imani, problems with visual perceptual skills were contributing to poor math performance, as well as significant frustration and helplessness with school. In addition to help in the everyday classroom, she benefited from accommodations in test situations as well. The following list provides the test accommodations that might be considered by an evaluator when assessing a student with visual perceptual processing difficulties:

- Calculator
- Extended time (with amount of time specified)

- Graph paper
- Lined paper
- Oral examination
- Scribe
- Speech-to-text software
- Talking calculator
- Test setting (private, semiprivate, small group)
- Word processor

Imani

Imani laughs loudly with her friends during lunch. She forgot how much fun it was to spend time with her friends! Since her evaluation, Imani is receiving extra help at school through her IEP, including occupational therapy and resource help for math. She is working with her occupational therapist to improve her ability to understand visual information and write more fluidly. She gets a copy of her friend's notes so she can just focus on the board in class and is allowed to type her assignments on the classroom computer. She still works slowly, but Mrs. Chandler is nice and allows her to go to the resource room to read quietly if she doesn't finish as quickly as the other students. Imani is allowed 50 percent extra time to complete her work on tests, which helps her to feel less nervous. When she gets a math worksheet, she immediately uses her ruler to draw a grid around each item. It's a trick she learned—and it helps her to put her answers in the right place. Imani is also allowed to use graph paper rather than notebook paper when she completes math problems from the textbook. Imani is starting to enjoy school again and is proud that she's found a way to see things that works for her!

A Word on Access to High-Stakes Examinations

IMANI

As she moves through high school, Imani maintains her passion for learning and recognizes her dream of becoming a kindergarten teacher so that she can help other children, like herself, who struggle to learn. Imani knows she will need to go to college and obtain a teaching credential. She also worries about the SAT. Imani has been allowed to use the computer and graph paper for many years. Imani is scared that she will fail the SAT without the accommodations.

IMANI'S MOTHER

Imani's mother is aware of her daughter's desire to attend college as well as her fears about the SAT. After talking to Dr. Patel and Imani's occupational therapist, she realizes that Imani may need additional testing in order to document the accommodations she needs to be successful on the SAT. Imani's mother begins to collect the necessary records and report cards for the neuropsychologist because she knows she must supply all the data she can to prove her daughter's need for additional support.

As described in Chapter 2, the need for accommodations for high-stakes testing must be based on a comprehensive evaluation of your child's current functioning. There may even be different accommodations for Imani, and an updated assessment could identify further areas of need. Imani's neuropsychologist considered the following options for educational accommodations for her SAT examination:

- Audio recording with large-print figure supplement
- Audio recording with raised-line (tactile) figure supplement
- Calculator
- Enlarged font on computer monitor
- Extended time at 50 percent
- Graph paper
- Large-block answer sheet (the student is not required to fill in the bubbles)
- Large-print answer sheet
- Large-print test
- Lined paper
- Scribe (recorder and writer of answers)
- Tape recorder for dictation
- Test setting (private, semiprivate, small group)
- Word processor

IMANI

As she finished the SAT, Imani felt confident that she performed at her best. The 50 percent extra time and the ability to use a computer helped her to stay organized and focused. Imani was grateful that she could show what she truly knew when provided with the accommodations. She thought, "I nailed it!"

Beyond High School

IMANI

"I'm now in college and I had my last surgery three years ago. All went well and my tumor has stopped growing. I still see my neurologist every five months or so, and she told me that my prognosis is good. I applied to several colleges and I want to get my teaching certificate some day. My goal is to become a kindergarten teacher. I feel like I have a lot to give and would like to work with kids with special needs, too. I learned all about assistive technology when I was in tenth grade and these tools 'opened the

door' for me in so many ways. I was evaluated at that time and told that I could benefit from several technologies. First, I learned to use a word processor with speech-to-text and text-to-speech software. This software really helped me to express my thoughts because I did not have to write. The software did it for me! I also benefited from the computer reading text to me. The text-to-speech software kept me interested in the chapters I was reading and I understood the information better, too. The assistive technology evaluator also told me about digitized text, which allowed me to access any type of book. All of these tools were helpful. I talk about them all of the time and I have helped other students who have challenges. I know that my future is 'wide open' now."

CHAPTER 9

Visual Processing Speed

WHEN YOU JUST CAN'T GET YOUR WORK DONE FAST ENOUGH

At School

Emma is 10 years old and taking a test in the fourth grade. She used to be nervous about finishing tests on time. Her teacher talked with her one month ago and told her she could have additional time to complete all tests. Emma felt so relieved! She is able to complete all tests now that she has the extra time. Emma doesn't have those butterflies in her stomach anymore! Tests no longer scare her.

EMMA'S TEACHER

Emma's teacher, Mrs. Franklin, teaches fourth grade at a private school. Mrs. Franklin was told that Emma was diagnosed with a reading disorder. She knows that Emma has trouble completing quizzes and tests on time. In fact, Emma sometimes had to finish her tests during recess or after school. Mrs. Franklin attended a recent meeting with the lower school director and Emma's parents in order to discuss what other options were available to help Emma finish tests. As a result of this meeting, Emma was granted the accommodation of 50 percent extended time for all tests and quizzes. Fortunately, Emma accepts the need for this accommodation and, in fact, has blossomed because of it. Mrs. Franklin is glad Emma truly understands her weaknesses and makes good use of the additional time. The teacher knows that this awareness is called "metacognition" (see Chapter 6). Understanding her weaknesses also helps Emma check the accuracy of her work (proofread), which has improved her test scores.

What Is Visual Processing Speed?

"Ari can't complete tests or quizzes on time. I wonder if he has problems with focusing."

"Brandon has trouble staying on task in order to complete assignments."

"My son takes about four to five hours a night to complete his homework and he is only 10 years old. I wonder what will happen when Brad is 16."

"Hannah gets so tired at night. It seems like homework takes so long. I feel like a 'helicopter parent.' I have to hover over her to make sure it gets done."

"My grandson John would rather use the computer than handwrite essays. I'm wondering if there is something wrong. It seems that using the computer is easier for him and his thoughts just flow out of his brain."

"My daughter never finishes her tests in time and, on top of that, she makes careless errors. Anna is really smart but her grades on tests do not reflect what she truly knows. It is different if you quiz her orally; then she knows the answer."

Processing speed refers to the quickness and efficiency with which you can process or take in information. The term "processing speed" can be conceptualized in many ways. For example, speed can refer to your reaction time when driving a car and stopping quickly in an emergency. It can also be thought of as cognitive efficiency, which refers to the accuracy in processing certain types of information. For example, many children with ADHD rush when taking a test and easily finish within the allotted time. However, they will make many errors. Weak cognitive efficiency undermines their overall test performance. Children who are cognitively efficient may be able to learn more accurately and rapidly. That, in turn, enhances their performance on many tasks because they expend less energy learning new material. As discussed in Chapters 7 and 10, processing speed and working memory are important for the understanding and production of spoken language.[1]

One aspect of processing speed is visual in nature. We define visual processing speed as the ability to quickly take in visual information and process it rapidly. Concentration and rapid eye-hand coordination (writing) are important factors for visual processing speed.[2] Visual-motor integration is eye-hand coordination. This is required for tasks such as handwriting, copying information from the board, and drawing. A child can have difficulties with either the visual or motor component of processing speed (see Chapter 8). Weaknesses in visual processing speed typically impact a student's speed on a timed test.

Difficulties with processing speed can coexist with other disorders such as SLI and disabilities in the areas of reading, written expression, and mathematics. Processing speed weaknesses can occur in children having medical conditions such as traumatic brain injury, very low birth weight, or very premature birth. Trouble with processing speed can also impact students who have been diagnosed with depression, attention, bipolar, and autistic spectrum conditions.[3–12]

Visual processing speed impairments typically coexist with thinking, behavioral, and emotional challenges. Researchers have found that most children on the autistic or bipolar spectrums or who have problems with attention and concentration also have learning disabilities and associated problems with processing speed, attention, and fine motor problems. They also found that the majority of children with ADHD and autism show weaknesses in the areas of learning, attention, graphomotor (coordination of small muscle movements in the fingers and eyes when writing), and processing speed.[10,11] These latter weaknesses are clustered predominantly in children who have ADHD or are high functioning on the autistic spectrum, as opposed to children who are anxious, depressed, or oppositional. Children having trouble with processing speed also manifest mental fatigue and exhibit problems with the rate and efficiency of learning, comprehension of new information, and speed of performance.[13]

Visual processing speed affects many thinking processes. Children like Emma with visual processing speed impairments usually have problems with executive functioning, such as working memory, because processing efficiency is critical for this function (see Chapter 6). Working memory is important for taking in language once language is acquired (see Chapter 7). In addition, working memory is critical for processing information quickly and for holding verbal information in short-term memory. Processing speed also overlaps with attention. Problems with attention and concentration probably exacerbate a child's troubles with completing tasks and tests in a timely manner. The processes of executive functioning, attention and concentration, and processing speed are synergistic and inseparable. Understanding the role of each of these functions will help you guide your child toward receiving the appropriate accommodations in school.

When Is the Problem a *Big* Problem?

EMMA'S MOTHER

Emma's mother knew there was a problem when her daughter was in the third grade. Emma had no trouble reading words. But she read slowly. In addition, Emma did not like to read and considered it boring. She avoided reading because it took so long to read a paragraph. Homework was a chore because it took Emma several hours to complete any assignment involving reading. She had Emma read to her every evening. It was even stressful to listen to her read. The problem seemed to worsen when her daughter was required to complete in-class work or a test within a specific time. It was the timed aspect of tests that distressed Emma because she could not read fast enough.

Emma has marked problems with visual processing speed. These problems occur *frequently* and are *pervasive* when completing assignments or tests in class or working on homework. Emma's troubles are also *severe* and affect her performance academically. Typically, the first sign that something is "a little off" is the inability to complete work in class and tests in the time allowed. You may also observe that your child has difficulty taking in new information and that he or she tires quickly. These children typically learn less material in the same amount of time as their peers and require additional time and prompting to learn the material. Children like Emma may become quite frustrated, anxious, and fatigued when working on a lengthy assignment. This fatigue can also result in them rushing to complete their work, or they may avoid it altogether. This may result in many errors even when they know the material.

If your child is experiencing problems with visual processing speed, you may have noticed the following signs:

- Problems completing tests on time
- Difficulties completing in-class work on time
- Lengthy periods of time to complete homework compared to peers
- Expressing frustration that homework and class work assignments are too long
- Staying in from recess to complete class work
- Being sent home with work not completed in class
- Incomplete assignment books
- Sloppy handwriting
- Complaining that copying from the board is too tiring
- Complaining that the class work is too hard
- Asking that new information be repeated
- Avoiding classroom work and homework
- Complaining of headaches, nausea, and stomachaches

Looking Ahead

WHAT DO YOU DO NOW?

Emma's Mother
Emma's mother was referred to a pediatric neuropsychologist by the director at her daughter's private school. This was a good idea because many different issues, such as weak focusing skills, could have been responsible for her daughter's problems with completing work in a timely manner. It seems like Emma is a happy kid. However, her mother wondered if there was something "going on" that she was not aware of. The neuropsychologist recommended that Emma have a vision examination from a pediatric ophthalmologist before coming in for her evaluation, because Emma had not had her vision checked recently. The examination found her vision to be normal. The neuropsychologist then assessed Emma and discovered that she was not a fluent reader

and had trouble with visual processing speed as well. Everything made sense! Emma had a real problem with speed and her problems with not finishing work were not because she was lazy or unmotivated. The mother decided to call the director at Emma's school to discuss the test results. The assessment provided her with tools to help her daughter.

THE ROADMAP

As mentioned previously, obtaining a roadmap is important for several reasons. For Emma, the assessment by the neuropsychologist was crucial in order to map out her strengths and weaknesses academically and cognitively. We have shown that visual processing speed disorders can be accompanied by problems with attention and concentration, executive functioning, graphomotor skills, and learning disabilities. Also, difficulties with visual processing speed can undermine a child's ability to show what he or she truly knows on a timed test. Children like Emma may be candidates for additional time to complete tests and class work at school when assessment reveals significant problems in this area.

By now, you probably understand that weaknesses in visual processing speed do not exist alone. For children on the autistic spectrum or those having difficulties with attention and concentration, an examination of attention skills, graphomotor skills, executive functioning, and processing speed is necessary. Researchers think these areas are of significant concern with respect to academic functioning, and early identification of problems is necessary to support effective intervention.[11]

The Accommodation Plan

WHAT TYPES OF ACCOMMODATIONS WOULD BE HELPFUL AT SCHOOL?

The following list identifies the classroom accommodations that Emma's neuropsychologist considered in light of her weaknesses in visual processing:

- Additional time to answer questions
- Additional time to process information
- Audiotaped lectures
- Books on tape
- Copies of homework assignments, lecture material, and notes
- Extended time on homework, in-class work, and projects
- Large assignments broken into smaller assignments

- Note taker
- Outline of instruction prior to class instruction
- Paraphrased information
- Preferential seating
- Proofreading assistance
- Read-alouds (electronic/human)
- Repetition of oral instructions
- Speech-to-text software
- Tape recorder for dictation
- Text-to-speech software
- Typist for dictation
- Visual tools (outlines/PowerPoint) used in conjunction with oral instruction
- Word processor
- Written directions

WHAT TYPES OF ACCOMMODATIONS WOULD BE HELPFUL FOR TESTS?

As discussed previously, visual processing impairments can occur with other associated weaknesses with working memory, attention and concentration, and graphomotor skills. These areas need to be assessed and considered when a student shows difficulty completing a test. Many of the test accommodations recommended for children exhibiting reading, writing, and math impairments also apply to those with visual processing impairments because these weaknesses may affect fluency (see Chapter 10). Emma's evaluator considered the following test accommodations:

- Breaks (additional, extended, frequent)
- Extended time (with amount of time specified)
- Read-alouds (electronic/human)
- Scribe
- Test setting (private, semiprivate, small group)
- Word processor

A Word on Access to High-Stakes Examinations

EMMA: SIX YEARS LATER

"I decided not to take the SAT test. My heart was not into it. My interests really involve hair and makeup for theater and television. That is the career I really want to dive into. I will be attending beauty school after graduation and I'm looking

forward to it. I know I will need to take the state board test in order to enter the business world in the television industry. I'm glad I can apply for extended time for the written part of the test. I know I need 50 percent additional time because of my problems with reading quickly and putting my thoughts down on paper."

Accommodations for high-stakes examinations are necessary so a student can show what he or she truly knows. Accommodations for reading, writing, and math fluency deficits are discussed in Chapter 10. As mentioned earlier, visual processing difficulties can affect these areas and directly impact a student's performance on timed tests. Several of the accommodations that are suggested, particularly extended time, are critical for students who have difficulties with decoding, understanding vocabulary, and understanding semantics because these problems slow down the reading process. Similarly, extended time for written expression is critical because of difficulties producing written text. Extended time for students with math disorders is necessary because of the associated deficits in working memory, processing speed, or even language that impact their rate of processing mathematical information.[14] Again, extended time is not a modification. It does not change any expectations with respect to the materials learned. In addition, as discussed in Chapter 2, extended time is not going to enhance a student's performance if he or she does not know the test material.

The following list of test accommodations was considered by Emma's evaluator:

- Breaks (additional, extended, frequent)
- Extended time (with amount of time specified)
- Multiple-day testing sessions
- Read-alouds (electronic/human)
- Scribe
- Speech-to-text software
- Test setting (private, semiprivate, small group)
- Text-to-speech software
- Word processor

Beyond High School

EMMA

"I attended a beauty school for makeup artist training. It was a great experience. I had to work for 1,600 hours in order to sit for my license. I discovered there is a written examination to become a licensed cosmetologist. The fact that I had to read scared me. However, I applied for extra time even though I was going to be taking the

test on a computer. I sent the board all of my documentation about my previous accommodations as well as the evaluation I had back in fourth grade. The board told me that I needed to be retested. The report from the neuropsychologist was very helpful. I found out that I improved in many areas but there were still problems with reading quickly. The bottom line is that I was allowed 50 percent extra time on the test, and that was a relief. This reminded me of school all over again. However, it was okay. I did well on the test and now I can work in television doing makeup. I'm doing really well because I work with my hands and I really enjoy working with people. It's so interesting."

CHAPTER 10

Achievement

READING: THE GATEWAY TO INFORMATION

At Home

Nine-year-old Jonathan slams the book on the table. He has had enough! Jonathan is really trying but he always has difficulty sounding out words that he has not memorized. He turns to his mother and says, "Mom. This is taking too long. Can you help me? I don't want to do this now. Can I go play?"

Jonathan's Mother

"It is always frustrating to help Jonathan with his homework. Thirty minutes of homework turns into two hours of homework. That's a lot for a third grader! He has trouble reading unfamiliar words and skips, substitutes, and misreads 'small' words such as 'an,' 'the,' and 'that.' Jonathan even skips entire lines of reading. He does not like to read out loud and avoids any type of reading. However, Jonathan loves to be read to. He even likes to talk about what the characters are thinking and feeling when I read to him at night."

Grade Three Teacher

Mr. Olson is concerned because Jonathan is still struggling with reading. He should be reading to learn and not learning to read at this point. Jonathan is falling further behind. Mr. Olson notices that Jonathan cannot finish tests on time and is having problems reading math word problems. His spelling is poor. Jonathan can only spell words that he has memorized. He has trouble completing in-class assignments and often has to stay behind during recess to complete them. However, Mr. Olson knows that Jonathan has excellent reasoning skills and understands the material when the text is read to him. Jonathan has no difficulties using a computer. He also has no trouble figuring out math (non–word problems). In fact, Jonathan's classmates ask for his help when they have problems with these areas.

What Is Reading?

Children need to develop three skills in order to become successful and independent readers. They must be able to sound out words (decoding), read rapidly and effortlessly (fluency), and understand the text (comprehension).

- Decoding: Children with decoding challenges lack the ability to distinguish sounds within spoken words or syllables. They have difficulty processing the sounds of speech or the units of language, called phonemes. For example, they may experience problems hearing the beginning "s" sound or last "n" sound of a word such as *sun*. They may also have trouble hearing the separate words that come together to make the words *airplane* and *pancake*. These children can struggle to blend sounds together or rhyme. They will experience difficulty sounding out unfamiliar words. Children with decoding weaknesses do not have the "key" to accessing the words on a page.
- Reading fluency: Children can have a reading disorder if they read accurately but not fluently. The word *fluency* refers to the ability to read words and text quickly and automatically. An "automatic reader" reads words without hesitation and at a quick pace. Fluency also involves anticipating what is coming next in the text. Fluent reading incorporates many factors such as executive functioning, as discussed in Chapter 6. Jonathan has significant difficulties with fluency on many levels. For example, he has problems reading single words in a fast and accurate manner. As a result, Jonathan is not an automatic reader. A child must be a fluent reader to grasp the meaning of text in an efficient manner. Those who are not fluent readers tire easily and become overwhelmed as text material increases in complexity. When the process of reading text is slow and effortful, it negatively affects reading comprehension because so much concentration and effort are spent on reading the words. Jonathan uses the context of a paragraph to help him decode words. This tedious process leaves him no energy to think about what he is reading. As a result, Jonathan has to reread text in order to understand the meaning of the words and text overall.
- Reading comprehension: Even accurate and fluent readers can suffer from deficits with reading comprehension skills. Conversely, some children have difficulty with reading comprehension skills because they are not accurate and fluent readers. All of these children experience problems understanding what they read and typically do not enjoy reading. Understanding the meaning of what they read is challenging because

they frequently miss the point of the text. These children may also have problems with self-awareness; they may not be cognizant of the fact that they do not understand what they are reading. This is referred to as *meta-cognition* (see Chapter 6). This process is critical because children with good metacognitive skills think about what they are reading and whether or not it makes sense to them.[1] If not, they will reread the material and try to make sense of the text. You can think of reading comprehension as a child's ability to understand the *big* picture of what he or she reads.

Children with a breakdown in any of these categories are classified as dyslexic. The term "dyslexia" refers to an *unexpected difficulty in reading*. What does unexpected mean in this instance? Dyslexia is not the result of a lack of motivation or sensory impairment such as vision problems. It is also not a consequence of inadequate instruction or other conditions, such as an emotional disturbance or a cultural or economic disadvantage. A reading disorder is "unexpected" in light of the child having adequate cognitive abilities and effective classroom instruction. In other words, a child who is healthy, motivated, and taught to read may still struggle with reading. The International Dyslexia Association defines dyslexia as follows:

> Dyslexia is a specific learning disability that is neurobiological in origin. It is characterized by difficulties with accurate and/or fluent word recognition and by poor spelling and decoding abilities. These difficulties typically result from a deficit in the phonological component of language that is often unexpected in relation to other cognitive abilities and the provision of effective classroom instruction. Secondary consequences may include problems in reading comprehension and reduced reading experience that can impede growth of vocabulary and background knowledge.[2]

It is estimated that reading disorders affect 5 to 17.5 percent of children, and approximately 75 to 90 percent of students with a learning disability have dyslexia. It is an inherited condition and affects both males and females. Brain imaging studies show neurobiological evidence for these difficulties. Researchers have examined how the brain functions while an individual reads, and differences have been detected between dyslexic and nondyslexic individuals.[3-5] Dyslexia is a broad-based learning disability that affects word reading, spelling, and written expression. One can only imagine the challenges that Jonathan faces on a daily basis in school. It seems that school targets every weakness he has, both in the classroom and in test taking.

Reading is a complex function that involves many processes, and children with reading difficulties will frequently exhibit weaknesses in other areas such as attention, concentration, language, motor skills, writing, spelling, and mathematics. Secondary difficulties such as anxiety or depression can arise since these children can become quite frustrated in the classroom. As with other functions, a reading disorder does not necessarily exist by itself.

When Is the Problem a *Big* Problem?

A reading disorder is chronic. A child will not "grow out" of a reading disorder. In fact, a reading disorder will worsen over time without intervention because text material and classroom expectations increase in complexity and quantity. Neuropsychologist Jack Fletcher and his colleagues describe children with reading problems as existing at the extreme end of a continuum from poor readers to good readers.[6] It is the *frequency, pervasiveness,* and *severity* of the reading problem that negatively impact a child's functioning at school. Early intervention is the key to *unlocking* the reading process for the child before frustration sets in.

You may suspect that your child has reading difficulties if you observe many of the following signs:

- Family history of reading difficulties
- Speaking late developmentally
- Difficulties pronouncing words
- Problems understanding rhymes
- Avoiding games involving rhymes
- Trouble sounding out unfamiliar words
- Problems coming up with the right word when expressing thoughts
- Using a word that sounds like the desired word
- Problems recalling the names of letters
- Difficulty understanding the sounds of letters
- Problems blending sounds
- Avoiding the reading process
- Relying on memorizing words
- Difficulties retaining more complex words that have been memorized
- Substituting, misreading, and skipping words in a reading passage
- Effortful reading with the child verbalizing frustration
- Difficulty spelling words
- Problems understanding a math word problem
- Difficulty writing an essay
- Problems with handwriting skills
- Excellent understanding of reading material when discussing the material with another individual

- No problems understanding text when read to orally
- Difficulties completing tests and quizzes that involve reading
- Rushing through a test
- Becoming easily overwhelmed when reading
- Becoming fatigued when reading lengthy text
- Inability to complete questions involving reading comprehension and spending too long on a problem
- Failure to grasp the main point of a story due to words that cannot be read
- Trouble analyzing text in depth
- Difficulty drawing conclusions from information not directly stated but suggested in the information presented
- No problems answering concrete questions about the material, but difficulties comparing and contrasting ideas and concepts as well as predicting future ideas and questions
- Problems with attention and concentration on tasks involving reading
- Feeling embarrassed when reading or presenting orally in front of a class
- Difficulties with foreign languages

Children with reading challenges also have multiple strengths. These strengths are frequently overlooked in the classroom because reading skills are critical for learning and, ultimately, academic success. You may observe that your child is able to grasp the big picture of material when the text is discussed *actively* with you. Your child may have excellent reasoning skills. He or she might show excellence in all areas not dependent on reading. Students with disabilities share, upon graduation from high school, characteristics such as resiliency, determination, and resourcefulness due to the struggles they have had with learning weaknesses.[7] These characteristics are critical for the successful implementation of interventions and accommodations.

THE ROADMAP

Jonathan's mother decided to visit the pediatrician for a physical examination. She initially thought that her son had vision problems. She was relieved when the pediatrician assured her that Jonathan's vision was fine. The physician then suggested the service of a neuropsychologist. A neuropsychological examination was sought to investigate Jonathan's strengths and weaknesses on measures of intellectual, cognitive, achievement, and social-emotional functioning. For Jonathan, this type of evaluation was a good second step in order to analyze his specific strengths and weaknesses so the team could identify suitable interventions. All of these areas needed to be assessed because Jonathan was also experiencing difficulties with handwriting, attention, and concentration. A comprehensive evaluation, exploring all processes, is critical for the child who presents with attention and learning challenges.[8,9]

The neuropsychological assessment revealed that Jonathan had a reading disorder, a writing disorder, and marked problems with attention and concentration. One of the things the neuropsychologist did was to have Jonathan read out loud. Jonathan read with effort; it was apparent that the reading process was not automatic for him. The *frequency, pervasiveness,* and *severity* of the weaknesses were of interest to the neuropsychologist. Jonathan was having problems with reading despite his high intellect, good reasoning skills, and competent classroom instruction. A psychoeducational evaluation was also done at school because Jonathan's parents and teachers were concerned that Jonathan was not successfully accessing the curriculum within the classroom. The school psychologist conducted his assessment of Jonathan. The achievement test results were consistent with those of the neuropsychologist. Jonathan was eligible for special education and other services at school based on his specific deficits and areas of need as documented in the reports. His needs were outlined in the IEP (see Chapter 1). Jonathan is given intensive and structured reading intervention at school four days a week, plus occupational therapy for his handwriting difficulties. The IEP documented the interventions that are implemented in the classroom, including the need for frequent monitoring of his reading skills as supported by research.[4] In addition, the educational therapist works with Jonathan on Saturdays for two hours to enhance study and test preparation skills.

Jonathan's Father

"We now have a plan. The reading specialist described Jonathan's program as explicit and systematic. She is teaching my son how letters relate to sounds step by step. He is starting to understand how different letters relate to each other, using pictures to help him. She is also helping Jonathan with spelling and vocabulary. There's lots of practice with reading and writing in the classroom and at home. In addition, my son is seeing an occupational therapist, who is helping him to write better. Jonathan used to grip his pencils very tightly to the point of making holes through the paper. We are going to continue both interventions through the summer. Jonathan feels a lot better now. He was always a smart, motivated kid. Now he is starting to shine!"

The Accommodation Plan

WHAT TYPES OF ACCOMMODATIONS WOULD BE HELPFUL AT SCHOOL?

Accommodations are critical for students with learning and cognitive disabilities to provide them *access* to classroom instruction and allow them to show what they know when taking a test (see Chapter 2). Evidence-based reading intervention is not the sole answer for helping a student with a reading disorder. It is the combination of evidence-based reading interventions and accommodations that provides the *bridge* to helping these students realize their potential to "level the playing field" when competing with nondisabled peers.

Dr. Sally Shaywitz and her colleagues propose three types of accommodations for the reading-disabled student. These accommodations are "(a) those that bypass the reading difficulty by providing information through an auditory mode, (b) those that provide compensatory assistive technologies, and (c) those that provide additional time so that the dysfluent reader can demonstrate their knowledge."[5] Examples of accommodations that compensate for reading difficulties include active discussion of the reading material and books on tape. Read-alouds, such as a human reader and text-to-speech software, provide auditory (spoken) information to the student. Many students prefer the use of read-alouds because the method encourages *active* reading and helps them to focus on the material. Read-aloud accommodations are commonly used for students with reading disabilities. However, read-alouds are controversial. Although many students use some type of assistive technology, there has been limited research investigating the impact of assistive technology on learning and test performance.[5,10,11] Options for assistive technology accommodations for classroom and test-taking contexts are presented in Appendix 3. Options for classroom accommodations are listed in Appendix 1.

Extended time is an accommodation frequently used by children with a reading disorder. The benefits of additional time for the child with decoding, fluency, and reading comprehension difficulties are well documented. Many students need extended time because of their use of additional tools, such as read-alouds and e-text.[5,11] It is also necessary because many students have co-occurring weaknesses such as problems with executive functioning and difficulties maintaining attention (see Chapters 6 and 4, respectively). These challenges fetter a child's ability to *manage* time effectively when completing homework and class work.

Jonathan's evaluator considered the following classroom accommodations as well as others (see Appendix 1):

- Abbreviation expander
- Books on tape
- Breaks (additional, extended, frequent)
- Digitized or electronic text
- Embedded e-text support
- Enlarged-print text
- Extended time on homework, in-class work, and projects
- Full/partial waiver of a foreign language class

- Grammar checker
- Minimal distractions
- Note taker
- Oral presentations prepared before class
- Orientation aids
- Outline of instruction prior to class instruction
- Peer assistance for in-class assignments
- Preferential seating
- Private learning space (when reading material out loud)
- Read-alouds (electronic/human)
- Speech-to-text software
- Spell checker
- Spelling not graded
- Tape recorder for dictation
- Teacher engagement (discussing material to enhance understanding)
- Text-to-speech software
- Typist for dictation
- Visual tools (outlines/PowerPoint) used in conjunction with oral instruction
- Word prediction software
- Word processor

WHAT TYPES OF ACCOMMODATIONS WOULD BE HELPFUL ON TESTS?

Testing accommodations are necessary for children with decoding, fluency, or reading comprehension challenges. Extended time is the *gateway* to *accessing* test material, which allows a student to show what he or she knows. Extended time is the most common accommodation for children having these problems, as well as for students with other learning disabilities. Read-alouds are controversial for test taking.[11,12] Options for test accommodations are listed in Appendix 2.

An evaluator may consider the following test accommodations for the student with a reading disability:

- Breaks (additional, extended, frequent)
- Extended time (with amount of time specified)
- One examination per day
- Read-alouds (electronic/human)
- Scribe
- Test setting (private, semiprivate, small group)
- Word processor

A Word on Access to High-Stakes Examinations

GRADE TEN: JONATHAN AND HIS TEACHER

Mrs. Gross met with Jonathan and suggested that he apply for extended time for the SAT examination. She explained to Jonathan that he would need extra time because of his difficulties with reading quickly. The fact that he needs additional time is not surprising, even though Jonathan reads words accurately. The reading program he took several years ago was productive for him. Jonathan is a dedicated student who works very hard and has benefited from extended time of 50 percent throughout the years on classroom tests and assignments. In fact, Jonathan has used this additional time fully on every test where reading is required. Jonathan got over his embarrassment of using extra time as he understands his reading disorder has nothing to do with his intelligence or motivation. But Jonathan will need to be reassessed because his previous assessment was conducted more than five years ago. Jonathan knows he will need the extra time because he would not be able to complete the SAT otherwise, as he is a very slow reader.

Extended time is a frequently requested accommodation for the SAT and other high-stakes tests for those students with reading disabilities. This accommodation does not alter the nature of a test. Several researchers have indicated that extended time does not improve a student's performance on a test if he or she does not know the material.[13] Jonathan had an IEP early on in his schooling and was later phased out of the IEP because he had made substantial progress in school. A 504 plan was then implemented and Jonathan was provided with accommodations for test taking and for classroom instruction within a general education–based classroom. Extended time for the SAT, ACT, and other ETS examinations are not considered a modification, but an accommodation.

The need for 50 percent extended time was based on Jonathan's reading disability (fluency) and its substantial impact on any task requiring reading, along with his long-standing history of using this accommodation. Unfortunately, there are no formal guidelines or tests for an evaluator to determine the exact percentage of time a student needs on an examination. It has been proposed that the percentage requested be based on a student's own experience over the years.[5] Other researchers have suggested that additional time, from time and a half (50 percent) to double time (100 percent), is a good place to start and should provide enough time for students with a learning disability to complete a test.[14] The determination of how much additional time is necessary as well as additional accommodations to access print material should be decided by an evaluator who reviews all aspects of a student's educational career, current testing results, and present functioning in test-taking and classroom situations. A thorough review of all previous accommodations is necessary to understand in what way the accommodations will serve to "level the playing field" in order for a student to compete fairly with peers. The evaluator also needs to provide a rationale for the requested accommodations. Requested accommodations must be reasonable, with the student's preferred accommodations considered based on the identification of a disorder and a disability, as discussed in Chapters 1 and 2. In fact, the examiner's fullest comprehension of a child's profile is necessary to identify the most appropriate and effective test accommodations.[11]

Jonathan's evaluator considered the following accommodations for the high-stakes examination:

- Breaks (additional, extended, frequent)
- Extended time at 50 percent
- Private room
- Read-aloud (human reader)

Beyond High School

Jonathan is now 19 years old. He is in his first year at college. Jonathan continues to struggle with reading material quickly and automatically. However, his grades have not been affected because he has been granted 50 percent extended time on all tests. The disability center also allows him the opportunity to take tests in a quiet classroom so distractibility is not a concern now. Jonathan uses electronic read-alouds for all texts and is learning to use software to help him outline texts. Everyone uses a computer at college, so Jonathan's handwriting is no longer a problem. Jonathan's organizational skills have improved. He prefers to organize all papers and review his work for the upcoming week daily. Jonathan has also learned to advocate (speak up) for his needs and is not afraid to ask questions during class. He plans on taking the Graduate Management Admission Test (GMAT) after college and would like to enter the field of marketing.

Students with reading challenges face difficulties after high school because a reading disability is chronic. However, the majority of students can be taught to read if they are provided with explicit and systematic instruction. This type of approach refers to a step-by-step preplanned and organized method of reading instruction based on research. Direct instruction techniques as well as the incorporation of strategies to enhance reading are typically used with the older student.[15] Accommodations should be based on a student's strengths and weaknesses as determined by comprehensive assessment. The overall interpretation of the assessment must take into account all aspects of a student's history and not just the current test scores (see Chapter 3). Linking assessment findings to interventions and accommodations will open the gateway to reading and the student's overall success within the educational system.

Written Expression: Getting It All Down on Paper

Sara: At School

Sara's hand hurts. It is 10:30 on Tuesday morning and she is taking a test in her fifth-grade Language Arts class. Sara's stomach also hurts and now her head is pounding. Everything is hurting! Sara looks to her right and sees that her good friend, Katie, is almost done with her essay. Sara doesn't like to write because, not only does it hurt her hand, but also it just takes too much time. She knows her penmanship is sloppy. Sara also has problems getting her thoughts down on paper. She knows the information and studied really hard for the test. It just seems like it comes out all wrong on paper. She really is trying to do her best. Sara feels paralyzed at this moment and starts to blink her eyes. Now she really feels stressed. This blinking is going to slow her down even more. Sara wishes that she could just talk to the teacher and tell him the answer to the essay question. That would be a lot easier. On top of that, Sara is now thinking about her basketball game tonight. Five minutes pass. "Time's up," Mr. Levinson states. Sara looks down at her paper. She did not get very far. Mom and dad are really going to be upset now. Sara's stomach hurts even more.

Sara's Teacher

Mr. Levinson gathers up all of the papers in the classroom. He notices Sara in the back of the classroom. She is the first student out of her chair and is running out of the classroom. Sara looks like she is in a big hurry. Mr. Levinson reviews Sara's paper. Sara wrote very little on the essay question. In fact, Mr. Levinson sees she wrote only one paragraph and her ideas are not organized or well developed. Mr. Levinson also observes that Sara's writing is sloppy and illegible. Although Mr. Levinson allowed fifteen minutes to write the essay, Sara did not finish. He has noticed a discrepancy between Sara's grades on multiple-choice examinations compared to essay examinations even though she is very intelligent. Mr. Levinson decides he must call Sara's parents. He doesn't quite understand how a student can have so many good ideas but can't write them down on paper.

Sara's Friend

Katie looks to her left. There was Sara blinking her eyes nonstop. Uh oh! That always means Sara is stressed. Katie wishes she could just take the test for her. Sara has complained to her that it is hard to get her thoughts down on paper. Sara has also said her father helps her too much with her homework. She would really like to be left alone. Katie decides to talk to her mother about it. Maybe her mother can talk to Katie's parents. Katie is her good friend. She has to help her.

What Is Written Expression?

"I had to buy different scissors. My son has had a lot of problems cutting with normal scissors and coloring inside lines."

"The only thing that Trisha can't do besides handwriting is button her shirts. I try to buy pullovers. It makes it easier for her."

"I'm so tired of this. I think it all has to do with motivation. Wendell's papers are always messy. It seems like he doesn't care to do well. Plus, he erases all of the time. Wendell even puts holes in the paper."

"Will can't copy from the blackboard. Maybe I should give him my notes."

"Homework takes forever. My daughter is spending two hours a night on homework. It should only take one hour."

"Aaron can't get it from his head to the paper. Not only does he have problems with spelling, but also his hand hurts all the time whenever he has to write."

"It's a stream of consciousness when Martha writes. She'll capitalize in the wrong spots in a sentence. There is very little organization throughout. My daughter just falls apart when she has to write an essay."

Written expression is important for learning and success in the classroom. Children who are unable to write well are at a considerable disadvantage. Students with difficulties in writing are unable to move forward with their learning. Their grades and their self-esteem can suffer. Approximately 10 to 15 percent of school-age children are estimated to have a learning disability. About 70 percent of these children have disabilities relative to reading and writing. In addition, 72 percent of fourth-grade and 69 percent of eighth-grade students cannot write at their grade level.[16,17] These statistics highlight that parents and teachers need to provide individualized attention to children who have challenges with written expression.

The writing process involves many functions, such as handwriting, spelling, and composition skills. A weakness in one area will hamper other areas of the writing process. For example, Sara has no difficulties expressing her thoughts orally, but she has trouble translating her thoughts into written form. Sara's difficulties with handwriting, planning, and organization impede her writing process. Her speed of handwriting is slow and she has trouble organizing her thoughts onto paper. Because of these difficulties, Sara gets distracted, which leads to a lack of motivation.

Underlying the aforementioned three major functions (handwriting, spelling, and composition) are spoken language, reading skills, attention and concentration skills, memory skills, and executive functioning skills. Composition may be affected by poor planning and organization, working memory, or self-monitoring (see Chapter 6). Poor time management can also affect a student's ability to write fluently during a timed examination. There is a symbiotic relationship between spoken language and written expression skills. Approximately two thirds of children who have difficulty expressing their thoughts orally also have problems with reading and writing.[18] A child's motivation can also affect the writing process. Some students do not like to write because it takes too much time to fully write down their thoughts. It is essential to identify the specific area(s) that impact a student's ability to demonstrate what they know through writing. Let us examine the major functions required for writing.

- Handwriting: Why is handwriting so important these days, since technology is dominating our world? Children are texting, e-mailing, and instant messaging all the time. However, students are still required to write at school. Writing is a basic and necessary skill in our day-to-day functioning that cannot be replaced entirely by technology. Fluent handwriting is a fundamental skill of written expression. The fluency (or pace) of handwriting determines your ability to write productively. Poor motor coordination can also slow writing. Children like Sara do not like to write. Sara must concentrate on *how* she writes, and that leads to frustration and fatigue. Difficulties in writing can be caused by poor motor abilities, poor visual-perceptual skills, or problems remembering the shapes of letters. Poor handwriting can also occur in the absence of a reading disorder.
- Spelling: Spelling refers to the ability to write a word in print. Problems with spelling frequently accompany reading disorders. Students with decoding problems have difficulties linking sounds to words and have not figured out the alphabetic code when spelling. Children in kindergarten are just learning about sound-letter relationships. They listen to speech sounds and spell as they hear the sound (invented spelling). By age 8, students understand sound-letter/word relationships and word patterns. Higher level instruction focuses on word meanings and word origins. Children with spelling challenges take more time to recall the motor and orthographic patterns needed to spell the words. *Orthography* is the spelling patterns that correspond to spoken words and also refers to the writing system of a language.
- Composition: This refers to the ability to write a sentence or compose an essay fluently. Writing is a multistep process. A child may struggle with handwriting, spelling, combining words to form sentences (syntax), or producing grammatically correct sentences. A child must be able to use words in context and understand the rules of grammar and mechanics, such as capitalization and punctuation. Writing at the composition level refers to the organization of a student's ideas when writing reports, essays, short stories, and poetry. Students like Sara can struggle to produce a well-written sentence and also lack the organizational skills required to create an essay that accurately conveys their thoughts. Essay writing depends on coordinating several interrelated processes. Students

have to initiate, plan, organize thoughts and sentences, remember what has already been written, anticipate future thoughts, and revise and self-correct errors. They also need to be aware of for whom they are writing (audience) and if their ideas are coming across in a logical manner. This awareness is referred to as *metacognition* (see Chapter 6). Students also need to understand the information they read before they can accurately write about it and correct their errors when proofing their work. Fluency is another part of writing composition. Sara's difficulties with handwriting skills and writing at the sentence level, along with her challenges with executive functioning, such as metacognition and attention, all play a part in her inability to complete her essays on time.

When Is the Problem a *Big* Problem?

SARA'S MOTHER AND TEACHER

Sara's mother spoke with Mr. Levinson that night. Without his call, she would not have known about the severity of her daughter's struggles at school. Sara's mother told Mr. Levinson that Sara was diagnosed with Tourette's syndrome (TS) when she was 6 years old. Sara was placed on medication initially because she would blink repetitively, especially in times of stress. Sara developed other tics (repetitive behaviors) involving throat clearing about six months ago. These tics wax and wane during times of stress. The neurologist, Dr. Reed, told her that Sara's problems with motor skills, such as using scissors and a pencil, and her difficulties with sustaining attention and keeping on task were related to the TS. He said Sara would probably have problems with executive functioning as well. The medication worked well, but Sara still has difficulties with handwriting and organizing her thoughts, especially on timed tests. Mr. Levinson suggested a school meeting to discuss how to help her. Sara's mother thinks that is a good idea. It seems that the tests, homework, and projects are getting more difficult. Recently Sara told her that she felt pressured all of the time, and her eye blinking is back.

Difficulties with written expression can occur with neurological conditions, such as TS. These difficulties typically co-occur with reading, math, and language-based disorders. It is not unusual for children with expressive and receptive language disorders to also have difficulties with written expression, as described in Chapter 7. Children with ADHD can struggle with written expression because some of them have difficulties with executive functioning and handwriting as well.

If your child has difficulties with handwriting, you may notice the following warning signs:

- Sloppy and illegible handwriting
- Letters of varying size, too small, or too large
- Crowding letters when writing

- Difficulty writing within the lines of the paper
- Trouble cutting with scissors and coloring inside lines
- Clumsy when using eating utensils
- Awkward pencil grip
- Excessive force/pressure on pencil when writing
- Clumsy in sports such as catching and throwing a ball
- Difficulty copying information from the board
- Computation errors due to poorly aligned numbers
- Complaints of hand and arm hurting when writing
- Too much time on any task requiring writing, including homework
- Requests for you to write for your child
- Brief essays; minimal sentences and text composition
- Complaints of being unable to finish tests on time
- Requests to use the computer for tasks requiring writing

If your child is experiencing difficulties with spelling and composition, you may notice the following warning signs:

- Letter additions
- Numbers and letters written backwards in a child who is 9 years of age or older
- Letters or key words left out when writing
- Reversed sequence of letters
- Vowel and consonant substitutions
- Poor letter formation and size
- Difficulties with initiating the writing process
- Difficulties with grammar and sentence structure
- Difficulties selecting the right word when using a spell checker
- Scanty sentence or essay composition
- Hastiness in getting the "job" done
- Problems developing and organizing ideas
- Difficulties staying on task
- Difficulties completing classroom assignments and tests on time
- Problems self-correcting when making an error
- Reliance on peers and adults to check work
- Difficulties with taking notes and keeping pace when listening to teacher's lecture
- Reliance on peers for notes
- Avoidance of any writing task
- Poor strategies for checking errors on written work
- Good verbal ability, but difficulty with reading

It is important to consider the age of the child when determining whether the problem is a *big problem*. Children go through several stages when learning to spell. A child may attempt to spell in kindergarten or even in preschool. Your preschool child may try to copy you when writing. You may see numbers and letters written backwards. This is not abnormal. In fact, your child may use invented spelling, which is encouraged at that age by educators, to enhance phonemic awareness. However, inaccurate spelling may be a warning sign of a problem in grade two. At this age, the teachers may notice a child is having trouble progressing in reading and in spelling familiar and unfamiliar words. The child may also have messy and illegible handwriting. Problems with speaking, such as difficulty pronouncing long words, may provide a clue that something is "a little off" with written expression.

Difficulties with written expression are not invisible. You will be able to see your child's challenges if he or she struggles with these areas. If you suspect a problem, seek an assessment to identify what is specifically underlying your child's struggles with written expression.

THE ROADMAP

Sara's mother decided to contact her daughter's teacher. She also made an appointment with the neurologist, Dr. Reed. He decided to review Sara's medications because of her additional co-occurring challenges with attention and concentration. He referred them to an occupational therapist for an assessment and to an educational therapist. The occupational therapist agreed with Dr. Reed that Sara had significant problems with handwriting and other motor skills, which affected daily activities such as buttoning clothes and using eating utensils properly. The occupational therapist determined that a six-month intervention plan would help Sara to enhance her handwriting. The educational therapist met with Sara twice a week and focused on written expression. She also taught Sara how to use speech recognition programs such as speech-to-text software. This software allows Sara to dictate into a headset microphone and her speech is then converted into print on her computer screen. This is a fantastic boon for Sara! The assistive technology also helps Sara to plan, organize, and produce her thoughts efficiently without her handwriting throwing a curveball into the process. In addition, the educational therapist gave Sara typing lessons to increase her typing speed because Sara prefers to use a computer when writing.

Sara's Mother
Mr. Levinson told Sara's mother that Sara did not need special education but would benefit from accommodations that would "level the playing field" for Sara. Sara's mother requested a 504 plan to formalize the accommodations. The 504 documentation listed several accommodations for Sara. Sara's parents are pleased that everyone is helping their daughter to do her very best at school. They also really appreciate Mr. Levinson's role in bringing this about. Without his call, they would not have known about the severity of Sara's struggles at school.

Coming up with the right plan is the key. Problems with written expression are typically interwoven with other weaknesses. It is up to you, as the parent-advocate, to establish what is underlying your child's challenges and to implement the suggested intervention or accommodation plan.

The Accommodation Plan

WHAT TYPES OF ACCOMMODATIONS WOULD BE HELPFUL AT SCHOOL?

Accommodations are necessary for students who have challenges pertaining to reading and math and also for those who have difficulties with written expression. Options for classroom accommodations are listed in Appendix 1.

Sara's evaluator considered the following list of classroom accommodations because of her difficulties with written expression skills:

- Abbreviation expander
- Alternate keyboard
- Audiotaped lectures
- Concept or knowledge maps
- Extended time on homework, in-class work, and projects
- Graphic organizers
- Note taker
- Preferential seating
- Proofreading assistance
- Recorder (digital/tape)
- Scribe
- Spelling not graded
- Speech-to-text software
- Text-to-speech software
- Visual tools (outlines/PowerPoint) used in conjunction with oral instruction
- Voice recognition software
- Word prediction software
- Word processor with spell checker
- Writing preference flexibility
- Writing tool flexibility

WHAT TYPES OF ACCOMMODATIONS WOULD BE HELPFUL FOR TESTS?

For students exhibiting difficulties with written expression, taking a timed test is frustrating and nerve wracking. This can increase test-taking anxiety.

Sara has problems with attention, concentration, motor skills, and executive functioning due to her TS. Sara's handwriting skills have improved because of the occupational therapy. Her hand no longer hurts when she writes because the therapist taught her the proper grip to use. The occupational therapist used handwriting instruction that enhanced her letter-naming, copying, and letter-writing pace.[19] But Sara still experiences the eye-blinking tics that hinder her ability to stay focused. Assessments from a pediatric neuropsychologist and educational remediation therapist indicated that she needed accommodations during tests so that she could truly show what she knew.

Sara's evaluator considered the following test accommodations because of her primary problems with written expression:

- Ability to point to answers
- Alternate keyboard
- Breaks (additional, extended, frequent)
- Calculator
- Extended time (with amount of time specified)
- Large-print answer sheet
- Large-print test
- Multiple-choice format
- Multiple-day testing sessions
- Preferential seating
- Read-alouds (electronic/human)
- Scribe (recorder and writer of answers)
- Speech-to-text software
- Tape recorder for dictation
- Test setting (private, semiprivate, small group)
- Text-to-speech software
- Voice recognition software
- Word processor
- Writing in test booklet

A Word on Access to High-Stakes Examinations

SARA: SIX YEARS LATER

"I need to get another assessment for SAT accommodations. The testing done when I was younger is out of date. I know exactly what I need to do well on the SAT. I have been getting almost straight A's at school. I will never be able to show what I know if I am not allowed extended time and the use of a computer on tests. I feel anxious, but everyone who takes these big tests feels that way, too. I know I will be able to complete the SAT with 50 percent additional time. I use every minute of the extended

time on tests. I could never finish it without the extra time. Thank goodness for accommodations!"

Accommodations are vital for students like Sara. Sara has a medical disorder along with co-occurring weaknesses that are typical of TS. Sara's challenges impede her from showing what she truly knows when she is tested without extended time. The neuropsychologist documented that Sara has disorders *and* disabilities. The accommodation of 50 percent extended time was granted to Sara on the high-stakes examination. Sara knows that colleges place a significant amount of weight on her SAT and ACT results. The extended time allows her to reveal her knowledge, rather than penalizing her because she cannot complete the test in the regular time allotted.

Extra time for adolescents with a learning disability is an appropriate and reasonable accommodation. There is strong empirical support for the accommodation of extended time for students with writing disabilities. There is also solid empirical evidence for the use of a word processor when taking a test.[11,20,21] Using a word processor decreases the frustration caused by slow and effortful handwriting. This slowness can hurt a student's ability to write thoughts down quickly and automatically. These students often report that "their thoughts are faster than their hands." Many students use a spell checker, word prediction software, voice (speech) recognition software, and text-to-speech software to help them express what they know on paper. These tools enhance the performances of those students with written expression disorders.[11]

Evaluators may consider the following accommodations for the high-stakes examination for a student with a written expression disability:

- Ability to point to answers
- Alternate keyboard
- Breaks (additional, extended, frequent)
- Calculator
- Extended time (with amount of time specified)
- Large-print answer sheet
- Large-print test
- Multiple-choice format
- Multiple-day testing sessions
- Preferential seating
- Read-alouds (electronic/human)
- Scribe
- Speech-to-text software
- Tape recorder for dictation
- Test setting (private, semiprivate, small group)
- Text-to-speech software

- Voice recognition software
- Word processor
- Writing in test booklet

Beyond High School

SARA: FIRST YEAR OF COLLEGE

"My college reviewed my neuropsychological testing results along with the letter from my educational remediation therapist. I was granted 50 percent extended time, one examination per day, permission to take a test in a private room at the learning support center, and the use of my computer for all tests requiring essays. I did not receive 50 percent extended time for math courses because those courses do not involve much handwriting. I will have these accommodations through college. I hope to attend graduate school someday. I'm glad that I will have the opportunity to do so even though I have disabilities."

Mathematics: When the Numbers Don't Add Up

Charlie

"Seven plus 4 is. . . 1, 2, 3. . . ." Charlie counted number by number up to seven and was about to continue when he heard, "Stop. Put your pencils down!" Mr. Wilson watched from the front of the classroom as Charlie sighed, looking at his paper. He had only completed eight of the twenty-five problems. He hated math. It took so long for him to count out each problem. "Now pass your paper to your partner," Mr. Wilson said. Charlie looked at his eight completed problems and wondered how many would get red X's from his partner.

Grade Two Teacher

Mr. Wilson collected all the papers and looked for Charlie's worksheet in the stack. He only finished eight problems—and four of them were wrong. Charlie's first-grade teacher had warned Mr. Wilson that math was a struggle for Charlie. She had noticed Charlie's difficulty understanding relationships between numbers as well as concepts related to subtraction and addition. When Mr. Wilson began to introduce basic math facts to his class, Charlie needed more repetition than the other children and always relied on counting with his fingers, which slowed him down on timed quizzes. Mr. Wilson knows that Charlie is quickly falling behind and he wonders how best to help Charlie to develop good basic math skills.

Charlie's Father

When Charlie walks through the door after school, his father knows something is wrong. "What's up, champ?" he asked. "I failed another math quiz, Dad. I hate math!" Charlie pouts, dropping his backpack on the floor and collapsing on the couch. Charlie's father worried—would his son struggle the way he had in school? He remembered how difficult school was for him and how it led him to get a job after graduation rather than pursuing college. He wanted more for Charlie, but how could he help him build his math skills?

What Is Mathematics?

"I can practice multiplication tables with Dylan for hours, but he forgets everything the next day during the test."

"My daughter doesn't understand how numbers relate to each other. She always needs to count on her fingers to figure out an answer. That won't work in real life."

"When Grant is working on his math homework, he forgets parts of the problem. It's like he can't hold all the information in his head."

"Word problems are overwhelming for Taylor. She gets bogged down in silly details and can't figure out which parts matter in order to solve the problem."

Difficulties in mathematics can be caused by struggles in a variety of different areas, both cognitive and academic. Children with *dyscalculia*, a mathematics learning disability (MLD), can grapple with aspects of mathematics itself, such as understanding how numbers relate to each other, or they can struggle in areas that are the foundation for understanding and completing math problems, such as attention, language, memory, and executive functions. A simple math problem requires you to read and understand the problem (this is even more challenging for word problems), select the appropriate strategy for solving the given problem, ignore aspects of the problem that are irrelevant, remember the essential details required to compute the answer, process the information in a rapid and organized fashion, and produce the answer in the appropriate format. Then you have to remember to double-check your work to make sure you performed everything correctly. Many children with poor executive functioning (see Chapter 6) often forget this last step, which contributes to poor performance. Solving a math problem is a complicated process!

To be successful in math, a child must master each of these skills and learn to use them appropriately. With so many potential pitfalls, it's no wonder that

5 to 8 percent of children have some form of mathematical learning disability. The 2008 National Mathematics Advisory Panel highlighted the need to improve mathematics instruction in the United States. A 2004 US Department of Education report found 27 percent of eighth-graders could not correctly shade one third of a rectangle and 45 percent could not solve a word problem that required dividing fractions. The panel noted that basic mathematical skills acquired during elementary school, such as fluent addition and subtraction of whole numbers and proficiency comparing decimals and fractions, are key building blocks for the acquisition of algebra skills. Charlie's father's concerns regarding his son's math difficulties affecting college are valid. Charlie's ability to complete high school Algebra II will improve his chance for enrollment in a four-year college.[22-26]

When Is the Problem a *Big* Problem?

David Geary, a psychologist at the University of Missouri, proposes that children with MLD have difficulties in three common areas: (1) learning to accurately use math procedures such as addition and subtraction, (2) retrieving math facts from memory, or (3) representing or interpreting spatial mathematical information such as geometry problems.[22,27] When children are first introduced to mathematics in kindergarten, they use procedures like counting on their fingers or number lines to solve simple math problems. As they grow older, they shift from a reliance on counting to the memorization of math facts and concepts that can be recalled and used fluidly to solve math problems.

Parents and teachers often recognize a child is struggling with mathematics in early elementary school, when instruction focuses on how numbers relate to each other as well as memorization of basic math facts. In kindergarten, poor performance is often associated with difficulty paying attention or poor instruction rather than a learning disability.[28] As mathematics instruction becomes more complex during first grade, teachers and parents notice that some children do not learn quicker or use more sophisticated methods for solving math problems. For example, although Charlie is in the second grade, he continues to count on his fingers, starting at the number 1, when trying to solve a basic math problem. He is also apt to make errors when retrieving the simple math fact "7 + 4 = 11" from memory. Charlie's ineffective and tiring problem-solving strategy causes him to move slowly through the quiz. This results in fewer questions completed in the allotted time. In addition, this process takes up "space" in his head that could be used for other tasks, such as holding the right information in mind (working memory) and checking to make sure he has completed the problem correctly.

Because mathematics is complicated, many children experience difficulties with some aspect of math during school. Such difficulties become concerning to parents and teachers when the problems occur *frequently*, are *pervasive* when solving different math tasks, and are *severe* enough to impact a child's school performance, self-esteem, and motivation. Charlie's difficulty with numerical relationships was noticed in kindergarten when his first-grade teacher observed consistently poor scores on assessments of basic math facts, such as simple addition and subtraction skills. His father also saw how Charlie's struggle affected his self-esteem and desire to learn mathematics. These are clear signs that something needs to be done to help Charlie succeed in math.

If your child is experiencing difficulty with mathematics, you may have noticed the following behaviors or signs:

- Does not quickly and accurately identify numbers
- Does not understand which number is "larger" or comes next in a sequence
- Continues to count on his or her fingers rather than counting silently
- Cannot retrieve math facts that have been learned previously
- Is unable to understand which details are relevant to solving a word problem
- Does not understand the language concepts when solving a word problem, such as size, volume, weight, or quantity
- Does not notice errors in calculation
- Makes "careless errors" when carrying numbers during more complex math problems
- Cannot line up numbers or keep steps organized when solving a long problem
- Avoids math

If you are concerned about similar behaviors in your child, an evaluation may be warranted to determine if these difficulties are *frequent, pervasive*, and *severe* enough to affect your child's ability to perform at grade level in mathematics. Asking your child's teacher and listening to your child will guide you as to whether an evaluation is the most appropriate next step.

GRADE TWO TEACHER

Mr. Wilson is not surprised when he receives a call from Charlie's father later that week. He agrees that Charlie is having significant difficulties with math and that he needs help in order to succeed. Mr. Wilson appreciates the father's concern about the effects of Charlie's poor math skills on his self-esteem. He describes Charlie's difficulties to Charlie's father and explains the process for obtaining a school evaluation to further assess Charlie's weaknesses. Mr. Wilson thinks Charlie's difficulties could be addressed by a 504 plan for the regular classroom. He also thinks Charlie needs extra time for quizzes, peer tutoring with flash cards, and direct instruction about problem-solving approaches. Direct instruction means that Mr. Wilson will break down the math problems into small steps and give Charlie immediate feedback on his progress. He also will use diagrams to help Charlie understand the basic math facts. He will meet with Charlie after school for thirty minutes to reinforce what was taught that day in math. Charlie's father is relieved to hear Mr. Wilson has a plan to help him.

THE ROADMAP

To develop a better understanding of your child's math difficulties, the first step is to obtain a roadmap of your child's strengths and weaknesses and a clear diagnosis from a comprehensive evaluation (see Chapter 3). Since math difficulties can affect a variety of areas of academic performance, it is essential to understand the specific areas in which your child is struggling—as well as what other factors could be contributing to the problem. Many children with MLD also have difficulty in reading or spelling. Almost half of children with one learning disability also struggle in another area.[29,30]

Problems with mathematics are often associated with weaknesses in other cognitive areas. Difficulties with attention, concentration, visual processing speed, language skills such as rapid decoding of words, visuospatial organiza tion, working memory, visual and verbal memory, or graphomotor skills can impact a child's performance on basic and higher level math. Although we do not fully understand which of these areas is the key deficit underlying MLD, we do know that weaknesses in these areas, and coordination of these skills across cognitive areas, contribute to poor math skills. The combination of these weaknesses underlies accommodations.[11]

A quarter of MLD children also have a diagnosis of ADHD.[31] Since attention and executive functioning are key components to mathematics success, it is easy to see how poor attention and organizational skills associated with ADHD can hinder a child's ability to perform well in math. It is important to get the appropriate evaluations for your child so you are equipped with a roadmap of his or her strengths and weaknesses. Because MLD often co-occurs with other learning and cognitive difficulties, a thorough evaluation is needed to support any necessary services, interventions, accommodations, or modifications as early as possible.

The Accommodation Plan

WHAT TYPES OF ACCOMMODATIONS WOULD BE HELPFUL AT SCHOOL?

Research supports the effectiveness of a variety of classroom interventions for mathematics. Most of them focus on early math skills. Acquiring basic math and problem-solving skills are key elements to future success in more complex forms of mathematics.[23]

For basic math facts, such as multiplication tables, the key is practice, practice, practice. Learning math facts is like learning a new language. You must learn the building blocks of the language, such as nouns and verbs, before you can speak fluently. A child can be naturally talented with languages but will not succeed without regular practice. Math facts are the basic building blocks for other math skills. Regular practice with math facts will help a child achieve automaticity, which is the core of math fluency. If a child is not fluent with basic math skills, his or her cognitive resources will be less available for higher math demands such as problem solving. As a result, the child will tire easily when faced with more complex problems, which can lead to distractibility and anxiety. Therefore, many accommodations for MLD focus on improving automaticity of math skills through practice and a variety of learning formats, such as reviewing new skills in groups with classmates.

The following list of classroom accommodations may be considered by evaluators who assess students with MLD:

- Calculator
- Concept or knowledge maps
- Extended time on homework, in-class work, and projects
- Graphic organizers
- Preferential seating
- Private learning space
- Quiet setting to work
- Read-alouds (electronic/human)
- Small group setting
- Talking calculator

WHAT TYPES OF ACCOMMODATIONS WOULD BE HELPFUL ON TESTS?

Charlie's difficulties with math skills contribute to poor performance on quizzes and tests. Therefore, he would benefit from accommodations in test situations. Poor math fluency and slower processing speed can significantly impede a child's performance on a test. The accommodation of extended time (usually between 50 and 100 percent) allows a child to effectively show what he or she knows on math exams.[32]

The following list provides the test accommodations that were considered by Charlie's evaluator because of his documented MLD:

- Calculator (for solving fractions)
- Extended time (with amount of time specified)

- Formula sheet
- Graph paper
- Read-alouds (electronic/human)
- Test setting (private, semiprivate, small group)

Charlie

Charlie smiled as he handed his quiz to his partner. Back in second grade, Mr. Wilson taught him many tricks to improve his math skills. For the past few years, Charlie and his father have spent time each night working with flash cards and now Charlie can do multiplication much faster. Now that he is in fifth grade, Charlie knows he needs to review his math homework each night, doing each problem two to three times to make sure he knows the steps. Charlie also asks his teacher or nearby classmate to show him the steps in solving a problem again if he doesn't get it the first time. On tests, Charlie is relieved that he gets extra time to complete his problems. The additional time allows him to slow down and think clearly. He doesn't feel pressured now. Charlie realizes that although he can't stand math, he can still do well on the quizzes and tests.

A Word on Access to High-Stakes Examinations

CHARLIE'S FATHER

As Charlie makes his way through high school, his father wonders how he will perform on the SAT. After speaking with the school counselor, he realizes that the school evaluation conducted a few years ago will not be sufficient documentation to obtain accommodations for the SAT. He knows that extra time for tests has been a critical component to Charlie's success in math in recent years. Charlie's father decides to contact the local college for suggestions on how to locate an evaluator for a comprehensive evaluation to find out which accommodations would be best for Charlie on such an important exam.

The evaluator must review all of your child's educational records as well as performance on a recent evaluation in order to determine which accommodations would be appropriate for your child on high-stakes examinations. It is suggested that the percentage of extra time requested be based on a student's previous accommodation of extended time fully used.[5] Research on extended time for students with math disabilities is limited and unclear. However, additional time is critical for those with MLD because they typically have associated difficulties with working memory, processing speed, or language. Other accommodations may be appropriate for your child, and these should be based on your child's specific needs. Charlie's evaluator considered the following accommodations for the high-stakes examination:

- Breaks (additional, extended, frequent)
- Calculator

- Extended time (with amount of time specified)
- Read-alouds (electronic/human)
- Test setting (private, semiprivate, small group)
- Writing in test booklet

CHARLIE

Charlie knows he would be overwhelmed and anxious taking the math section of the SAT without accommodations. The neuropsychologist recommended, and Charlie was granted, the accommodations of 50 percent additional time and a private room. One of the tools he had learned from Mr. Wilson's direct instruction was reading his math problems aloud. This helps him to slow down. A private room is necessary so he does not disturb other students. The math section of the SAT is still an unpleasant challenge for him but, because of the accommodations, the day ahead of him feels manageable.

CHAPTER 11

Emotional Functioning

ANXIETY: WHEN OUR FEARS GET THE BEST OF US

David

As the car stops in front of the school, David can see the other children laughing and playing as they run toward the front door. He can hear their laughter inside the car—it's so loud. David feels scared. None of the kids like him, he just knows it. His hand is resting on the door and it starts to tremble. He just can't get out of the car. His stomach churns and he begins to feel sick. He turns to his mother, "Mommy, I feel sick." David's mother sighs loudly, "Again? What's wrong today? Out you go!" Reluctantly, David exits the car and trudges toward school.

David's Mother

David has just started grade one and he's already missed five days of school for "illnesses" that disappear when he returns home. He never seems excited about school. His mother also notices that he prefers to stay with her rather than play with children in the neighborhood. David is such a sweet, gentle soul. He's always been a bit reserved and timid. His mother observes that he likes to stay by her side when they are out. Even at family gatherings, David chooses to stay near his mother rather than playing with his cousins. David's mother never goes out to a movie because he refuses to stay alone with a babysitter. He will just cry and cry if she even mentions going somewhere without him. David's clingy nature never used to bother her. She just saw him as more fragile than other children. Now David is 7 years old and she sees there is a problem, but she isn't sure what it is. David always seems scared of school and stressed when he comes home. He often complains of headaches and stomachaches, wakes up with nightmares, and refuses to be alone. Was David afraid of school because she was in the classroom too much when he was in kindergarten? Was that a mistake? David looks like he is about to cry. She pulls away from the curb to head home, wondering what she did wrong. It's so hard to see him struggle like this!

Grade One Teacher

Ms. Westin is worried about David's repeated absences from school. When he does come to school, she notices that David is very quiet and keeps to himself. He will interact when other children approach him, but he always seems so nervous. David never offers answers during class discussions and looks terrified when asked to come up to the board for a math problem. Ms. Westin isn't sure what to do. David's class work shows that he understands the concepts, but the stress of a quiz or test seems to overwhelm him. David takes a long time to complete his worksheets, because he erases and changes his answers multiple times. She is afraid to push him too far. At this point, she would just be happy if he could make it through a full week of school! If David keeps missing school, it will begin to affect his grades. She decides to wait in the front of school tomorrow morning and try to catch David's mom.

David

David feels scared when he sees Ms. Westin standing in front of the school the next day and his anxiety builds as he sees her walk toward their car. Did he break a rule? His thoughts start to race and his heart beats loudly in his chest. David knows he's in trouble—he did something wrong, but what was it? Ms. Westin hates him! His head begins to pound and his eyes start to water. David looks at his mother, who is waving back to Ms. Westin. David is worried about what they will say to each other. He doesn't want them to be mad at him. He just wants to go home, where he feels safe and calm.

What Is Anxiety?

> "My child has no friends. She is always so scared at parties and refuses to go on play dates unless I agree to stay. I can't always be with her."
>
> "Sam is terrified of crowds. I tried to take him to the mall and he just cried the whole time."
>
> "It's the morning before a spelling test and Adrianna says she has a headache or a stomachache. At first, I took it seriously. Now I think she's just avoiding things."
>
> "I'm so tired. Eliot refuses to sleep alone because he's scared of the dark. He's always in our bed."

Feelings of fear and anxiety are a natural response to a perceived threat in our environment. This causes the body to gear up its "fight or flight" response in order to protect you from danger. Fear is useful when it allows us to run quickly to safety if we are confronted by an angry bear. Although most of us are not threatened by angry bears during everyday modern life, our bodies are still "wired" to respond in this manner when we perceive a threat in our environment. For some children, like David, the world is a scary and unpredictable place. These children experience fear and anxiety in response to everyday situations, and this causes them to struggle. It is this extreme response to normal situations that alerts us that our child is struggling with anxiety.

Children with anxiety experience a wide variety of fears and worries related to school or their lives. Many students with anxiety experience physical symptoms, such as headaches or stomachaches, when confronted with stressful or feared situations. Anxiety emerges when they worry about school performance, which typically is associated with a need for perfection in all tasks. Such performance anxiety may lead children to avoid schoolwork or refuse to complete assignments. Some children spend too much time on their work—anxiously trying to make everything perfect. They may worry needlessly about the safety and well-being of family members and feel overwhelmed. As a result, these children may refuse to separate from their parents upon arrival at school or refuse to attend school altogether. Anxiety can also be associated with intrusive and bothersome thoughts about cleanliness or orderliness. This leads children to perform time-consuming compulsive behaviors that decrease their anxiety but also prevents them from completing tasks or enjoying playtime. Some children may also fear social judgment or rejection because they are afraid they might make a mistake or embarrass themselves in front of peers or teachers. This may lead some children to avoid interacting socially with peers or participating in group or classroom activities.

When Is the Problem a *Big* Problem?

Some amount of anxiety is normal and healthy. Anxiety before a big test or school play is normal. Anxiety about meeting new people is normal. Anxiety about traveling to a new place is normal. Healthy feelings of anxiety will come and go with the stressor and help us to be careful and do things right. In contrast, too much anxiety or fear prevents us from doing the things we want to do. As a result, we may be too afraid to try new things or meet new people, or we may be so scared of making a mistake that we won't even try. At this point, the level of fear and anxiety is causing us problems in our life, and that's the signal that we need help and support.

Anxiety disorders are the most common type of psychological disorder for children and adolescents.[1] Many children suffering from anxiety are not identified because the symptoms are "internalized" rather than "externalized." Internalizing disorders, such as anxiety and depression, are typically associated with feelings of fear and sadness as well as behavioral signs such as crying, avoidance, and withdrawal. In contrast, "externalizing" disorders, such as ADHD and oppositional defiant disorder (ODD), are associated with clearly observable behaviors that typically cause problems at school or at home. A child can also exhibit both internalized and externalized symptoms. David shows many signs of anxiety, including avoidance of school and crying when overwhelmed. David's mother is in the dark about his worries, because David is not able to explain what is bothering him. Since anxious children tend to hide their fears rather than lash out, they rarely cause problems at home or in school. They tend to slip through the cracks. David's anxious behaviors at school were not noticed until his grades started to slip. Fortunately, there are effective interventions for addressing anxiety and improving your child's ability to cope at school and at home.

DAVID'S MOTHER

After speaking with Ms. Westin, David's mother knows for sure there is something wrong. She has always thought that David was just a sensitive boy. When he started kindergarten, he was so timid and would cry in the face of the smallest challenge. She volunteered a few times a week in David's classroom and he seemed to be more comfortable when she was around. She knew her son was different from her other children, but hoped that he would grow out of his fears before elementary school. Now that she is going back to work full-time, David's mother cannot be in the classroom anymore and she was hoping that David could make it on his own. She sees that his fear of school is even worse than before kindergarten. Why hadn't she noticed it before? She is frustrated with herself for missing David's signals. David's mother wishes she had known what to look for.

While anxiety and fear are normal feelings, you should become concerned if your child's anxiety is *frequent, pervasive,* and *severe* and significantly affects his or her ability to function in everyday tasks. Anxiety or fear is *excessive* when it goes beyond what is reasonable for a certain situation. It is normal to be nervous before a big test, but anxiety is *excessive* if the student is sweating, trembling, and feeling nauseous for every test. Anxiety is pervasive and consistent if it occurs in all situations in which your child is being tested or evaluated, even for brief quizzes. Anxiety is affecting your child's functioning if your child is so nervous that he or she leaves the room and refuses to take the test or can't remember what was learned. We can evaluate symptoms of anxiety and fear to determine if they are severe enough to warrant concern and intervention.

If your child or adolescent is experiencing anxiety, you may have noticed the following behaviors or signs:

- Fearful when asked to separate from you or other loved ones
- Repeatedly checking things to "make sure they were done right"
- Excessive fear of certain situations, such as dark places, heights, or crowds

- Worrying about "too many" things, such as family finances, schoolwork, friends, or the future
- Trouble concentrating during school
- Physical symptoms when upset, such as a headache or stomachache
- Trouble getting to sleep or staying asleep
- Repetitive thoughts about germs or cleanliness, which may be associated with constant hand-washing
- Becoming overwhelmed in the face of even minor stress such as a homework assignment
- Nightmares

You need to evaluate whether the behaviors are *frequent*, *pervasive*, and *severe* and if they affect your child's ability to function on a daily basis to determine if you should seek an evaluation.

Anxiety is often associated (comorbid) with other difficulties. In the previous list, you will notice that "trouble concentrating" and "trouble sleeping" are typical signs of anxiety in children. As discussed in Chapter 4, attention problems can come from many sources. An anxious child like David may be so worried about his parents' safety that he cannot concentrate in class. Conversely, anxiety can appear when a child is struggling in another area. Many children with difficulties, such as language impairments (see Chapter 7), poor attention or executive functioning (see Chapters 4 and 6), or slow processing speed (see Chapter 9), also experience significant anxiety if they feel overwhelmed and cannot cope with the demands from their environment. A child with reading difficulties (see Chapter 10) may become very anxious when asked to read aloud because he or she has problems sounding out unfamiliar words or reads so slowly. In this situation, both the reading problem and the anxiety are harming the child's performance in school. It is important to get the appropriate evaluations for your child so you are equipped with a "roadmap" of his or her strengths and weaknesses. Because of potential associated conditions with anxiety and other difficulties, obtaining the correct diagnosis is vital to ensure that you choose the correct "tools" to support your child.

Looking Ahead

WHAT DO YOU DO NOW?

David's Mother

Ms. Westin asked David's mother to come to a parent meeting after school that day. During the meeting, Ms. Westin described her concerns about David's behavior and said she worried about its effect on David's grades. She shared some ideas about various accommodations that could be made to decrease David's anxiety about school. As a result of the meeting, a 504 plan was implemented. David did not need special education classes, but he did need accommodations. The plan documented accommodations such as preferential seating that allowed David to be closer to Ms. Westin, as well as moving his desk next to his close friend, Sam. David's mother hopes that this will help him feel more secure in the classroom, but she is not sure how to deal with David's fears about separating from her in other situations. Ms. Westin encouraged David's mother to talk to David's pediatrician to obtain a referral for a clinical psychologist or psychiatrist who could work with David and his mother outside of school to ensure that David was receiving the appropriate support and guidance for his problems.

Early intervention is critical for those children who exhibit marked anxiety. In David's case, his mother wondered what was causing the anxiety. She also felt that David needed support outside of school. A consultation with the pediatrician would be a good starting point to get her son the help that he needed.

THE ROADMAP

As discussed throughout this book, obtaining a roadmap is crucial. David's mother wondered what other factors were possibly affecting David at this point. The visit with his pediatrician, Dr. Parli, was helpful. A physical examination indicated that David was a healthy little boy. His vision and hearing examinations were normal. The pediatrician referred David and his mother to the local psychiatrist for an evaluation.

The psychiatrist, Dr. Kath, met with David and his mother. He interviewed each separately and also gave David a few inventories to fill out. Dr. Kath found out that David was struggling with his father's death. David's father had passed away due to lung cancer when David was only 3 years old. David's mother had never remarried. Dr. Kath suggested that David meet with him once a week. He decided that cognitive-behavioral therapy (CBT) would be the most effective approach for the treatment of David's anxiety and sadness.[2,3] Dr. Kath also referred David to an educational therapist to assess his achievement. He was not sure whether David had additional problems with reading, spelling, or writing. The psychological/educational report revealed that David was at the appropriate age level for all areas of achievement. David's mother was relieved that he had no problems with those areas.

The Accommodation Plan

WHAT TYPES OF ACCOMMODATIONS WOULD BE HELPFUL AT SCHOOL?

David's mother was not sure what sort of changes could help David to feel more comfortable in class. During her conversation with Ms. Westin, she learned there are many ways to help children cope with anxiety at school, depending on their strengths and weaknesses. In addition to therapeutic help outside of school, Ms. Westin thought that some basic changes in David's location in the classroom could help him to feel "safe" and connected with people he feels close to.

The following list provides some of the most common classroom accommodations for children with anxiety:

- Additional time to answer questions
- Additional time to process information
- Advance warning on projects/tests
- Assistance with focusing from teacher
- Breaks (additional, extended, frequent)
- Extended time on homework, in-class work, and projects
- Large assignments broken into smaller assignments
- Oral presentations prepared before class
- Preferential seating (allow child to sit by the teacher or preferred classmates)
- Routines and rules displayed visually
- Tape recorder for dictation
- Teacher engagement:
    - Develop a de-escalation procedure to cope with stressful feelings. For example, when worried, the student will (1) take ten deep breaths; (2) identify how a preferred "hero" would handle the situation; (3) access designated teacher or "safe person" on the staff; (4) complete alternative, less stressful work; (5) read for five minutes in a designated area (corner of room, library).
    - Discuss any problem behaviors outside of the classroom. Do not "call out" or punish the child in front of classmates.
    - Identify a "safe place" in the classroom or hallway where the child can go to use coping strategies, such as squeezing a stress ball, reading quietly, deep breathing, or using progressive muscle relaxation.
    - Let the child know he or she can seek out a teacher when feeling overwhelmed to talk about feelings.
    - Offer praise for the *effort* applied to the task, with less emphasis on accuracy.
    - Provide encouragement after completion of small pieces of the task to build confidence toward the completion of the whole task.
    - Remind child about *realistic* expectations for performance.
- Typist for dictation
- Word processor
- Written directions

David: Two Years Later

David runs toward his mother's car at the end of the day. As he hops into the car, he smiles and hands his mother his multiplication quiz. He only missed two out of twenty! David is in grade three now and has weekly math facts quizzes. Rather than rushing through quizzes within the time limit, David has extra time so he can stay calm and think clearly. David is receiving accommodations in school and meets with his psychiatrist once a month now. He loves to meet with Dr. Kath, and they talk about everything. David is no longer scared. Dr. Kath has taught him ways of dealing with his father's death. David has a "hole in his heart" but he knows how to cope. His mom has been really helpful and now they talk about things. David's mother used to avoid any discussion of his dad. It is different now. As a result, David is finally enjoying school and has met many new friends.

Depression and Mood Instability: The Ups and the Downs

Kimia

Kimia is 16 years old. It is 6:00 on Thursday morning. She rolls over in bed, covering her head with a pillow. Kimia is so tired. She can't face another day at school. No one likes her. She feels so stupid. On top of that, she thinks about the homework that she did not finish last night. It's going to be a bad day. Well, what's another F? She is failing most of her classes anyway. She feels like giving up and wishes that she wasn't on this planet.

Kimia's Mother

The sound of Kimia's alarm resonates down the stairwell and into the kitchen. Kimia's mother listens quietly, wondering if her daughter is going to make it out of bed today. She reflects on the past year and feels worried. Kimia has changed so much since starting high school. Once a bright, bubbling girl, Kimia is now quiet and withdrawn. She always looks sad and, at night, her mother hears her crying. Other days, Kimia is sarcastic and screams at her mother over small disagreements. Her mood is unpredictable. She no longer is interested in friends or shopping or music—or school. She just sits up in her room, doing nothing. Kimia's grades have dropped drastically and her mother worries that she might not pass her sophomore year. Will she be able to graduate? What about college? Kimia's mother considers these issues and wonders about the best way to talk to Kimia. Last time her mother asked what was going on, Kimia yelled at her and stomped out of the room. Kimia's mother worries that things will get worse if something doesn't change soon.

What Is Depression and Mood Instability?

"Kobe never comes out of his room. When I check on him, he's sleeping—and it's 4 o'clock in the afternoon."

"Sari always looks sad. She used to be such a happy girl."

"My daughter is happy one minute and in a rage the next minute. It's like her mood flips and it's completely unpredictable. I feel like I'm walking on eggshells."

"My son is just so moody! I thought that was normal for a teenager."

"My grandson never wants to do anything anymore. He used to love fishing and skateboarding. Now he just sits in front of the television. His friends call and ask him to do things, but he never feels like going. It's like he's a ghost."

Similar to anxiety, many children and adolescents keep their feelings of depression inside. On the inside, a child may be feeling worthless. On the outside, parents may only see their child cry, give up easily on tasks, or say negative things about him- or herself. The child may even withdraw quietly from his or her peer group. It is rare that a child or teenager will walk up to his or her parents and say, "I'm depressed." Kimia's mother noticed that changes in her daughter occurred gradually over time and she became more concerned as Kimia's difficulties persisted and led to a drastic drop in her grades. Therefore, as a parent, you need to be on the lookout for warning signs, which we discuss later in this chapter.

When Is the Problem a *Big* Problem?

Symptoms of depression and mood instability lie along a continuum from normal to abnormal. One would expect a child to be sad after the death of a pet or losing an important ball game. Similarly, it would be normal to be angry if teased by classmates. For children like Kimia, the feelings of sadness are overwhelming and not necessarily in response to a particular problem or stressor in their lives. Some children develop mood symptoms quickly, perhaps in response to a major stressor or change, while others experience a slow progression of mood difficulties. In extreme cases, these feelings can lead to thoughts of hurting oneself. This requires immediate medical attention. Kimia sometimes wishes she could "go to sleep and never wake up." Such thoughts are an early warning sign that a child is at risk for hurting him- or herself and should be addressed immediately with the pediatrician.

Children and adolescents with mood difficulties can demonstrate a wide variety of symptoms, from depressed mood to irritability to euphoric mood. It is important for you to determine if your child's symptoms of depression and mood instability are *frequent*, *pervasive*, and *severe* and affecting his or her ability to function in everyday tasks. When periods of depression or mood instability are extreme and associated with changes in sleep, energy, appetite, and motivation, it is clear that attention is warranted. Children and adolescents with mood problems often experience a decline in school performance and begin to withdraw from family and friends.

If your child or adolescent is experiencing depression, you may have noticed the following behaviors or signs:

- Prolonged periods of sadness
- Crying
- Feelings of worthlessness
- Very low self-esteem
- Decreased energy, feeling "tired all the time"
- Trouble sleeping
- Significantly increased *or* decreased appetite
- Decreased motivation for school and extracurricular activities
- Decreased interest in fun or pleasurable activities, including sports, art, or play time
- Withdrawal from friends and family
- Spending more time alone in room
- Difficulty making decisions about everyday problems
- Trouble maintaining attention or processing information quickly
- Problems remembering tasks that need to be completed
- Avoidance of complex or effortful tasks, such as schoolwork or chores

Some children with mood difficulties may appear irritable or angry. These symptoms of irritability can persist over a prolonged period or may appear in short, unpredictable bursts. These feelings may occur simultaneously with the feelings of depression noted previously. Children with mood difficulties may:

- Engage in more conflicts with family, friends, and teachers
- Have trouble controlling their emotions in response to limit setting
- Have difficulty tolerating frustration in the classroom setting
- Avoid complex tasks
- Refuse to comply with teacher's or parent's requests

A small proportion of children may experience periods of manic mood, which are characterized by clear periods of prolonged euphoria or elation that are quite different from a "good mood" or being "hyper." This elation can last for several days. To be considered unusual, the change in mood has to be more than you would see when a child goes to Disney World or has a birthday party. In other words, the child would seem distinctly different from normal, to the point where a parent or teacher would notice and be very concerned. In addition, the change in mood is accompanied by a variety of other changes in sleep, appetite, and behavior. These children:

- Have periods of mood instability, alternating quickly between periods of depression, irritability, and excitable mood. Such children may be sad one moment and out of control the next. When they are upset, they are inconsolable and the period of emotional upheaval seems to last much longer than it should.
- Have periods of increased activity, which may lead them to start new projects or move from task to task without finishing anything.
- Seem "over the top" silly or giddy when it does not fit the situation.
- Have decreased need for sleep with *no* complaints about being tired.
- Talk more quickly.
- Feel "on top of the world."
- Believe that they have special powers or abilities.
- Exhibit increased sexual behaviors.
- Have racing thoughts or "flight of ideas."
- Engage in risk-taking or dangerous behaviors that put them or others at risk for injury, such as attempting dangerous stunts on their bike, chasing a sibling with a knife, or driving at high speeds.
- Are completely unaware of how their behavior is affecting others.
- Have trouble focusing on one task.

Looking Ahead

WHAT DO YOU DO NOW?

It is difficult to see your child in pain. Many parents tend to underestimate their child's difficulties when he or she is depressed. Kimia's mother did. Kimia's sadness, periods of crying and anger, and withdrawal from her friends were now a concern. It was obvious that Kimia's sadness had "touched" every part of her life. She was noticeably different and other individuals such as her teachers and friends had made comments throughout the year.

Kimia's mother asked herself the following questions: What was the sadness all about? Was this inherited? Kimia's mother had never told her daughter that her grandfather had committed suicide. This was something that the family did not talk about. Perhaps there was a connection. Kimia's mother also thought that the sadness was not related to any learning problem because Kimia had always been a straight A student since kindergarten. However, she wondered whether Kimia had been bullied or teased at school. Kimia had gained fifteen pounds within the past year. Maybe that had something to do with it.

THE ROADMAP

To develop a better understanding of your child's mood difficulties, the first step is to obtain the roadmap of your child's strengths and weaknesses and a clear diagnosis. For Kimia, consultation with her pediatrician was a logical starting point. Kimia and her mother met with her pediatrician and he suggested a visit with the child psychologist in their community. He also gave them the names of child psychiatrists. The pediatrician advised them that both professionals would be a good starting point in developing her roadmap.

Depression and mood disorders can be accompanied by cognitive issues, including poor attention, memory, and processing speed. Problems in basic cognitive domains, such as attention (see Chapter 4), executive functioning (see Chapter 6), or language (see Chapter 7), can lead to poor self-esteem and depression in children.[4] Difficulties associated with depression—or anxiety— can be subtle and significantly impact a child's ability to perform in school.

Kimia's mother decided to start with the child psychologist, Dr. Wong. The psychologist met with Kimia and her mother. Dr. Wong referred them for a psychological assessment to clarify the degree of the sadness. The assessment was also important to understand if there were any other psychological difficulties that were getting in Kimia's way. The examiner, Dr. Wood, indicated that Kimia was depressed. The depression was severe and needed to be treated as soon as possible. It was also clear that there was a family history of depression. Kimia was not reacting to any stressors at home or at school. Kimia's mother was relieved that her daughter was not suffering from other psychological, cognitive, or achievement difficulties. In addition, Dr. Wood suggested educational accommodations for the school as well as a 504 plan. The 504 plan was scheduled very soon after Dr. Wood talked with the counseling director at Kimia's school.

The Accommodation Plan

WHAT TYPES OF ACCOMMODATIONS WOULD BE HELPFUL AT SCHOOL?

Feelings of depression or mood instability can be overwhelming for a child or adolescent. The good news is that changes in the school environment can go a long way toward helping a child feel more effective at school. Through your roadmap, you will have a clear understanding of your child's mood difficulties. The following list shows the classroom accommodations that an evaluator will consider for those children who exhibit depression and mood instability:

- Breaks (additional, extended, frequent)
- Educational facilitator to encourage proofreading and remaining on task
- Extended time on homework, in-class work, and projects
- Extra set of books at home (to allow the child to work when he or she has energy)
- Large assignments broken into smaller assignments
- Minimal distractions
- Note taker
- Pass that allows a student to leave the classroom at his or her discretion for emotional reasons (bathroom breaks, allowance of physical movement)
- Peer assistance for in-class assignments
- Preferential seating
- School day plan (shorten the school day if necessary to address fatigue)
- Scheduling plan (schedule more demanding classes or exams during the period of day for the older child when he or she has the most energy)
- Teacher engagement.
  - Allow the student to return to a frustrating task when he or she is more calm.
  - Help the student to focus (develop a signal to inform the child that his or her attention is drifting or energy is waning).
  - Let the student know that he or she can talk with a designated teacher to regroup when feeling moody or upset.
  - Monitor the child's progress throughout the day.
  - Provide the child with support in prioritizing assignments.
  - Provide time at the beginning and end of the day for the student to meet with a facilitator or counselor to organize assignments and review upcoming deadlines.
- Water bottle/snacks
- Word processor

If your child's physician or psychiatrist suggests medication, be sure to speak to him or her about any side effects of the medication. Some common side effects are dry mouth, frequent urination, drowsiness, and blurred vision. The American Academy of Pediatrics Council on School Health published specific guidelines about the administration of a child's medications in school. It is important that your physician speak to school staff to ensure that your child is receiving the proper level of support around his or her medication and its side effects.[5] Mani Pavuluri, associate professor in Child Psychiatry and director of the Pediatric Mood Disorders Clinic at the University of Illinois at

Chicago, provides a helpful checklist that can been used to coordinate a tele-conference between your child's physician and the school staff.[6] Your physician may want to consider the following accommodations if your child is coping with medication side effects:

- Books on tape (for the child experiencing blurred vision)
- Breaks (additional, extended, frequent: for the child who is coping with fatigue or sleepiness)
- Pass to leave classroom at student's discretion for physical/emotional reasons (bathroom breaks, occurrence of tics, management of pain)
- Preferential seating (to allow better viewing of the board or easy exit from classroom)
- Read-alouds (electronic/human)
- School day plan (allow the student to arrive late to school or shorten the school day if the child has trouble waking early in the morning)
- Tape recorder for dictation (for the child with tremors or fatigue)
- Teacher engagement (reminders to use the bathroom and cues to indicate the need to use the bathroom for the younger child)
- Typist for dictation (for the child with tremors or fatigue)
- Water bottle/snacks (allow in the classroom to cope with thirst or hunger)
- Word processor (for the child with tremors or fatigue when writing)

Kimia: One Month Later

Kimia began to see the child psychologist two times a week. The psychologist suggested a consultation with a psychiatrist, Dr. Loo, at the university near their home. The reason for this consultation was Kimia's severe depression. Kimia was placed on medication by Dr. Loo and participated in CBT with Dr. Wong. The psychologist told Kimia that CBT was the "gold standard" so that her depression could be treated effectively. Kimia's mother questioned this approach. She even decided to get a second opinion on the use of CBT and medication. However, she soon found out that all of the professionals were on the same page. The specialists told her that the medication and CBT were needed because of the severity of Kimia's depression—Kimia wanted to injure herself, withdrew from family and friends, and had significant problems functioning in school.

Kimia: Six Months Later

"I have been meeting with Dr. Wong and Dr. Loo. I feel so much better. I feel no side effects from the medication and I have been learning how to think differently. I see

things differently now and when I have a bad thought I know now how to change it. You see, my mind is made up of different channels, like on a television. I have a different scene, or I call it a 'happy place,' for each channel. I never get bored that way. Well, it works! I know I'm not done yet but I feel lighter, like I'm not carrying a big weight on me."

Coping with Poor Frustration Tolerance and Oppositional Behavior

Tom's Teacher: At School

"Tom is a difficult student. He doesn't do anything in class. He won't do anything that I request of him. He also argues with me. Tom does not complete any of the class work. Instead, he will just get a book out and read. Tom is 12 years old and in my sixth grade class. I'm not sure what is going on but I want to help him."

What Are Poor Frustration Tolerance and Oppositional Behavior?

"My student John refuses to complete any written work. It's like he puts the brakes on and shuts down."

"Barbara threw her book at me the other night. It wasn't even a school night. She is so angry all the time."

"Tessa should have a T-shirt made for her that says 'No!' She responds with a 'no' every time my husband and I ask her to do chores. It's turning our house upside down."

"I'm just angry. If I get frustrated my daughter just shuts down. Once she does that you can't bring her back to the homework."

Children with cognitive and emotional difficulties are apt to "shut down" or "give up" when confronted with a new or challenging task. Some children have difficulty tolerating frustration when they are not able to complete the task quickly and easily. Other children realize that a certain task will be hard for them and they would rather give up than fail. As a result, the child may become angry or defiant, refusing to continue with the task. This pattern is described in Chapter 7, where trouble with expressive language caused Deeksha to give up in social situations. Some children with low self-esteem or depression may become discouraged and give up too quickly. Any punishment or removal of privileges in school due to the child "shutting down" can increase anxiety or depression around the task and worsen the problem. For example, David's anxiety made it hard for him to go to school each day and his teacher was worried that he would not be able to tolerate the stress of an examination or quiz.

Poor frustration tolerance can affect a child's ability to handle difficult or stressful tasks, contributing to avoidance of schoolwork or chores. These children may experience difficulty in social situations because of their impatience with others (see Chapter 12). When frustrated, they can become oppositional or aggressive. As these children become fatigued, their ability to tolerate stress can diminish quickly. This can lead to withdrawal or oppositional behavior. Kimia would scream at her mom over minor problems, such as not being able to find her favorite shirt or being asked to do simple chores. This is a common example of poor frustration tolerance for a teen struggling with mood problems. Other children can go quickly from being calm to becoming irritable and angry, which leads to arguments with teachers and fights with peers.

When Is the Problem a *Big* Problem?

TOM'S FATHER

Tom's father is clearly frustrated. The teacher and the principal called him the other night and voiced their frustration. Tom is shutting down in the classroom but seems fine on the playground with his friends. Tom's father is very concerned because Tom's grades are being affected.

If your child shows low frustration and oppositional behaviors, it is important to try to understand why he or she might be acting this way. Oppositional or defiant behavior often represents a child's attempt to take control over his or her circumstances. This may occur when the child feels overwhelmed by the demands of a current situation. Alternately, such behavior can occur because of the attention that the child receives from caregivers in response to his or her difficult behaviors. Oppositional or avoidance behavior may also reflect another underlying problem, such as a learning disability or motor problems, because children are apt to avoid tasks that are difficult for them.

Oppositional behaviors can lead to *bigger* problems down the road. Oppositional children are often seen as "difficult" by peers, parents, and teachers. As a result, they are apt to experience social isolation and may seek friendships with peers who are also defiant and difficult in order to feel a sense of belonging. Adults often respond to such children with criticism and punishment, and that can contribute to the child's development of low self-esteem. These children continue to act out either because they receive attention for their poor behavior or because they believe that they are "no good."

THE ROADMAP

Tom's Father
Tom's father called the teacher and principal for a second meeting. They were just as
confused as he was. The principal, Dr. Hart, decided to request a psychoeducational
evaluation within the school district. She thought that the problems were severe
enough and it looked like Tom had some special needs that required help in the class-
room. Tom's father thought that was a wonderful idea. At least they would get to the
bottom of the problem.

In Tom's case, an assessment was necessary to pinpoint what exactly was underlying his oppositional behaviors in the classroom. As with the other challenges discussed in this book, an assessment is critical in order to identify a student's strengths and weaknesses and to further address intervention, services, and accommodations, if needed. In Tom's case, the school psychologist indicated that Tom had learning disabilities in the areas of written expression and organization that needed to be addressed. Therefore, Tom had a reason to "shut down" in the classroom. Although Tom did not require special education classes, accommodations were suggested in the 504 plan. In addition, counseling and educational therapy were recommended as documented in the 504 plan to address Tom's issues.

The Accommodation Plan

WHAT TYPES OF ACCOMMODATIONS
WOULD BE HELPFUL AT SCHOOL?

Many of these problems—as well as problems with cognition and learning—are often intertwined with other problems. Cognitive difficulties can contribute to emotional difficulties, and vice versa. As your team develops your child's plan based on the evaluation results, they will reflect on your child's cognitive *and* emotional needs in the classroom.

Researchers William Jenson, Elaine Clark, and Jason Burrow-Sanchez at the University of Utah in Salt Lake City discuss how to understand and manage difficult behaviors in the classroom.[7] The following list includes common classroom accommodations for children with poor frustration tolerance and oppositional behavior:

- Breaks (additional, extended, or frequent to prevent fatigue or frustration)
- Extended time on in-class work, projects, and homework
- Large assignments broken into smaller assignments (to decrease frustration and promote success)
- Peer assistance for in-class assignments

- Teacher engagement:
  - Avoid putting the student in competitive situations.
  - Choose to ignore small problem behaviors (for example, talking out of turn during class discussion). If the child does not get your attention for the smaller behaviors, he or she will be less likely to show such behaviors in the future.
  - Provide logical and consistent consequences for inappropriate behaviors. Inform the student of the potential consequences of misbehavior. Quickly apply such consequences as soon as the inappropriate behavior is demonstrated.
  - Consider using a token economy or other rewards system, whereby the child earns points or privileges for a specified set of appropriate behaviors and loses points or privileges for a set of inappropriate behaviors.
  - Provide praise consistently as progress is made; this will encourage the child to seek attention and support through positive behaviors rather than seeking attention through problem behaviors.
  - Provide clear expectations for appropriate behavior.
  - Provide praise for the child's ability to continue with a task even when frustrated, rather than his or her ability to complete the task quickly or accurately.
  - Provide supervision during unstructured times at school, such as recess, to decrease the possibility of acting out, and facilitate your child's ability to problem-solve through a conflict situation.
  - Redirect inappropriate behavior to a more appropriate behavior or task.
  - Select a clear set of inappropriate behaviors to address first and move through the list as the child makes progress.
  - Remind child to use "time-outs" or relaxation techniques to calm down and regroup when frustrated.

Tom's Father: Two Months Later

"I will always thank the school district for coming to the rescue. The counseling has been very important for my son because he has someone he can talk to about his frustrations in getting his thoughts down on paper. The educational therapist is helping Tom plan and organize his thoughts by using concept maps. I was told from the school psychologist that my son is very visual. The educational therapist used the information from the psychoeducational report to plan her intervention. Also, Tom got extended time on all of his classroom projects and assignments. We also worked it out that he could leave the classroom when he was feeling angry or frustrated. Tom can now talk to the school counselor anytime when he gets in this 'space.' The school district also told me that Tom may not need his 504 plan in the future if he gets better."

My Mind Is Playing Tricks on Me: Coping with Unusual Thoughts or Experiences

Dorit: At Home

Dorit is 14 years old. It is 9:00 at night and she is trying to sleep. Those soldiers keep stomping up the stairs. Dorit runs to her bedroom door stretching her neck to hear the sounds. Are they real? Maybe she is just "hearing things." There they go again. She then runs to her parents' bedroom. Her mother and father look at her, puzzled. Her dad says, "What's up, Dorit. Is everything okay?" Dorit responds, "No problem, dad. I just wanted to see if you and mom were here." Dorit walks back to her bedroom slowly. She hopes that she can fall asleep tonight. Those soldiers aren't scary but they keep talking to her.

Some children experience unusual thoughts or sensory experiences. These can occur during times of anxiety or mood symptoms, or they can occur as part of disorders like schizophrenia. Such children may have unusual beliefs, including fears that others are out to harm them or that events happening around them have a special meaning just for them. Other children may repeatedly hear sounds when no one is there or see shadows or people out of the corner of their eye on a regular basis. Some believe they possess very special gifts or talents, which can lead them to pursue unrealistic goals or engage in dangerous behaviors. These experiences can be troubling or overwhelming for the child and lead to them to withdraw from friends, family, and school.

These children may seem distracted and have trouble staying focused on longer tasks. Difficulties with attention, executive functioning, and memory are common in these children and are associated with trouble in school and peer relationships.[8-10] They can be fearful in school, which leads to isolation or absenteeism. Similar children may have difficulty tolerating normal stress and likely become easily overwhelmed in situations they previously handled with ease. Such children may avoid schoolwork or chores because they have become "too stressful." As the stress of these experiences increases, they can develop symptoms of anxiety or depression and can become irritable when teachers or family encourage them to complete tasks or assignments.

When Is the Problem a *Big* Problem?

DORIT'S MOTHER: ONE YEAR LATER

"Boy, this is difficult. Dorit was doing so badly in school. She really withdrew from her girlfriends and all of our family activities. Because of the sudden withdrawal from friends and pleasurable activities, we took her to a counselor, Dr. Feldman, who was highly recommended by one of our friends. He told us that Dorit was very anxious and

had been hearing things at home. I couldn't believe this. I mean, all kids hear things at night. I did when I was a young girl. However, Dr. Feldman also told me that Dorit had been hearing voices for some time and, in fact, had been hearing whispers initially. The good thing was that Dorit felt that the voices were not necessarily real. However, she was frightened because the voices were getting louder and not going away. To make a long story short, we ended up in a national study at the medical school and Dorit met with a psychiatrist and a psychologist and had assessments done there. We found out that she was 'prodromal' and that the voices she was hearing were the early warning signs of schizophrenia. We were also told (before I almost passed out) that early intervention was everything and that Dorit would be okay. We are doing everything to help her now."

As with the other cases presented in this book, early intervention is critical. Dorit's mother sought help as soon as she was advised to do so by Dr. Feldman. The warning sign of her daughter withdrawing from her friends was an important indicator that there was a *big* problem. If your child or adolescent is experiencing unusual thoughts or sensory experiences, you may have noticed the following behaviors or signs:

- Declining grades in school
- Difficulty concentrating
- Gradual withdrawal from classmates, parents, and teachers
- Hearing voices
- Inappropriate expression of emotion
- Irrational ideas
- Poor frustration tolerance
- Poor self-care such as poor eating habits, sleep patterns, and personal hygiene
- Seeing visions
- Suspiciousness of others

THE ROADMAP

To obtain the roadmap for these children, you should seek an evaluation by a clinical psychologist or child psychiatrist to obtain the appropriate diagnosis for your child. With the appropriate diagnosis, the psychologist or psychiatrist can give you guidance on the correct treatment and accommodations to help your child succeed in school.

The Accommodation Plan

WHAT TYPES OF ACCOMMODATIONS WOULD BE HELPFUL AT SCHOOL?

Because of their decreased tolerance for stress and tendency to be distracted by internal experiences, these children often require accommodations to decrease demands within the home and classroom. Therefore, many accommodations suggested for anxiety and mood instability can also be useful for these children. It is important to provide the child with a manageable workload and the ability to relax and rest if necessary. The following list provides additional classroom interventions that may be considered by your child's evaluator:

- Extended time on homework, in-class work, and projects
- Pass to leave classroom at student's discretion for physical/emotional reasons (allow the child to leave the stressful situation and seek a quiet place to calm down and regroup when overwhelmed), on an as needed basis
- Teacher engagement (encourage the child to talk about his or her experiences and use more effective coping strategies, such as deep breathing)

In addition, modifications may be needed to cope with medication side effects. Placement in a special classroom or school that can provide more one-on-one attention and support may be needed.

Dorit's Mother

Dorit's mother decided to meet with the director at her daughter's school. She felt that this was necessary so that the reports from Dorit's medical team could be shared with the director. The director suggested accommodations to decrease the pressure that Dorit had at school. These accommodations involved extended time for all class work and the ability to leave the classroom to talk with the school counselor when she felt stressed. Dorit was a very important part of this entire process. Dorit talked freely now and communicated her feelings to the director and her parents.

NOTE FROM AUTHOR: The material below is for ALL students with Emotional Disorders as the accommodations for tests and high-stakes examinations will be the same.

WHAT TYPES OF TEST ACCOMMODATIONS WOULD BE HELPFUL FOR STUDENTS WITH EMOTIONAL DISORDERS?

For children with emotional difficulties, testing situations can be very stressful, leading to poor performance and the inability to demonstrate what they have learned. The following list provides test accommodations that an evaluator may consider:

- Alternative testing format (a word processor if perfectionism creates multiple erasures; oral response if tics impede ability to turn pages or write; allowing student to speak oral responses into a tape recorder, in front of a small group, or with just the teacher rather than presenting aloud in front of class)

- Breaks (additional, extended, frequent)
- Different test day or time (allow testing on another day if the student is symptomatic)
- Extended time (with amount of time specified)
- Multiple-day testing sessions
- Scratch paper (the ability to take notes in the margins of the test book or on scrap paper)
- Test setting (private, semiprivate, small group)

A Word on Access to High-Stakes Examinations for Students with Emotional Disorders

The College Board allows testing accommodations for students with psychological difficulties that affect test taking. As discussed in Chapter 2, the College Board permits reasonable testing accommodations for those students who have a *disorder* and a *disability*. Documentation of a student's *current* functioning is critical to pinpoint in what ways the disability is limiting a student in a substantial way compared to *most* students. In addition, a student's continued impairment despite the use of medication and the anticipated impact of such medications on the student at the time of the testing should be reported. A rationale must be provided for each accommodation that is requested. While a student may have had IEPs or 504 plans in the past, these do not guarantee accommodations for high-stakes examination purposes.

A diagnosis of a psychological disorder or note from a doctor is not sufficient to obtain accommodations on College Board or ACT examinations for psychological difficulties. Many students with psychological difficulties take these tests without accommodations. As previously discussed, the fact that a student has a clinical disorder does not mean that he or she disabled. The College Board and ACT require documentation to support the rationale for a requested accommodation in order to demonstrate that the student's disability will prevent him or her from demonstrating what he or she truly knows unless such accommodations are provided.

The following accommodations may be considered by your child's evaluator for high-stakes examination purposes:

- Breaks (additional, extended, frequent)
- Different test day or time (may be considered for the student who has trouble waking up in the morning due to medication effects)
- Extended time (with amount of time specified)
- Multiple-day testing sessions
- Test setting (private, semiprivate, small group)
- Word processor

CHAPTER 12

Social Skills

WHY CAN'T WE BE FRIENDS?

At Home

Amanda and Julia are having a play date at Amanda's home. They are 6 years old and in the first grade. Amanda's mother can hear them arguing in the next room as they play with dolls. She decides to quietly walk to the room and peek in. Amanda is yelling at Julia for taking her doll away from her, and she's not "letting up." Julia is quiet and does not say anything. Amanda continues to yell at Julia, telling her that she is play-ing their game all wrong. Julia can't get a word in and looks like she is about to cry. Amanda's mother wonders why her daughter isn't picking up the cue that her friend is upset.

AMANDA'S MOTHER

The next day, Julia's mom calls. Mrs. Pederson's voice sounds very angry. Mrs. Pederson says, "Julia will not be able to have any more play dates with Amanda." Amanda's moth-er's heart is pounding and she feels very confused. "I'm not sure I understand," she states. Mrs. Pederson says, "Amanda is too rude and I heard that she recently hit another classmate. All the mothers are talking about it. I can't have Julia around a child who is mean." Mrs. Pederson also tells her that perhaps their daughters can have a play date next fall "if she's better." Amanda's mother hangs up the phone and bursts into tears. She feels hurt and upset. Did Amanda really hit another child? No one told her about this. She decides to talk with her husband and the director of the school to get to the bottom of the situation. There may be something going on here. Is everyone talking about her Amanda? She feels alone. They live in a small community. This is not good!

What Are Social Skills?

"Kendra often spreads rumors about her peers and she is losing friends because of it. I think she does it to get attention."

"My son doesn't really play with his play dates when they are over. He sort of just plays in the same room."

"Jin brings his belongings to class and gives them away to the boys he wants to be friends with. However, they just take them and don't want to play with him."

"My daughter was recently told that she was a snob because she never seems to show an interest in what her friends want to talk about."

"I feel like my son is a great kid, but I just found out that he teases children at school. He seems to be attracted to the kids who are troublemakers."

"My teenage daughter is going through a rough time. She doesn't have any friends. It seems like she has no idea how to make friends despite my telling her how to go up and introduce herself to people."

"Jeremy tends to get in people's faces and does not know when to back off."

"Mia often interrupts other children and doesn't let them finish what they are saying."

"When the other boys are rude to Blake, he just looks like a 'deer in the headlights' and doesn't understand what is going on."

"Max is really into videogames now. I mean he can play them for hours and hours. All of his friends do the same thing. Max used to be into World War II stuff."

You probably have an idea of what social skills are, but you might be surprised to learn just how much is involved and the consequences of difficulties in this area. Social skills enable us to interact with others in an agreeable manner. They involve both verbal and nonverbal (visual) communication and the ability to follow "unwritten rules" of behavior. Anytime your child is in the presence of another person, social skills are active. Social skills are evident when a baby makes eye contact and smiles at another child, when a school child can take turns in a board game with a friend, when a child knows how the rules of behavior change from the playground to the dinner table, and when a teenager understands how to have a two-way conversation with a friend.

Social skills are present very early in children's lives, but these skills evolve as they age.[1] For the majority of children, good social skills come naturally and are further shaped through their environment, such as by mother's and father's parenting. We are more forgiving of younger children's social gaffes because we know they may not yet be mature enough to understand the complexity of their social world. Requirements of social interaction get more complicated as children age. Problems may not necessarily be noticed until the child is in early elementary school, when social interaction becomes complex and we expect children to be socially successful on their own.

Interestingly, research suggests that some social patterns, such as aggression, are evident as early as infancy and are predictive of similar patterns later on.[2] By approximately age 2 through preschool, children begin to show a preference for particular friends over others. They also start to gravitate toward playing with children of the same gender and are interested in playing together in groups. Social awareness starts to develop and at this point, social deficits *may* become visible. Beginning in preschool, language also begins to play a very important role in socialization. As discussed in Chapter 7, language is a part of social communication. Children who have trouble with speaking or understanding others typically are at a great disadvantage in making friends. This shows how the struggle in social functioning may begin very early for children with language impairment. While it is typical for a preschooler to enjoy spending a great deal of time playing alone, this type of play decreases around ages 6 to 8. The absence of friends for this age group can result in isolation, rejection from their peer group, and feelings of loneliness. By age 9 through adolescence, "best" friendships emerge based on commonalities (approximately fourth grade) and children begin to engage in mature conversation versus simply talking about likes and dislikes (approximately sixth grade).[3] Children will begin to befriend the opposite sex beginning in grade five to early middle school. Students also form groups of close friends, called *cliques*, as early as first and second grade. Cliques can cause emotional distress in some children if they are excluded. Although some children may prefer to play with one or two best friends, membership in a clique is healthy social behavior. Either way of bonding with friends is beneficial for children.[3,4]

In peer groups, children may be popular, accepted, neglected, or rejected.[1,5] Popular children tend to be highly socially competent. These children are perceived as friendly and helpful to others and they engage in conversations appropriately, understand what others think and feel, and have good friendship and sportsmanship etiquette. Students with high levels of social competence are frequently favored by their peers and sought out for companionship. On the other hand, a popular child may not be well liked by most of his or her peers. For example, a popular student may be one who is known by most peers and gets attention for inappropriate (negative) behaviors. However, this child may not necessarily be liked by them.

Accepted children are well liked by the majority of peers but may not be the most popular. How does a child become an accepted peer? The following characteristics are typical of children who are accepted by their peers:

- Join a group of friends at play with no effort
- Initiate conversation easily
- Maintain conversation in a give-and-take manner
- Offer personal information disclosing their own feelings
- Are cognizant of boundaries such as not crowding others' space

- Correctly interpret visual signals such as understanding and responding to different facial expressions and gestures
- Initiate and maintain eye contact with others
- Self-correct their errors in behavior or conversation
- Show good sportsmanship in games and at play
- Show caring, interest, and trust in others
- Support their friends
- Resolve conflict smoothly with problem-solving techniques that work

Neglected children may or may not have high levels of social competence. These children can be shy, can lack confidence when interacting with peers, and tend to keep a low profile in school. However, these students may have friends outside of school, indicating that they have adequate social skills. On the other hand, neglected children can also be anxious and fearful and lack the give-and-take needed to sustain a conversation. These children are seen as lacking in social competence, which results in their limited involvement with others.

Lastly, rejected children are typically characterized as having low frustration tolerance and difficulties managing or regulating their attention. They may be verbally or physically aggressive with others. For example, these students may tease and fight with their peers without provocation. Behaviors such as tattling, bragging, and telling others how they should think and feel are some of the other characteristics that "turn off" their peers. It is estimated that approximately 15 percent of children are rejected.[6]

Parents often expect that their child will "grow out of it" or "work it out" when they have social difficulties. Although some of these behaviors are characteristic of the younger typically developing child, other children who have poor social skills have marked deficits that are not a result of motivation or age. These children, if not helped, may eventually be neglected or rejected by their peer group. In addition, children with skill deficits typically will show a "downward spiral" as they age because social interactions become more complicated.

Children with weaknesses in social skills may not be aware of what is wrong. As previously discussed in Chapter 6, metacognition involves an awareness and insight into one's own behavior and thought processes. At the same time, it involves an understanding of how one's behavior affects other people. Children with good metacognition will be cognizant of the impact their actions have on others and will repair or fix their action if it is a problem. If children lack this executive skill, they may not view their social behavior as troublesome, ineffective, or problematic. They may be confused by their lack of friends or being left out of interactions or activities with peers. Typically, these are the children who are rejected or neglected by their peers. There is a stark difference between having a friend versus an acquaintance, and children with social difficulties may not appreciate this distinction. Children with deficits in social skills may report they have "friends" or even a "best friend," but their parents will report the friendship is not mutual from the perspective of the peer or that the peer is merely an "acquaintance."

The initiation and maintenance of friendships are important for many reasons. First, friendships can buffer stress and are viewed as protective. Second, relationships with peers teach children the skills necessary to solve and cope with conflict resulting in higher self-esteem, more independence, and fewer mental health issues compared with children who lack them. Third, friendships contribute to a child's sense of happiness, adjustment, and self-worth.[1,7,8]

Social functioning often suffers for children with developmental challenges.[1,5,9,10] These challenges include problems with attention (see Chapter 4), executive functioning (see Chapter 6), language (see Chapter 7), and emotional functioning (see Chapter 11). Therefore, you will often see social skills impairments in children with ADHD, autism spectrum disorders, fetal alcohol spectrum disorder, selective language disorders, and emotional disorders. In the absence of friends, existing cognitive, academic, or emotional challenges are more difficult to manage. Lack of friends in preadolescence has been shown to extend to later psychological problems in adulthood. Problems such as depression and anxiety, antisocial behavior, delinquency, or school failure may result from poor social abilities or peer isolation. Unfortunately, children with difficulties in social skills tend to gravitate toward other kids with the same issues, which can exacerbate their weaknesses in social skills.[1,5,6,8,11]

What about bullying? How does this relate to social skills? A bully is described as a child who, through verbal, physical, or "relational aggression," intentionally and repeatedly inflicts harm (directly or indirectly) toward another person in which there is an imbalance of power.[12,13] Examples include calling one names and teasing (verbal), hitting (physical), and spreading rumors or saying things like, "If you are friends with Lauren, I won't be friends with you" (relational aggression). Interestingly, children who are bullies can be popular, whether liked or disliked.[14,15] Bullying is of concern both to parents of children who bully and to parents of victims of a bully. Some children find themselves in the role of both bully and victim.

Children having problems with managing their emotions, impulsivity, and understanding of others are often more vulnerable to being teased or bullied, or of becoming a bully themselves.[1] Popular or accepted children often resolve conflict on their own, or they know when it is appropriate to seek help from an adult to intervene with the bully. As mentioned previously, these children are socially competent. In contrast, neglected and rejected children may have a poor sense of danger when being teased, threatened, or bullied and not know when to seek help from an adult.[16] This suggests that children with social skill deficits require *explicit* instruction on how to handle and report bullying.

By explicit instruction, we mean that these children need to be taught the skills in a step-by-step manner.

Bullying must be taken seriously and addressed immediately by an adult. The severity of the situation is illustrated by the fact that both bullies and victims are at risk for mental health problems, including thoughts of suicide and harming themselves.[17,18] Sharyn Burns and her colleagues, Donna Cross and Bruce Maycock, report that support or lack of support by friends in one's social circle can strongly influence whether or not one bullies.[14] Children with a strong sense of self (both bullies and peers who are friends with the bully) may switch to a more positive friendship group when they realize the bullying is wrong.

"Cyberbullying" is a relatively recent phenomenon that involves nonphysical forms of bullying such as name calling, spreading rumors, making threats, posting private images, and using verbal aggression through the use of the Internet and cell phone text messaging that intends to cause harm to another person.[19,20] What does cyberbullying look like? Consider this transcript of a text message that Jenn received from a peer (Angie) in the fifth grade:

> ANGIE: *Hey booger brain*
> ANGIE: *you r so ugly*
> JENN: *Y ru tryn 2 make me feel bad*
> ANGIE: *sorry butt it is so true*
> JENN: *It is not true*
> JENN: *Y u talk bad about me? I am not a brat I am not spoiled and I hve PLENTY of frnds*
> ANGIE: *I don't care about you. Ur such a loser*
> JENN: *Y ru a hater? U need to learn how 2 treat a friend*
> ANGIE: *I hate you soooooo much*
> JENN: *Wow whatd I do 2 u 2 make u feel ths way*

Would you consider the text message harmful if your child was in Jenn's position? Conversely, would you see a "red flag" if Angie was your child? The dangerous thing about cyberbullying is it is more removed or anonymous for the bully than traditional bullying. This affords greater distance and makes it feel less serious or real for the bully, thus encouraging further abuse.[21] Cyberbullying can be devastating, scary, and dangerous for the victim. It can also lead to anxiety and school avoidance and negatively affect grades. In spite of this, children (victims) may not report instances of cyberbullying for fear of losing access to their computer or lack of confidence in school personnel to be able to stop it.[22] This highlights the importance of *active* parent involvement with a child's access to electronic social communication. Electronic media allows information to be disseminated quickly on a widespread level, and it can be accessed by numerous people. It is difficult to remove some information, such as that posted on social websites.

Much of a child's social development occurs in the school setting beginning at a very young age. Intervening as early as possible is critical because the child's success in making and keeping friends is so important.

When Is the Problem a *Big* Problem?

AMANDA'S MOTHER

Amanda's mother is distraught and confused about her daughter's behavior during her play date. She did see that Amanda was being bossy and insensitive to her friend Julia. However, she thought it was normal for that age. Don't children need to learn to work out conflicts on their own? After the phone call with Julia's mother, she became so concerned about Amanda that she lost sleep over it. Are these social issues permanent? Does Amanda have a real problem? Was it her parenting that caused the problem?

Amanda was eventually diagnosed with ADHD by the pediatrician a few months later. Her impulsivity and difficulty managing her emotions (emotional regulation) interfered with her ability to have quality relationships with peers. Children with ADHD are more likely to have fewer or no friends, poorer quality friendships, and social problems that may last into adulthood.[5] Amanda's mom learned that the behaviors associated with ADHD could negatively affect friendships. She was also told that marked difficulties with attention and concentration could impact schoolwork, the ability to follow directions, and the ability to "listen" to her parents. Amanda's pattern of "emotional dysregulation," including impulsivity, bossiness, aggression, and argumentative behavior with peers, is typical of children diagnosed with ADHD and is known to negatively impact social skills as documented by Russell Barkley, professor in the Department of Psychiatry at the Medical University of South Carolina.[9] As such, Amanda's symptoms extend beyond academics and into social dynamics. Social skills problems for children with ADHD may be visible very early on, or they may not really become apparent until around third grade, when the demands increase both socially and academically.

When is a social problem a *big* problem? Think of social abilities as lying on a continuum. Even children on the "acceptable" side of the continuum, having good social skills, will experience some conflict, have a bad play date, decide that they aren't friends anymore with someone, call someone a negative name, or have an "off day" when they are cranky and impolite. On the other end of the continuum are children who have these issues on a regular basis or *more often than not*. Furthermore, having a social skills deficit doesn't mean all aspects of social functioning are problematic. It may be that some, but not all, social abilities are affecting your child's adjustment. If you find yourself thinking your child does not seem to have quality relationships and these problems are impacting family relations, schoolwork, or your child's overall adjustment and happiness, then your child's social skills should probably be assessed and addressed. Parents may be primarily concerned with academic performance, but equal emphasis should be given to social skills. As mentioned earlier, lack of friendships is linked to mental health problems that can exacerbate or create difficulties in school. Therefore, early detection of problems is critical. Children who bully typically "justify" their behavior and lack insight into the consequences of their actions.[21] This lack of metacognition (see Chapter 6) further underscores that your involvement is necessary when you notice that something is "a little off."

CARTER: AT SCHOOL

Carter is 14 years old. He feels like an "outsider" at school although he knows everyone in his class. He never did fit in and feels left out of most school activities. It is as if things are happening in front of him like on a movie screen and that it is impossible for him to "get in." Carter has one good friend, Evan, from his science club and they eat lunch together in the science lab every day. Carter is a straight A student in his math and science classes but struggles a bit in Language Arts. The problem is that he feels vulnerable outside of classes. Carter feels awkward whenever he sees the popular guys in the hallways laughing and "horsing around." He just doesn't understand what they are doing differently. Was he supposed to do that stuff, too? He feels his stomach churning and wants to flee from the scene. Yet, it is these same guys who call him whenever there is a science or math project due.

Although Carter never feels quite right in school, he always receives great grades and he "gets by" in social situations because he just stays out of the way. He has heard that peers describe him as "pleasant." He doesn't really desire more friends because he is very content with Evan and the other guys from the science club. However, Carter can't escape from his uneasiness.

You may have noticed the following behaviors in your child if he or she has difficulties with social skills:

- Does not have a friendship that is reciprocated (your child is not "liked back" by the peer)
- States that everyone is his or her friend even though he or she does not know the friend well
- Does not have a best-friend relationship (fourth grade and beyond)
- Behaves in inappropriate ways in order to make friends (gives away belongings or is always making practical jokes for attention and approval)
- Tends to repeat the same unwanted behaviors with peers and doesn't learn from experience
- Chooses to play predominantly with other children a few years older or younger than himself or herself

- Chooses to play with peers who have other behavioral or developmental challenges
- Prefers to spend time with adults versus same-age peers
- Spends time with friends almost exclusively playing video games or watching TV (no face-to-face interactions)
- Often interrupts conversations with peers
- May be physically aggressive with peers
- Is considered mean, rude, or selfish by peers
- Does not understand facial expressions or gestures
- May only get invited to parties when the entire class is invited
- Criticizes others
- Does not recognize physical boundaries with others (crowds their space)
- Is ignored or excluded by peers at school
- Thinks that everyone feels as he or she does
- Does not know how to join in with peers during play or in conversation
- Often cannot keep new friends that he or she makes
- Avoids situations where he or she may meet new same-age peers
- Is typically lonely
- Often says he or she wants to be alone
- Is bossy and domineering in play
- Has trouble knowing what not to talk about in a certain setting
- Gets confused when others are talking because he or she does not understand the intent or goal of the conversation
- Talks over people or talks too loud
- Talks too much about himself or herself; engages in one-sided conversation
- Only has social interactions with peers through websites and not face to face

What are the signs that you should look for if your child is a victim of bullying?

- Anxiety about attending school
- Anxiety about normal route to school or riding the school bus
- Avoidance of social situations
- Avoidance of after-school places to "hang out" with peers
- Stomachaches or headaches and other physical ailments
- Difficulty getting to or staying asleep at night
- Tearfulness
- Difficulty managing anger at home
- Abandoned Internet or mobile devices
- Recess or lunch time spent in class
- Decreased sense of self-esteem
- Sudden change in interest in school or extracurricular activities

- Declining grades
- Belongings damaged with no explanations
- Comments that life is not worth living anymore
- Running away from home
- Alcohol or drug use
- Unexplained physical injuries, such as bruises

What are the signs that you should look for if your child is bullying others?

- Often makes negative comments about selective peers
- Exhibits aggressive behavior
- Some peers are avoiding your child
- Has low frustration tolerance and bad temper
- Has difficulty managing anger at home
- Complains that no one plays with him or her
- Likes to be dominant over others

While friendships are incredibly important, please note that the goal is not necessarily to become a "social butterfly." The basic goal for children with social difficulties is to know how to navigate social situations successfully and to develop at least a couple of quality reciprocal relationships. To achieve this goal, parents need to be *actively* involved with helping their child make friends and helping to coach them in appropriate and effective social behavior. As mentioned earlier, children will not "grow out of" nor learn how to "work out" social skills problems with peers without explicit (step-by-step) instruction. As a child becomes older, parental involvement changes but is still necessary. This may involve making sure the child has opportunities to make new friends, such as extracurricular activities, and helping to manage the child's schedule so he or she has unstructured or free time with friends. Some children, such as those on the autistic spectrum, may not have the motivation or the potential to move beyond the basics of social interaction. Therefore, expectations must match the individual characteristics of your child.

THE ROADMAP

For children with poor social skills, it is important to obtain an assessment to identify the child's strengths and weaknesses cognitively, emotionally, and behaviorally. This process will reveal the *big picture* of your child's abilities. Social skills can also be measured by observations of your child in unstructured situations by parents, teachers, and others close to the child. Typically, these individuals will complete inventories designed to assess a child's ability to navigate socially in many situations such as home and school. An interview with the teacher(s) may clarify additional questions after the inventories are reviewed by the evaluator. In addition, the examiner will want to interview the child, depending on his or her age. Lastly, the evaluator will have an in-depth interview with the parents to review their child's development, early social interactions with the family and others, and ability to use language effectively. The quality and types of peer relationships are also probed by the examiner. To help the evaluation process, you may want to think about the following questions:

- Does your child initiate play with other children?
- Does your child desire friendships?
- Does your child prefer to play one on one versus in a group situation?
- How does your child resolve conflict?
- Does your child have a best friend?
- Does your child have many friends?
- Does your child have many acquaintances?
- Does your child prefer to play with children either older or younger than him- or herself?
- How does your child manage rejection?
- Is your child argumentative with others and does not "let up"?
- Does your child understand nonverbal (visual) signals such as different facial expressions?
- Does your child look at others when they talk?
- If your child is not included in an activity, does he or she take it as a personal attack or become emotionally hurt?
- Is your child drawn to children that you do not approve of and are a bad influence?
- Does your child enjoy interactions with others?
- Is your child withdrawing from others? If yes, has this been a recent occurrence?
- Can your child communicate personal feelings to others?

Amanda's pediatrician also referred her to the local neuropsychologist, Dr. Goodman, for a more in-depth evaluation of her strengths and weaknesses. The pediatrician wondered whether Amanda was depressed or anxious at that time. The neuropsychologist also wondered whether Amanda was suffering from a learning disorder. All of these factors needed to be considered because of Amanda's trouble with managing her anger. Dr. Goodman told the mother that Amanda did not have a learning disorder. She was not depressed or anxious. However, she explained that Amanda had trouble managing her emotions. In particular, Dr. Goodman indicated that Amanda had a low frustration level, seemed to get impatient easily, and was very impulsive. The neuropsychologist called this "emotional impulsiveness," as coined by prominent researcher Russell Barkley.[9] These factors impacted Amanda's ability to regulate her emotions and socialize with others both in and out of school. The neuropsychologist recommended that Amanda and her mother take part in a social skills training group offered by a clinical psychologist in the community. They signed up to take part in the next twelve-week program that was offered.

Carter's mother took him to a clinical psychologist to discuss his nervousness and difficulties socializing with the other students at his school. The psychologist met with Carter and his mother together and separately. She also had them, his father, and even a couple of Carter's teachers fill out several inventories. Much to Carter's and his mother's surprise, the psychologist reported that Carter's symptoms of social discomfort, social confusion, and anxiety were consistent with an autistic spectrum disorder. In addition to individual therapy, the psychologist suggested social skills training as well as speech therapy to work on pragmatics/social communication skills (see Chapter 7).

As described previously, behaviors associated with attention (see Chapter 4), executive functioning (see Chapter 6), language (see Chapter 7), and emotional weaknesses (see Chapter 11) can cause or contribute to social skills difficulties. It is particularly important to include the assessment of social skills in the evaluation of children with suspected ADHD, autistic spectrum disorders, fetal alcohol spectrum disorder, specific language impairment, or emotional disorders. In addition, assessment for those children with genetic disorders such as neurofibromatosis type 1 (see Chapter 8) and medical conditions such as head injury also include a routine check of a child's social functioning. Comprehensive assessments including social skills are typically conducted by professionals such as pediatric neuropsychologists, child clinical psychologists, and pediatric psychiatrists.

Following a comprehensive evaluation, an IEP or a 504 plan may be indicated to implement goals and objectives to help your child in unstructured or social situations at school (see Chapter 1). If bullying or victimization is an issue with your child, preventive measures should be taken, including participation in a school bullying prevention program.

Looking Ahead

WHAT DO YOU DO NOW?

Amanda: Six Months Later
Amanda was angry at first when she had to see a doctor to talk about her friends. She had better things to do! When she began attending the group on making friends at the suggestion of her doctor, she did not want to get to know the other kids. But when the

therapist began asking questions in a group setting, she saw they were a lot like her. Amanda was able to "practice" with these kids she did not know. It was okay to do something incorrectly. No one became upset with her. When Amanda was ready, she began to do some of the things her therapist showed her at school. She learned that, instead of just barging in to play a game with other girls, she should watch and wait to get invited in. One day at recess she tried it for the first time. And guess what? Her classmates invited her to play. That little event made Amanda's day! Amanda had twelve group sessions with the therapist and now she goes in individually to help support what she has learned. Amanda has made several new friends from class whom she plays with regularly outside of school.

Amanda's Mother

Amanda's mother couldn't be more relieved. She never fooled herself into thinking her child would be "Miss Popularity," but she always expected Amanda would at least find children like herself to bond with. The past several months were painful and heart-breaking to watch once she recognized the signs of her daughter's social difficulties. Finally, after Amanda received some professional help, she can see a difference in her daughter. She saw where Amanda's impulsivity, inattentiveness, and low frustration tolerance were interfering with her ability to make and keep friends. Amanda's mother met with the therapist several times to discuss how to support her daughter's efforts. With her knowledge of what Amanda has been learning, she can confidently help her daughter create meaningful friendships.

The Accommodation Plan

WHAT TYPES OF INTERVENTIONS AND STRATEGIES WOULD BE HELPFUL?

Parental involvement in the identification and remediation of social skills problems and weaknesses is of critical importance. Parent-assisted social skills interventions have demonstrated gains in social functioning for children with ADHD, fetal alcohol spectrum disorder, and autistic spectrum disorders. One intervention, consisting only of parent coaching, resulted in improved social functioning for children with ADHD. For children on the autistic spectrum, various social skills training studies have demonstrated positive results. After-school programs aimed at improving social skills are shown to increase positive social behaviors and decrease problem behaviors.[5,7,23–28] Professionals such as clinical psychologists, social workers, and speech-language therapists may offer individual or group sessions targeting improvement in social skills. Local therapists or university counseling centers may be able to help you find where these services are offered.

Researchers Fred Frankel, Robert Myatt, and Elizabeth Laugeson at the University of California, Los Angeles, have suggested the following key principles to help your child or teen make and keep friends[29,30]:

- Parent involvement is necessary to support the development of friendships; children with social skills weaknesses cannot achieve this on their own.
- Children and teens should have regular one-on-one play dates or get-togethers with same-age peers in order to develop best friendships.
- Parents must make time for their children and teens to have friends over.
- Parents should be present to supervise play dates or get-togethers.
- Parents should not make play dates with children whom they know to have negative feelings toward their child even if their child is requesting it; the goal is a successful play date.
- Parents should keep play dates or gatherings with new friends short to ensure success.
- If a child or teen is not finding friends in the school setting, parents need to help the child or teen by expanding his or her social circle through extracurricular activities such as team sports, art class, or drama.
- How to handle teasing or bullying needs to be taught explicitly, not necessarily just "walk away" or "tell a teacher."
- Conversational skills and joining groups of friends in conversation or at play need to be explicitly taught and practiced.

To follow are tips for parents whose child is a victim of bullying, including cyberbullying, as suggested by psychologist Richard S. Newman and pediatrician and health journalist Gwenn Schurgin O'Keeffe[20]:

- Talk to your child about the differences between normal conflict and bullying.
- Help your child to understand when an incident is intentional versus accidental.
- Have your child distance him- or herself from a peer known to be overly aggressive.
- Prior to acting (or retaliating), your child should think about the severity of the incident and calmly formulate a plan of what to do.
- Your child should practice being assertive (confidently telling the bully "no" or "stop").
- Instruct your child not to overreact in aggressive ways that make the incident worse.
- Always have your child seek help from a peer or adult when the situation is repetitive or potentially dangerous.

- Decide with your child under what circumstances he or she should seek help and when he or she should try to resolve a conflict on his or her own.
- Both you and your child should inform an adult at the school (or the setting where it occurs) so that your child feels comfortable seeking help from that adult in order to reduce his or her anxiety or fear about encountering the perpetrator.
- Remember that threats and physical aggression always require adult intervention.
- Role-play and model how to handle verbal and physical bullying with your child at home.
- Educate your child and role-play with him or her about bullying *before* it happens (such as early elementary school) in order to prepare your child for such situations should they occur.
- Foster the development of quality friendships because they are protective against effects of bullying.
- Block out the bully on all social media including phone and e-mail carriers.
- Print out records of cyberbullying behavior and assess for degree of harm.
- Become involved with and support school programs aimed at combating bullying.
- Ensure that school programs incorporating bullying prevention also address cyberbullying and education regarding self-harm and suicide prevention.

With respect to cyberbullying, parents must educate their children about the Internet, e-mail, and mobile text-messaging use and safety. Some things to remember and educate your child about include:

- Cyberbullying requires parental intervention and ongoing *active* monitoring by the adult.
- Any written comment via electronic media, including humor, can be misinterpreted and create anger and retaliation.
- Any written comment can be read by anyone at any time.
- You cannot take back or erase a comment that you regret.
- Know that your message can be sent to anyone by the recipient.
- Your child should not reveal personal information such as a phone number or address for safety purposes.
- Posting a photo or private family information on the Internet is not confidential.
- Invest in software that allows parental control of online activities.
- Be actively involved in helping your child understand and use security features on Internet sites.
- Place your child's computer in a common area in the home to discourage inappropriate computer use.

- Keep an open line of communication with your child's school principal or director regarding cyberbullying if your child is victimized.

WHAT TYPES OF ACCOMMODATIONS WOULD BE HELPFUL AT SCHOOL?

For students eligible under classifications such as "other health impaired," "emotional disturbance," "autism," and "speech or language impairment," specialized services and accommodations for social skills may be included in their overall IEP or 504 plan. For example, individual counseling is a common school-based service for students with social skills deficits. Accommodations are typically suggested to "level the playing field" for those students who show substantial limitations in their ability to learn and in their ability to navigate during unstructured activities such as recess and lunch periods. As mentioned previously, social communication deficits are comorbid with other challenges. Deficient pragmatic skills in the context of language functioning may contribute to social skills impairment. The latter will warrant accommodations (see Chapter 7). Pragmatics can also impact reading comprehension and written expression, which require corresponding accommodations (see Chapter 10). In addition, children with ADHD may have problems with social communication skills (see Chapter 4). All accommodations should be matched to the needs of the individual child based on the results of a thorough evaluation. Additional classroom accommodations for children with social communication impairments may include:

- Advance warning on projects/tests
- Assistance with focusing from teacher
- Breaks (additional, extended, frequent)
- Check for understanding of information
- Checklists (self-monitoring forms)
- Concept or knowledge maps
- Educational facilitator (such as a supportive assistant/shadow for the younger child)
- Educational facilitator to encourage proofreading and remaining on task
- Large assignments broken into smaller assignments
- Minimal distractions
- Oral presentations prepared before class
- Pass to leave classroom at student's discretion for physical/emotional reasons (management of anger and other emotions to be discussed with a trusted staff member)
- Peer assistance for in-class assignments
- Private learning space

- Scheduled day plan (participation in after-school programs targeting social skills; scheduled time with the school counselor, principal, or director to discuss social problems or bullying incidents)
- Teacher engagement:
  - Allow student to have his or her own "space" when stressed.
  - Be prepared for periods of anxiety with stress-reducing activities.
  - Encourage eye contact.
  - Facilitate or supervise play during unstructured activities such as recess or lunch.
  - Guide other classmates in interacting with the child.
  - Interpret situations for the student.
  - Maintain consistency in your approach.
  - Show the child what is expected by providing explicit examples.
  - Simplify language and keep abstractions to a minimum (concrete, direct, and explicit instructions should be given).
  - Support the child in physical activities if coordination is a problem.
  - Support the parents with daily information about any behavior that is of concern.
- Visual tools (outlines/PowerPoint) used in conjunction with oral instruction

WHAT TYPES OF ACCOMMODATIONS WOULD BE HELPFUL FOR TESTS?

Because of pragmatic difficulties (see Chapter 7) and associated written expression and reading comprehension weaknesses (see Chapter 10), accommodations on tests are often recommended for children with social skills difficulties.

The evaluators assessing Amanda and Carter considered the following options for test accommodations:

- Advance warning on tests
- Breaks (additional, extended, frequent)
- Different test day or time
- Extended time (with amount of time specified)
- Familiar test administrator
- Oral examination
- Test setting (private, semiprivate, small group)

Carter: Beyond High School

Carter was shocked to learn that what he was experiencing was due to an autistic spectrum condition. Because he was more aware, Carter remembered that he used to get quite anxious. With the help of a counselor, he accepted his disability and realized that he was not crazy after all! As a matter of fact, the knowledge gave him power and increased his self-confidence. Carter continued to make more friends through the science club and was even elected president of the club for the following three years. He also developed a peer-mentoring society to help children who had difficulties with math and science. Carter realized that his feelings were normal and he learned how to advocate for himself. The counselor gave him tools from her "toolbox" so that he could understand the world around him. Although he always felt comfortable with his "science" friends, Carter also met others who were not in his "circle" because he had the "tools" to read body language. He also understood his body language better. Carter now has the confidence to walk around his new campus without feeling like he is just part of "the audience."

THE BIG PICTURE

CHAPTER 13

Things to Remember

PUTTING IT ALL TOGETHER

By now, you have either read this entire book or read selective chapters to help you understand your child's challenges. You can see that each child is truly unique and that each family will take a different route based on their child's distinct "roadmap." It is the *roadmap* that is the key to understanding your child's individual learning needs. This roadmap will identify specific directions that will allow your child *access* to all learning and test-taking situations.

Knowledge is power! Despite well-meaning intentions, some parents are fearful of the assessment process because of their angst about the unknown. Not acting because of these fears can be costly. For example, your child may be experiencing problems with depression, and this can affect his or her performance in school. However, teachers may interpret this behavior as your child being lazy without really knowing the reason why he or she is not motivated. You, in turn, may be equally disappointed because your effort to engage your child leads to anger and frustration. The lesson here is obvious. Knowledge of your child's strengths and weaknesses will have deep and profound implications as your child matures in the years to come.

We propose that you consider the following salient points as you embark on your journey:

- Early detection of weaknesses is crucial in order to prevent problems from increasing over time.
- Do not wait for your child to age to see if the problems "go away."
- Make sure that your child's physical, vision, and hearing examinations are current.
- Call your local university or pediatric clinic if you need assistance in finding an evaluator.
- Don't be afraid to seek an opinion from more than one professional if needed.

- Always ask questions if you do not understand what the evaluator is telling you.
- There is no such thing as an inappropriate question.
- There is a difference between behavior that happens once in a while versus behavior that is *frequent*, *pervasive*, and *severe*.
- It is the *frequency*, *pervasiveness*, and *severity* of the behavior that make it a *big* problem.
- The goal is not to label a child, but to address the behaviors that are negatively impacting him or her.
- A student can have a disorder and not be disabled.
- Disorders and disabilities can wax and wane, depending on their nature.
- A comprehensive evaluation is necessary when evaluating a student's strengths and weaknesses and for identifying appropriate accommodations in classroom and test-taking situations.
- Stay involved with the assessment process and gather information from your family members and teachers in order to obtain different points of view concerning your child's behavior at home and at school.
- Remember that teacher perspectives are important in order to understand a child's behavior in classroom environments and in test-taking situations.
- A disorder *and* a disability must significantly impact your child's *current* academic functioning in test-taking situations in order to be considered for test accommodation(s) for high-stakes examinations.
- Not all disabilities negatively impact test performance.
- Don't be angry with the evaluator if he or she does not confirm your opinion.
- Accommodations need to be tailored to each disability with a rationale provided to explain *why* the accommodations are necessary.
- Remember that accommodations allow *access* to classroom and test-taking situations.
- Accommodations do not alter a test or give preference to a student when taking a test.
- Accommodations for the SAT and ACT tests are not guaranteed even though the student has had accommodations for test-taking situations in elementary, middle, or high school.
- Envision the *big picture* as you seek out answers.
- Remember that you are your child's advocate and manager.
- Support and encourage your child.

One student, Alex, had this to say:

"I'm 26 years old and I was tested when I was 6 and 16. Why? Well, I was a bit hyper when I was 6 years old. My parents felt that I would 'grow out of it.' I was the 'class clown.' Eventually, I got anxious and felt lonely because play dates were not happening. I felt lousy. I did not grow out of it. I knew that I was smart but something wasn't right. I eventually got the help that I needed. That help made all the difference. I got into college and was allowed accommodations like extended time for tests and a note taker for classes. I did well. My dream is to attend business school. It is clear that I need more education to do what I want to do. I will need to be tested again for GMAT accommodations. I'm pretty confident that I will be allowed additional time for the test. I'm grateful that I will be able to show what I know with the extended-time accommodation. I also know that I will be successful with the support of my parents, professors, and friends."

CHAPTER 14

A Success Story

A STUDENT'S PLEA FOR HELP

Diane

Diane was previously assessed by a clinical psychologist when she was in the second grade. Her parents were told that she had a reading disorder because she had significant difficulty sounding out words that she could not memorize. Because of her decoding problems, Diane had trouble reading quickly and smoothly (see Chapter 10). Her parents were also told that, although she was very bright (her intellectual level was within the superior range), problems with attention and concentration were affecting her ability to complete tests and work in class. They were informed that her reading and focusing problems were two separate disorders. The psychologist suggested educational accommodations for her in school. Diane's parents gave the report to the school director, Dr. Lightwood, and she agreed that Diane needed classroom and test accommodations. Her parents made it clear to the director that they did not want any special treatment for Diane. Dr. Lightwood explained to them that Diane would still take the same tests as her classmates but she needed accommodations so her grades would not be penalized because of her disabilities. As a result of the conference with the director, Diane was allowed 100 percent extended time on all tests, oral examinations when necessary, preferential seating, and breaks to allow her to get up and move around during lengthy tests. The teachers met with Diane after class to review what she had learned during the day and helped her study for quizzes and tests. These accommodations continued throughout elementary, middle, and high school. Diane's mother read to Diane every evening and actively discussed any assigned reading with her as well. This took a lot of time, but her mother was devoted to her daughter and was not aware of any other way to help her. Unfortunately, Diane's parents and teachers were not aware of any reading interventions at that time. However, Diane did very well throughout her schooling despite her daily challenges with reading and focusing.

2009 Day One: In My Office

It is October 2009. Diane is 19 years old and in her freshman year at college. Diane is not thrilled to see me. She knows the results from the previous assessment are too "old" for college purposes. Diane admits to me she is dreading the reassessment because she is still experiencing problems with reading and focusing and has additional problems with organizational skills. She does not want to be embarrassed again in front of someone she doesn't even know. However, Diane is motivated to do her best. Because Diane worked day and night on her studies to get good grades and because she excelled in basketball, she was offered scholarships at some of the top universities in the country. The college requested a current assessment to document her disabilities. Diane was told accommodations at college could not be considered without the required documentation.

I interviewed Diane extensively. I also interviewed her parents for two hours to understand what Diane's challenges were in school and at home now and in the past. Diane tells me that taking tests in college is stressful. She also tells me that she has written in her journal about a recent test-taking experience in college. I decide to include her journal entry in the documentation as an example of what a challenged student experiences when taking a test. Here is what Diane wrote:

Although I knew a college midterm would be different than any midterms back home, I prepared the same way I would for any high school midterm or final. I used my techniques and methods that have made me successful in the past. These tricks have been modified and perfected over the course of 7 years. Why change when something is working for you? If I could compare this the testing and studying dynamic to anything I would compare it to running a race. I start training before the others. I learn ways to perfect my 'running technique' because for some reason I just don't run exactly like the rest of kids. I train the hardest not when the race is around the corner, because for me that doesn't work. Once I get to starting line I am ready to go and take off with the rest of the group. And in the end I finish with honors, or at least I place very high. Tonight I walk into the classroom, prepared for a race that I knew was going to be hard, and they placed a 30 lbs weight around my waist. The funny thing is I knew the weight was coming, but there was no way for me to prepare for it. This is where my analogy ends.

I started the exam at 6:10. I started my watch and began to work on the multiple choice. I read the question once through to get a baseline. Except once I had finished reading it, the words just look like symbols on a page. It's easy to understand why that didn't work: At least 50% of the multiple choice questions had 2 or 3 contingencies that affected one another in different ways. Okay round two: I reread the question even slower, quietly mouthing the words, and then I reread the part that seems the most important and highlight it. Finally I repeat in my own words what the question is specifically asking and what clauses are affecting the main point of the question. Then I look at the answers. I read through the answers. Ok once again I have to reread them. If the answer has a concept with an action I write on the side what it is. For example if one possible answer is: an increase in income, leading to a decrease in the demand for good X. I would write on the side (with up arrow) and next to it an equal sign with a question mark beside it and then Dx (with downward arrow). After doing this to usually 6 or 7 multiple choice options I reread the question. I then cross out the multiple choice that I know are wrong. Finally I try and process the answer or draw a picture or possibly think of a prior example it relates to. But today I did all these things and then I realized it had taken me 5 minutes to get this far. I had to move on to the next question if I wanted to come remotely close to finishing. I answered about 7 of the multiple choice questions fully and marked a few more because I knew I was on the right track but didn't have time to do those last vital steps. Once I was half way through I realized that I wouldn't be finishing. I tried to speed up my methods but that didn't work. In fact it made me more anxious and more distracted. I grew more and more frustrated with myself because there was no way for my brain to move faster.

Then I started working on the free response question. However, I misread the first part of the question and did parts 2 and 3 wrong because of it. I then was told I had ten minutes left. Only ten minutes to go back to all the questions I either skipped or worked 50% on. Only ten minutes to review my entire exam. Only ten minutes to find the usually large amount of silly mistakes I make. Only ten minutes to finish this one question. Needless to say in those ten minutes I didn't finish the free response question, and moreover I didn't review my exam at all. The most frustrating part is flipping through page of unanswered questions and seeing a multiple choice question I know I can solve but don't have the time to. With 2 minutes left I went through guessed on 13 multiple choice questions. At 7:55 I turned in my exam. For the first time I can honestly say I crossed the finish line, with a 30 lbs of burden, and never having felt so defeated. And I can honestly say I will forever remember how the first time I signed the college honor code, I cried.

2009 Day Two: In My Office

I am completing the assessment of Diane and decide to ask Diane to write an essay exploring the reasons why she needs extended time on tests. It is very clear to me that Diane has significant problems with reading, writing, and focusing and that these difficulties are negatively impacting her ability to show what she truly knows on a test. Diane is obviously very, very bright and has an amazing "heart." However, she is still struggling due to her disabilities compared to her nondisabled peers. Diane wrote the following letter to the director of the Office of Disability Services:

To Whom It May Concern:

My own disability inhibits me from being able to articulate my disability. If I could say it in a conversation it would make sense, but putting it on paper is what makes it so hard.

I write this in order to explain my request for 100% extended time. One hundred percent extended time is key to my academic success for the following reasons: The way I take tests and process the material on tests is a time consuming and energy expensive endeavor. My whole life I have always had trouble completing tests in the time constraints given. At a young age I remember taking literature or history tests and failing to complete them in time, but teachers luckily gave me extra time. At that time I had not been diagnosed with any learning disabilities or ADHD therefore I had not learned any tools which would help me. I simply thought that I wasn't smart enough. I would sit and take tests and get frustrated because it was almost as if I couldn't take the test but knew the information. Taking tests was traumatic experience for me.

Once I was diagnosed I was able to learn tools which helped get the information out. This helped with my frustration and I began to understand that I wasn't stupid. The tools I have learned enabled me to take on the test but the process of completing the task still takes much longer than it would for students without disabilities. Taking tests is a daunting task for me. Because I have so much trouble reading and deciphering words, and making meaning of the words, tests are very difficult. In addition to the difficulties of deciphering words, retrieving information from my brain relating to the words during the exam time is another task that is extremely energy and time consuming.

When I take a test, most of the time I struggle to find out what the questions are before I even think about the answers. If the questions are really complex, or if I need to read an essay or an article, this takes me a long time and sometimes I need to take notes or reorganize key information. Sometimes I need to make notecards or an outline to work from. It is so frustrating, because all of this comes before I even start to try to answer the question. But then when I try to answer the questions I need to reach to the back of my brain and retrieve the information and the process is even harder. The words and ideas are almost stuck in the back of my head. It feels like as I search for the answer I am leafing through every part of my brain. Sometimes I can stare at a test and see my notes about that topic in my head, but have no idea what they mean. I literally can see the words, but not understand what to do with them. Tests have to be taken in small parts so I can work with all of the words and ideas that relate to the question or the answer. On top of this, when asked to consider different perspectives, I have never been able to consider the multiple sides of a question. I have to pick one side and work really hard to come up with a good answer.

Not to mention it is extremely hard to sit and work when everyone around you has finished and can do the test in the allotted time. It takes me longer to process the information and recall it. When I have the extra time I am able to better understand the test and retrieve the information I know. 100 percent extended time is what allows me to use the tools I know and complete the test. Without the 100 percent extended time I am not able to adequately understand or finish the test.

Once I begin the test I do a "mind dump." This is where I write down key points which I remember. This mind dump is useful because it helps me clear my thoughts and get started. Then I start the test. Every question poses a different challenge for me. For example on a multiple choice question I first read the question. However, it takes me so long read the question and each word that by the time I get to the end of the question I have forgotten what the questions was even asking. Therefore I read the question again and sometimes make notes about the question to help me remember. If there is a word I have never seen before this poses a new challenge for me. I can't break down words into small parts, and I have to understand new words based on the sentence that they appear in. So when a new word is in front of me I work to understand how important the word is, and then need to figure out how it relates to the question and the answer that I am working. Now I read it again and highlight the key parts in the question. I repeat out loud to myself in my words what the question is asking.

I have a hard time with multiple choice questions. When I get them on a test I have to read each question a few times in order to figure out exactly what information I need to find in my brain about the specific topic being asked about. Then I start to look at the multiple choice options. I read the possible answers once through and then reread the answers. Then I examine each answer and how it relates to the question. I go down and each answer I reread and cross it out or leave it. Then I again read through the ones that I think could possibly work. If I have trouble understanding the options I write next to it in my own words what I think it means or a symbol. Then I eventually answer the question. If I still don't know the answer I will mark it and move on. One of the reasons tests are so hard are because they aren't just regurgitation of facts. The tests I take are the application of the concepts I have learned. I no longer face tests that are the simple memorization. Retrieving facts is already difficult for me. It's hard because if I study I know the material. The hardest part is trying to retrieve facts and then establish relationships and inferences. And those are the questions I face on tests. While this is going on it's also a difficult process because of my ADD. Since the test taking process as a whole is consuming, it is important I don't get distracted. My concentration has to be regular and consistent if I want to be able to retrieve facts. Therefore it is very hard to take tests as I fight myself in concentrating and remaining focused. This battle to stay focused becomes harder as the test progresses because I start to get really tired. I think of this as my brain fatigue. As I get more mentally tired I remember less and begin to make even greater stupid mistakes. This is when extended breaks come into play.

Other types of questions I face are essay questions. I delve into an essay question almost in the same fashion as a multiple choice question. I read the question through and then reread it three times. When I read essay questions although I see the words, can read them, and know what each word means individually, there is still a disconnect and I don't understand what the question is asking. In order to help me with this disconnect my learning support teacher would read the question aloud to me and then I would read it silently as she read it out loud. We would highlight certain parts of the question and break down each part. I would explain to her in my own words what the question was asking. Once it "clicked" it was very easy for me to answer the question and understand what it was asking. The next challenge was organizing my thoughts. While I knew how to answer the question, articulating my thoughts in an organized way is very difficult. I tend to forget to answer a large part of the question or my thoughts are very discombobulated. Therefore any time I answer a question that is in essay form (this includes short answer questions as well) I make an outline. In this outline I try and organize all my thoughts and make sure I am answering all parts of the question. I also use a computer to make this process easier. When I'm finished making this outline I begin to type the essay.

Including having trouble on tests I have always had trouble with reading. In 1st and 2nd grade I remember having to read with my mom because I couldn't read the books that were required for school. Throughout my grade school career I greatly struggled with reading and because of this every time I had reading my mom had to do it with me. As I got older my mom continued to read with me to ensure I understood all the material. On average, the amount of time it took me to do my work was double that of my peers. I used to feel very inadequate because I couldn't just sit in class and read like my classmates could. I was so embarrassed.

Something that I have always struggled with on all kinds of tests is the amount of time that I have for each section. I think that I get caught up in trying to understand the questions and the test itself, and in deciphering new words, and lose track of time. When I start to answer questions I concentrate so hard that I lose track of everything around me. When I was in upper school I was fortunate enough to have a Learning Support Department and caring teachers who would remind me to be careful about time. I will always appreciate their help, and how much they obviously cared about my education. They always told me that I could perform at the top.

It made me feel like I had accomplished something really important when they also asked me to talk with younger students who had been newly diagnosed with learning disabilities about how I was able to be so successful. I am so honored that I was also asked to speak to some parents about this, too.

Diane: In My Office

Based on my review of the psychologist's report from second grade, previous educational records, neuropsychological assessment, interviews with Diane and her parents, review of the inventories completed by Diane and her parents and teachers, and the documentation of her functioning during high school, I recommended Diane be granted the following test accommodations: 100 percent additional time for all tests at her college, a human reader, one examination per day, use of a word processor, and the ability to take tests in a small group setting. The college granted these accommodations to her. During the process of evaluating Diane, I noted that she had never had any remediation directed to her problems. I told Diane and her parents that there were evidence-based programs that could help Diane with her reading and gave them some referrals to people who could help her.

Diane

"I'm so happy that the college agreed with Dr. Schiltz that test accommodations were necessary because of my severe learning disabilities. I have taken two tests now and passed them both. I can't wait to tell my parents! I know that I will do well in college and I look forward to living my dream of entering sports medicine in the future. Dr. Schiltz also referred me to a reading specialist. I saw her four times a week over the summer, and the words began to look different to me and made sense. I can now see the words in my brain. It's as if my brain has been rewired! I wish we had found out about this help back when I was 10!"

Diane's Mother

Diane and her mom are visiting Diane's Aunt Jane who is in the hospital for a minor procedure. They have brought a stack of paperbacks for her. Because Jane has misplaced her glasses and can't see to read without them, she asks Diane what one of the paperbacks is about. Diane flips open the cover and reads the jacket blurb to her. Diane's mom excuses herself and goes into the bathroom and quietly weeps tears of joy for a minute. At age 20, her daughter has learned to read. She splashes water on her face, takes a deep breath, and rejoins her family with a big smile.

Appendix 1

CLASSROOM ACCOMMODATIONS

- Abbreviation expander (a software program that allows a student to type an abbreviation for commonly used words and phrases with the program completing the word or phrase)
- Adaptive tools/conditions (chair, desk, special lighting, acoustics, listening devices)
- Additional time to answer questions
- Additional time to process information
- Advance warning on projects/tests
- Alternate keyboard
- Alternate mouse system
- Assignment sheets (daily, weekly, monthly)
- Assistance with focusing from teacher
- Audiotaped lectures
- Books on tape
- Braillers (system of communication for visually impaired students to read and write)
- Breaks (additional, extended, frequent)
- Calculator
- Check for understanding of information
- Checklists (self-monitoring forms)
- Clear and consistent instruction
- Closed-captioned television
- Color cues to reduce confusion between easily reversed numbers and symbols
- Communication board (visual tools to facilitate expressive communication)
- Computer
- Concept or knowledge maps (diagrams to help organize knowledge)
- Copies of homework assignments, lecture material, and notes
- Digitized or electronic text (e-text is text-based information available in a computerized format, such as Recording for the Blind & Dyslexic)

- Educational facilitator (such as a supportive assistant/shadow for the younger child) to encourage remaining on task
- Embedded e-text support (organizational aid to highlight and summarize text, etc.)
- Enlarged font on computer monitor
- Enlarged-print text
- Examples of what is expected
- Extended time on homework, in-class work, and projects
- Extra set of books at home
- Eye contact established and maintained with student
- Formula sheet
- Full/partial waiver of a foreign language class
- Grammar checker
- Graph paper
- Graphic organizers
- Handheld digital voice recorder
- Increased amount of space between items on a worksheet to reduce the amount of extra information on a page
- Large assignments broken into smaller assignments
- Large monitor
- Medical devices (not attached to the body) such as asthma inhalers, crutches, diabetic equipment, eye drops, or a wheelchair
- Minimal distractions
- Note taker (a student who takes lecture notes for the disabled student)
- Oral and written instructions regarding announcements/assignments
- Oral presentations (prepared before class)
- Orientation aids (markers to block out unnecessary information, rulers to help student maintain place on a page, highlighters for key words in the work directions, reduced number of items on an in-class/homework assignment)
- Outline of instruction prior to class instruction
- Paper divided into distinct sections to help maintain focus on an item
- Paraphrased information
- Pass to leave classroom at student's discretion for physical/emotional reasons (bathroom breaks, occurrence of tics, management of pain) on an as needed basis
- Peer assistance for in-class assignments (discussing material to enhance understanding)
- Preferential seating
- Private learning space
- Proofreading assistance
- Quiet setting to work

- Read-alouds (electronic/human)
- Recorder (digital/tape)
- Reduced items on a page
- Repetition of oral instructions
- Routines and rules displayed visually
- Scheduling plan
- School day plan
- Screen magnification software
- Screens to block out distraction
- Scribe (recorder and writer of answers)
- Service animals
- Shortened class day
- Sign language interpreter
- Small group setting
- Speech-to-text software (allows a student to dictate and speech is converted into print)
- Spell checker
- Spelling not graded
- Study guides for quizzes/tests
- Talking calculator (calculators with speech options)
- Talking word processor
- Tape recorder for dictation
- Teacher engagement
- Text-to-speech software (spoken version of text)
- Typewriter
- Typist for dictation
- Videotaped class sessions
- Visual tools (outlines/PowerPoint) used in conjunction with oral instruction
- Voice notepad
- Voice recognition software (for dictation purposes)
- Water bottle/snacks
- Wheelchair access
- Wide-lined paper or paper with raised lines
- Word banks
- Word prediction software (software that anticipates a word the student intends to type)
- Word processor
- Word processor with spell checker
- Writing preference flexibility (allows a student to choose printing or cursive)
- Writing tool flexibility (allows a student to choose his or her writing tool, such as a pencil or pen)
- Written directions

Appendix 2

TESTING ACCOMMODATIONS*

- Abbreviation expander (a software program that allows a student to type an abbreviation for commonly used words and phrases with the program completing the word or phrase)
- Ability to point to answers
- Adaptive tools/conditions (chair, desk, special lighting, acoustics, listening devices)
- Advance warning on tests
- Alternate keyboard
- Alternate mouse system
- Alternate non-Scantron answer sheet
- Alternative testing format, such as multiple-choice formats
- Alternative testing site (home, hospital)
- Assistance with multiple-choice answer sheet (Scantron sheet)
- Audio recording of test questions
- Audio recording with large-print figure supplement
- Audio recording with raised-line figure supplement
- Braillers (system of communication for visually impaired students to read and write)
- Breaks (additional, extended, frequent)
- Calculator
- Closed-captioned television
- Communication board (visual tools to facilitate expressive communication)
- Computer for entire test (administration and response)
- Computer for essay
- Computer with spell checker for essay
- Dictionary
- Different test day or time
- Digitized or electronic text (e-text is text-based information available in a computerized format, such as Recording for the Blind & Dyslexic)

- Enlarged font on computer monitor
- Extended time (with amount of time specified)
- Familiar test administrator
- Formula sheet
- Grammar checker
- Graph paper
- Lamp(s) to control light conditions
- Large-block answer sheet
- Large monitor
- Large-print answer sheet
- Large-print digital clock
- Large-print test
- Lined paper
- Medical devices (not attached to the body) such as a wheelchair, crutches, eye drops, asthma inhalers, or diabetic equipment
- Monitoring by teacher
- Multiple-choice format
- Multiple-day testing sessions
- One examination per day
- Oral examination
- Orientation aids (markers to block out unnecessary information, rulers to help maintain place, highlighters to emphasize key words, reduced number of items on page)
- Preferential seating
- Proofreader
- Read-alouds (electronic/human)
- Recording of responses in test booklet
- Scratch paper (to work out math problems, to take notes)
- Screen magnification software
- Screens to block out distractions
- Scribe (recorder and writer of answers)
- Service animals
- Sign language interpreter (for directions and test items)
- Sit/stand during examination
- Speech-to-text software (allows a student to dictate and speech is converted into print)
- Spell checker
- Talking calculator (calculators with speech options)
- Talking word processor
- Tape recorder for dictation
- Test administrator to paraphrase test directions
- Test setting (private, semiprivate, small group)

- Text-to-speech software (spoken version of text)
- Typewriter
- Typist for dictation
- Voice recognition software (for dictation purposes)
- Water bottle/snacks
- Wheelchair access
- Word banks
- Word prediction software (software that anticipates a word the student intends to type)
- Word processor
- Word processor with spell checker
- Writing in test booklet
- Written directions

*Some of these accommodations may be considered a test modification depending on what the test is measuring and in what state the examination is administered (see Chapter 2). Also note that the following are not considered accommodations and can be used during examinations: eyeglasses, hearing aids, pillows for neck or back support, neck braces, adjustable chair, adjustable personal computer, ear plugs or head phones to screen out noise, and adjusting the brightness of a monitor.

Appendix 3

ASSISTIVE TECHNOLOGY

What is assistive technology? Assistive technology is any service, piece of equipment, or tool that helps a disabled student gain access to learning and test-taking situations. Examples of assistive technology can include mobility devices such as wheelchairs or software that helps a student to access computers or other information technologies. For our purposes, we will discuss accommodation software and its applications for classroom, test-taking, and homework contexts.

- *Abbreviation expanders* are "short-hand" programs that allow a student access to word phrases with single or dual keystrokes. These programs are typically used with word prediction programs and are beneficial for those students who struggle with writing. Options are as follows:
  - EZ Keys (www.words-plus.com)
  - Gus! Access Keyboard (www.synapseadaptive.com)
- *Alternate keyboards* are helpful for those students who have difficulty using a standard keyboard. The keyboards may include differing layouts, sizes, etc., or even key guards that prevent accidental key activation. The following could be considered:
  - IntelliKeys (www.intellitools.com)
  - ZoomText Keyboard (www.aisquared.com)
- *Alternative mouse systems* such as trackballs of different sizes and shapes can be considered for greater mobility and to decrease hand and wrist fatigue. The following trackballs are options to consider:
  - Kensington Expert Mouse (www.kensington.com)
  - Slimblade Trackball Mouse (www.kensington.com)
- *Digitized or electronic text (e-text)* refers to text-based information that is available in a computerized format. There are an increasing number of books that are now available in e-text format. The experience of reading can be

enhanced for the disabled student because the font and color of the text can be adjusted for a student's comfort level. In addition, the e-text can be easier to hold and fun to use, which, in turn, will help the student stay motivated so that he or she remembers what he or she has read. Digitized text is typically accessed through an e-book reader, also called an e-book device or e-reader. In addition, the text can be displayed on a handheld computer also known as a personal digital assistant (PDA). The following options may be considered if you choose to access text digitally:

- Bookshare (www.bookshare.org)
- eReader will read the text on web pages (www.CAST.org)
- Home Page Reader Version 3 will also read web-based information (www.spectronicsinoz.com)
- Recording for the Blind & Dyslexic (www.rfbd.org)
- Selective middle and high school textbooks can be accessed through Prentice Hall SuccessNet (www.pearsonschool.com)

- *Magnifying aids* include screen magnification software for a student's computer screen. The color, contrast of the font and the background, and level of magnification can be modified depending on the student's comfort level. The following options could be considered:
  - Keys U See Keyboard Yellow Keys with Black Print (www.spectronicsinoz.com)
  - ZoomText Magnifier English CD Version 9.18 (www.aisquared.com)
- *Portable word processors* are light in weight and are easy for a child to carry from classroom to classroom. It is ideal for the student who has trouble with penmanship and struggles with writing. It is also beneficial for the student who prefers to use a keyboard. The following options could be considered:
  - Alphasmart: NEO (www.neo-direct.com)
  - Fusion: with text-to-speech and word prediction (www.writerlearning.com)
- *Speech-to-text (STT)*, also called voice/speech recognition software, allows a student to dictate into a headset microphone and speech is automatically converted into print that is visible on a computer screen. Programs offer continuous speech (a student dictates and does not pause between words) or discrete speech (a student pauses between each dictated word). The discrete speech software is best for the student who speaks at a slow pace and whose voice is not strong. Options for continuous speech are as follows:
  - Dragon NaturallySpeaking (www.nuance.com)
  - iListen (www.nuance.com)
  - ViaVoice Millennium (www.nuance.com)

A software program that may be considered for discrete speech is as follows:

- Dragon Dictate (www.nuance.com/naturallyspeaking/)

- *Spell checkers* aid those students who have trouble with spelling. There are several programs that are available as well as software applications that are integrated into writing programs. You may choose to consider the following programs:
  - Franklin HW-1216 Children's Speller and Dictionary (www.franklin.com)
  - Franklin Spelling Ace 20th Anniversary Phonetic Spell Corrector (www.franklin.com)
  - Franklin Spelling Corrector (www.franklin.com)
  - Simon Spells (www.Donjohnston.com)
  - SpellingRules (www.spellingrules.com)
- *Talking calculators* refer to calculators with speech options. This device is ideal for those students who have low vision. The following full-functioning "talking calculators" may be considered:
  - Orion T1–36X Talking Scientific Calculator (www.Lissproducts.com)
  - Talking Calculator-Version 3.0 (www.readingmadeez.com)
  - Talking Calculator with Earphone (www.Lissproducts.com)
- *Talking word processors* are programs that speak aloud what the student has typed into the computer. These programs play back what you have just dictated. Some programs such as WordSmith not only read aloud the word that has been typed but also provide the spelling and definition of the word as well as other words that sound the same. Besides WordSmith, other programs such as Co-Writer 4000 also help the student with constructing sentences by offering the most common words that would make sense as the student writes. Options for this type of assistive technology are as follows:
  - Co-Writer 4000 (www.Donjohnston.com)
  - IntelliTalk II (www.synapse-ada.com)
  - Kurzweil 3000 (www.kurzweiledu.com)
  - Read & Write (www.texthelp.com)
  - Type & Talk (www.texthelp.com)
  - WordSmith (www.texthelp.com)
  - Write: Outloud (www.Donjohnston.com)
- *Text-to-Speech (TTS)* converts scanned printed material into a computer text file that can be read aloud by a student's computer. This software in turn facilitates active reading, which will enhance the meaning of the text for the student and keep him or her interested in the material. Some available software options are as follows:
  - Job Access with Speed (JAWS) (www.freedomscientific.com)
  - Kurzweil 3000 (www.kurzweiledu.com)
  - NaturallySpeaking Preferred (www.nuance.com)
  - NaturalReader (www.naturalreaders.com)
  - Read&Write GOLD (www.texthelp.com)
  - ReadPlease (www.readplease.com)

- SpeakOut (www.screenreader.co.uk)
- ViaVoice (www.nuance.com)
- WYNN 3.1 (www.freedomscientific.com)
- ZoomText (www.aisquared.com)

Additionally, for text-to-speech software, DAISY.org sets standards so that individuals with "print disabilities" can access and navigate digital talking books with greater ease. DAISY books are ideal for textbooks since the student can move around the book, insert "bookmarks," and study as if he or she was using a hard copy of the text. Their website offers information on accessibility to DAISY-approved books and products. They also provide information on how to access software to convert text into a text-to-speech file on your home computer.

- *Transcription and read-aloud accommodation software* that work together are as follows:
  - ScreenSpeaker along with NaturallySpeaking will read aloud back to the student what NaturallySpeaking has just transcribed. A student can dictate an essay, have it transcribed into print, and then listen as the dictated text is read back to him or her. This allows a student to proof and review what he or she has written.
- *Voice recognition software* is also available that allows a student to listen to what the computer has just transcribed from his or her voice dictation:
  - SpeakOut (www.screenreader.co.uk)
  - TextHelp Screen Reader (www.texthelp.com)
  - ViaVoice (www.nuance.com)
- *Word prediction programs* are used with word processors to help a student form the words and think of the correct words to use when writing text. For example, a student can begin typing one or two letters, with the program then creating and completing the word. Some programs may even anticipate what the next word or sentence may be, which allows a student to continuously review what he or she has written. The following programs are options when considering this type of technology:
  - Co-Writer 4000 (www.Donjohnston.com)
  - EZ Keys (www.words-plus.com)
  - Gus! Word Prediction (www.gusinc.com)
  - Kurzweil 3000 (www.Kurzweiledu.com)
  - WordQ (www.wordq.com)
- *Writing programs* may help students increase their vocabulary and organize their thoughts, and may aid them in the writing process. Options for software programs are as follows:
  - Draft: Builder (www.Donjohnston.com)
  - Inspiration (www.inspiration.com)

Appendix 4

ORGANIZATIONS

American Academy of Child and Adolescent Psychiatry: www.aacap.org

American Academy of Family Physicians: www.aafp.org

American Academy of Neurology: www.aan.com

American Academy of Pediatrics: www.aap.org

American Association for Pediatric Ophthalmology and Strabismus: www.aapos.org

American College Testing: www.act.org

American Dietetic Association: www.eatright.org

American Medical Association: www.ama-assn.org

American Occupational Therapy Association: www.aota.org

American Physical Therapy Association: www.apta.org

American Psychological Association: www.apa.org

American Speech-Language-Hearing Association: www.asha.org

Association of American Medical Colleges: www.aamc.org

Centers for Disease Control and Prevention: www.cdc.gov

Children's Defense Fund: www.childrensdefense.org

College Board Services for Students with Disabilities: www.collegeboard.com/ssd

Council for Exceptional Children: www.cec.sped.org

Educational Records Bureau: www.erblearn.org

Educational Testing Service: www.ets.org

Graduate Management Admission Council: www.gmac.com

Independent Educational Consultants Association: www.iecaonline.com

Keeping Kids Healthy: www.keepingkidshealthy.org

Law School Admission Council: www.lsac.org

Learning Ally (formerly Recoding for the Blind & Dyslexic): www.learningally.org, www.rfbd.org

Learning Disabilities Association of America: www.ldanatl.org

National Alliance on Mental Illness: www.nami.org

National Association for Gifted Children: www.nagc.org

National Disability Rights Network: www.napas.org

National Education Association: www.nea.org

National Institutes of Health: www.nih.gov

National Institute of Mental Health: www.nimh.nih.gov

National Institute of Neurological Disorders and Stroke: www.ninds.nih.gov

National Institute on Alcohol Abuse and Alcoholism: www.niaaa.nih.gov

National Institute on Drug Abuse: www.drugabuse.gov/

North American Society for Childhood Onset Schizophrenia: www.nascos.org

Technical Assistance ALLIANCE for Parent Centers: www.taalliance.org

U.S. Department of Education: www.ed.gov

REFERENCES

Chapter 1: The Law

1. Individuals with Disabilities Education Act of 2004, Public Law 108–446.
2. No Child Left Behind Act of 2001, Public Law 107–110.
3. Educational Testing Service. (2007). *Policy statement for documentation of a learning disability in adolescents and adults* (2nd ed.). Princeton, NJ: Author.
4. American College Testing. (2010). *Frequently asked questions about ACT.* Retrieved March 29, 2010, from http://www.act.org/aboutact/faq.html
5. American Psychiatric Association. (2000). *Diagnostic and statistical manual of mental disorders* (4th ed., text revision). Washington, DC: Author.
6. Loring, D. W. (Ed.). (1999). *INS dictionary of neuropsychology.* New York: Oxford University Press.
7. Americans with Disabilities Act Amendments Act of 2008, Public Law 110–325.
8. Americans with Disabilities Act of 1990, Public Law 101–336.
9. Hughes, S. J. (2008). Comprehensive assessment must play a role in RTI. In E. Fletcher-Janzen & C. R. Reynolds (Eds.), *Neuropsychological perspectives on learning disabilities in the era of RTI: Recommendations for diagnosis and intervention* (pp. 115–130). Hoboken, NJ: John Wiley & Sons.
10. Rathvon, N. (2008). *Effective school interventions: Evidence-based strategies for improving student outcomes.* New York: The Guilford Press.
11. McDougal, J. L., Graney, S. B., Wright, J. A., & Ardoin, S. P. (2010). *RTI in practice: A practical guide to implementing effective evidence-based interventions in your school.* Hoboken, NJ: John Wiley & Sons.
12. National Joint Committee on Learning Disabilities. (2005). Responsiveness to intervention and learning disabilities. Retrieved April 10, 2011, from http://www.ldonline.org
13. Rehabilitation Act of 1973, Public Law 93–113.

Chapter 2: The Tools

1. Klingberg, T. (2009). *The overflowing brain: information overload and the limits of working memory.* New York: Oxford University Press.
2. Gregg, N. (2009). *Adolescents and adults with learning disabilities and ADHD: Assessment and accommodation.* New York: The Guilford Press.
3. Sireci, S. G., Li, S., & Scarpati, S. (2003). *The effects of test accommodations on test performance: A review of the literature* (Research Report No. 485). Amherst, MA: Center for Educational Assessment.
4. Sireci, S. G., Scarpati, S. E., & Li, S. (2005). Test accommodations for students with disabilities: An analysis of the interaction hypothesis. *Review of Educational Research, 75,* 457–490.

5. Fuchs, L. S., & Fuchs, D. (1999). Fair and unfair testing accommodations. *School Administrator, 56*, 24–29.
6. Taymans, J. M., Swanson, H. L., Schwarz, R. L., Gregg, N., Hock, M., & Gerber, P. J. (2009, June). *Learning to achieve: A review of the research literature on serving adults with learning disabilities.* Washington, DC: National Institute for Literacy.
7. Press Release, College Board. (2002, July 17). *The College Board and disabilities rights advocates announce agreement to drop flagging from standardized tests.* Retrieved April 11, 2011, from http://www.collegeboard.com/press/article/0,1443,11360,00.html
8. Ofiesh, N. S. (2000). Using processing speed tests to predict the benefit of extended test time for university students with learning disabilities. *Journal of Postsecondary Education and Disability, 14*, 39–56.
9. Gordon, M., & Keiser, S. (2000). *Accommodations in higher education under the Americans with Disabilities Act (ADA): A no-nonsense guide for clinicians, educators, administrators, and lawyers.* New York: The Guilford Press.
10. Leong, N. (2005). Beyond Breimhorst: Appropriate accommodations of students with learning disabilities on the SAT. *Stanford Law Review*, 2135.
11. Educational Testing Service. (2004). *Accommodations on high-stakes writing tests for students with disabilities.* Princeton, NJ: Author.

Chapter 3: The Team

1. The Association of Educational Therapists. (2007–2009). *Educational therapy defined: Definition of the educational therapist.* Retrieved April 11, 2011, from http://www.aetonline.org
2. Schiltz, K. L., Humphrey, L. A., & Pappas, K. B. (2000). Neuropsychological applications to remediation planning in children. *The Educational Therapist, 21*, 12–18.
3. Gregg, N. (2009). *Adolescents and adults with learning disabilities and ADHD: Assessment and accommodation.* New York: The Guilford Press.
4. Silver, C. H., Ruff, R. M., Iverson, G. L., Barth, J. T., Broshek, D. K., Bush, S. S., et al. (2008). Learning disabilities: The need for neuropsychological evaluation. *Archives of Clinical Neuropsychology, 23*, 217–219.
5. Siegel, L. (2009). *Nolo's IEP guide: Learning disabilities* (4th ed.). Berkeley, CA: Nolo.
6. Lindstrom, J. H. (2007). Determining appropriate accommodations for postsecondary students with reading and written expression disorders. *Learning Disabilities Research & Practice, 22*, 229–236.

Chapter 4: Attention and Concentration

1. Barkley, R. A. (Coauthored by Benton, C.). (1998). *Your defiant child: Eight steps to better behavior.* New York: The Guilford Press.
2. American Psychiatric Association. (2000). *Diagnostic and statistical manual of mental disorders (DSM-IV-TR)* (4th ed., text revision). Washington, DC: Author.
3. Hallowell, E., & Ratey, J. (1994). *Driven to distraction: Recognizing and coping with attention deficit disorder from childhood through adulthood.* New York: Touchstone.
4. Barkley, R. A. (2003). Issues in the diagnosis of attention-deficit/hyperactivity disorder in children. *Brain & Development, 25*, 77–83.
5. Barkley, R. A. (2010). Deficient emotional self-regulation: A core component of attention-deficit/hyperactivity disorder. *Journal of ADHD & Related Disorders, 1*, 4–36.
6. Mikami, A. Y. (2010). The importance of friendship for youth with attention-deficit/hyperactivity disorder. *Clinical Child and Family Psychology Review, 13*, 181–198.
7. Blachman, D. R., & Hinshaw, S. P. (2002). Patterns of friendship among girls with and without attention-deficit/hyperactivity disorder. *Journal of Abnormal Child Psychology, 30*, 625–640.
8. Individuals with Disabilities Education Act of 2004, Pub. L. No. 108–446.
9. Siegel, L. (2009). *Nolo's IEP guide: Learning disabilities* (4th ed.). Berkeley, CA: Nolo.

10. Roodenrys, S. (2006). Working memory function in attention deficit hyperactivity disorder. In T. P. Alloway & S. E. Gathercole (Eds.), *Working memory and neurodevelopmental disorders* (pp. 187–211). New York: Psychology Press.

11. Gregg, N. (2009). *Adolescents and adults with learning disabilities and ADHD: Assessment and accommodation*. New York: The Guilford Press.

12. Taymans, J. M., Swanson, H. L., Schwarz, R. L., Gregg, N., Hock, M., & Gerber, P. J. (2009, June). *Learning to achieve: A review of the research literature on serving adults with learning disabilities*. Washington, DC: National Institute for Literacy.

13. Sireci, S. G., Scarpati, S. E., & Li, S. (2005). Test accommodations for students with disabilities: An analysis of the interaction hypothesis. *Review of Educational Research, 75*, 457–490.

Chapter 5: Memory

1. Huang-Pollock, C. L., Mikami, A. Y., Pfiffner, L. J., & McBurnett, K. (2009). Do executive functions explain the relationship between attention deficit hyperactivity disorder and social adjustment? *Journal of Abnormal Child Psychology, 37*, 679–691.

2. Barkley, R. A. (2010). Deficient emotional self-regulation: A core component of attention-deficit/hyperactivity disorder. *Journal of ADHD & Related Disorders, 1*, 4–36.

3. Baddeley, A. D. (2004). The psychology of memory. In A. D. Baddeley, M. D. Kopelman, & B. A. Wilson (Eds.), *The essential handbook of memory disorders for clinicians* (pp. 1–13). West Sussex, England: John Wiley & Sons.

4. Dehn, M. J. (2008). *Working memory and academic learning: Assessment and intervention*. Hoboken, NJ: John Wiley & Sons.

5. Gillam, R. B., Montgomery, J. W., & Gillam, S. L. (2009). Attention and memory in child language disorders. In R. G. Schwartz (Ed.), *Handbook of child language disorders* (pp. 201–215). New York: Psychology Press.

6. Wendling, B. J., & Mather, N. (2009). *Essentials of evidence-based academic interventions*. Hoboken, NJ: John Wiley & Sons.

7. Kramer, J. H., Knee, K., & Delis, D. C. (2000). Verbal memory impairments in dyslexia. *Archives of Clinical Neuropsychology, 15*, 83–93.

8. Mattson, S. N., & Vaurio, L. (2010). Fetal alcohol spectrum disorders. In K. O. Yeates, M. D. Ris, H. G. Taylor, & B. F. Pennington (Eds.), *Pediatric neuropsychology: Research, theory, and practice* (pp. 265–296). New York: The Guilford Press.

9. Ozonoff, S. (2010). Autism spectrum disorders. In K. O. Yeates, M. D. Ris, H. G. Taylor, & B. F. Pennington (Eds.), *Pediatric neuropsychology: Research, theory, and practice* (pp. 418–446). New York: The Guilford Press.

10. Yeates, K. O., Ris, M. D., Taylor, H. G., & Pennington, B. F. (2010). *Pediatric neuropsychology: Research, theory, and practice* (2nd ed.). New York: The Guilford Press.

11. Vargha-Khadem, F., Gadian, D. G., & Mishkin, M. (2001). Dissociations in cognitive memory: The syndrome of developmental amnesia. *Philosophical Transactions of the Royal Society of London Biological Sciences, 356*, 1435–1440.

12. Kondo, A., Saito, Y., Seki, A., Sugiura, C., Maegaki, Y., Nakayama, Y., et al. (2007). Delayed neuropsychiatric syndrome in a child following carbon monoxide poisoning. *Brain & Development, 29*, 174–177.

13. Weaver, L. K. (2009). Carbon monoxide poisoning. *New England Journal of Medicine, 360*, 1217–1225.

Chapter 6: Executive Functioning

1. Meltzer, L. (Ed.). (2007). *Executive function in education: From theory to practice*. New York: The Guilford Press.

2. Meltzer, L. (Ed.). (2010). *Promoting executive function in the classroom*. New York: The Guilford Press.

3. Powell, K. B., & Voeller, K. K. S. (2004). Prefrontal executive function syndromes in children. *Journal of Child Neurology, 19,* 785–797.

4. Jurado, M. B., & Rosselli, M. (2007). The elusive nature of executive functions: A review of our current understanding. *Neuropsychology Review, 17,* 213–233.

5. Dawson, P., & Guare, R. (2010). *Executive skills in children and adolescents: A practical guide to assessment and intervention* (2nd ed.). New York: The Guilford Press.

6. Sowell, E. R., Thompson, P. M., Holmes, C. J., Jernigan, T. L., & Toga, A. W. (1999). In vivo evidence for post-adolescent brain maturation in frontal and striatal regions. *Nature Neuroscience, 2,* 859–861.

7. Sokol, B., Muller, U., Carpendale, J. I. M., Young, A. R., & Iarococci, G. (Eds.). (2010). *Self and social regulation: Social interaction and the development of social understanding and executive functions.* New York: Oxford University Press.

8. Christ, S. E., Kanne, S. M., & Reierson, A. M. (2010). Executive function in individuals with subthreshold autism traits. *Neuropsychology, 24,* 590–598.

9. Bigler, E. D. (2008). Neuropsychology and clinical neuroscience of persistent post-concussive syndrome. *Journal of the International Neuropsychological Society, 14,* 1–22.

10. Belanger, H. G., Spiegel, E., & Vanderploeg, R. D. (2009). Neuropsychological performance following a history of multiple self-reported concussions: A meta-analysis. *Journal of the International Neuropsychological Society, 16,* 262–267.

11. Kofman, O., Larson, J. G., & Mostofsky, S. H. (2008). A novel task for examining strategic planning: Evidence for impairment in children with ADHD. *Journal of Clinical and Experimental Neuropsychology, 30,* 261–271.

12. Klingberg, T., Fernell, E., Olesen, P.J., Johnson, M., Gustafsson, P., Dahlström, K., et al. (2005). Computerized training of working memory in children with ADHD–A randomized, controlled trial. *Journal of the American Academy of Child and Adolescent Psychiatry, 44,* 177–186.

Chapter 7: Language

1. National Institute on Deafness and Other Communication Disorders (2010). *Statistics on voice, speech, and language.* Retrieved July 6, 2010, from http://www.nidcd.nih.gov

2. Stromswold, K. (1998). Genetics of spoken language disorders. *Human Biology, 70,* 297–324.

3. Bishop, D. V. M. (2001). Genetic and environmental risks for specific language impairment in children. *Philosophical Transactions of the Royal Society of London Series B-Biological Sciences, 356,* 369–380.

4. Tomblin, J. B. (2009). Genetics of child language disorders. In R. G. Schwartz (Ed.), *Handbook of child language disorders* (pp. 232–256). New York: Psychology Press.

5. Hook, P. E., & Haynes, C. W. (2009). Reading and writing in child language disorders. In R. G. Schwartz (Ed.), *Handbook of child language disorders* (pp. 424–444). New York: Psychology Press.

6. Shaywitz, S. E. (2003). *Overcoming dyslexia: A new and complete science-based program for overcoming reading problems at any level.* New York: Knopf.

7. Ward-Lonergan, J. M. (2010). Expository discourse in school-age children and adolescents with language disorders: Nature of the problem. In M. A. Nippold & C. M. Scott (Eds.), *Expository discourse in children, adolescents, and adults* (pp. 155–189). New York: Psychology Press.

8. Scott, C. M. (2010). Assessing expository texts produced by school-age children and adolescents. In M. A. Nippold & C. M. Scott (Eds.), *Expository discourse in children, adolescents, and adults* (pp. 191–213). New York: Psychology Press.

9. Shulman, C., & Guberman, A. (2007). Acquisition of verb meaning through syntactic cues: A comparison of children with autism, children with specific language impairment (SLI), and children with typical language development (TLD). *Journal of Child Language, 34,* 411–423.

10. Myles, B. S., Trautman, M. L., & Schelvan, R. L. (2004). *The hidden curriculum.* Shawnee Mission, KS: Autism Asperger Publishing Company.

11. Windsor, J., & Kohnert, K. (2009). Processing speed, attention, and perception in child language disorders. In R. G. Schwartz (Ed.), *Handbook of child language disorders* (pp. 424–444). New York: Psychology Press.

12. Ramsden, G. C., & Botting, N. (2004). Social difficulties and victimization in children with SLI at 11 years of age. *Journal of Speech, Language, and Hearing Research, 47,* 145–161.

13. Gray, S. (2005). Word learning by preschoolers with specific language impairment: Effect of phonological or semantic cues. *Journal of Speech, Language, and Hearing Research, 48,* 1452–1467.

14. Bellini, S., & Akullian, J. (2007). A meta-analysis of video modeling and video self-modeling interventions for children and adolescents with autistic spectrum disorders. *Exceptional Children, 73,* 261–284.

15. National Autism Center. (2009). *National Standards Project: Addressing the need for evidence-based practice guidelines for autism spectrum disorders.* Randolph, MA: National Autism Center.

16. Frankel, F., Myatt R., Sugar, C., Whitham, C., Gorospe, C. M., & Laugeson, E. (2010). A randomized controlled study of parent-assisted children's friendship training with children having autism spectrum disorders. *Journal of Autism and Developmental Disorders, 40,* 827–842.

17. Dweck, C. S. (2009). Foreword. In F. D. Horowitz, R. F. Subotnik, & D. J. Matthews (Eds.), *The development of giftedness and talent across the life span* (pp. xi–xiv). Washington, DC: American Psychological Association.

Chapter 8: Visual Perceptual Ability

1. Spreen, O., Risser, A. H., & Edgell, D. (1995). *Developmental neuropsychology.* New York: Oxford University Press.

2. Hyman, S. L., Shores, A., & North, K. N. (2005). The nature and frequency of cognitive deficits in children with neurofibromatosis type 1. *Neurology, 65,* 1037–1044.

3. Moore, B. D. (2009). Potential influences on mathematical difficulties in children and adolescents with neurofibromatosis, type 1. *Developmental Disabilities Research Reviews, 15,* 45–51.

4. Martens, M. A., Wilson, S. J., & Reutens, D. C. (2008). Research review: Williams syndrome: A critical review of the cognitive, behavioral, and neuroanatomical phenotype. *Journal of Child Psychology and Psychiatry, 49,* 576–608.

5. Mervis, C. B., & John, A. E. (2010). Intellectual disability syndromes. In K. O. Yeates, M. D. Ris, H. G. Taylor, & B. F. Pennington (Eds.), *Pediatric neuropsychology: Research, theory, and practice* (pp. 447–470). New York: The Guilford Press.

6. Davis, D. W., Burns, B. M., Wilkerson, S. A., & Steichen, J. J. (2005). Visual perceptual skills in children born with very low birth weights. *Journal of Pediatric Health Care, 19,* 363–368.

7. Taylor, H. G. (2010). Children with very low birthweight or very preterm birth. In K. O. Yeates, M. D. Ris, H. G. Taylor, & B. F. Pennington (Eds.), *Pediatric neuropsychology: Research, theory, and practice* (pp. 26–70). New York: The Guilford Press.

8. Stiles, J., Nass, R. D., Levine, S. C., Moses, P., & Reilly, J. S. (2010). Perinatal stroke. In K. O. Yeates, M. D. Ris, H. G. Taylor, & B. F. Pennington (Eds.), *Pediatric neuropsychology: Research, theory, and practice* (pp. 181–210). New York: The Guilford Press.

9. Kozeis, N., Anogeianaki, A., Mitova, D. T., Anogianakis, G., Mitov, T., & Klisarova, A. (2007). Visual function and visual perception in cerebral palsied children. *Ophthalmic and Physiological Optics, 27,* 44–53.

10. Dietrich, K. N. (2010). Environmental toxicants. In K. O. Yeates, M. D. Ris, H. G. Taylor, B. F. Pennington (Eds.), *Pediatric neuropsychology: Research, theory, and practice* (pp. 211–264). New York: The Guilford Press.

11. Muscal, E., Bloom, D. R., Hunter, J. V., & Myones, B. L. (2010). Neurocognitive deficits and neuroimaging abnormalities are prevalent in children with lupus: Clinical and research experiences at a US pediatric institution. *Lupus, 19,* 268–279.

12. Grandin, T. (2008). *The way I see it: A personal look at autism and Asperger's.* Arlington, TX: Future Horizons.

13. Grandin, T. (2006). *Thinking in pictures: My life with autism* (expanded ed.). New York: Vintage Books.

14. Ozonoff, S. (1999). Cognitive impairment in neurofibromatosis type 1. *American Journal of Medical Genetics, 89,* 45–52.

15. Hachon, C., Iannuzzi, S., & Chaix, Y. (2011). Behavioural and cognitive phenotypes in children with neurofibromatosis type 1 (NF1): The link with the neurobiological level. *Brain and Development, 33,* 52–61.

16. Moore, B. D., Ater, J. L., Needle, M. N., Slopis, J., & Copeland, D. R. (1994). Neuropsychological profile of children with neurofibromatosis, brain tumor, or both. *Journal of Child Neurology, 9,* 368–377.

17. Eliason, M. J. (1986). Neurofibromatosis: Implications for learning and behavior. *Journal of Developmental & Behavioral Pediatrics, 7,* 175–179.

18. Krab, L. C., Aarsen, F. K., de Goede-Bolder, A., Catsman-Berrevoets, C. E., Arts, W. F., Moll, H. A., et al. (2008). Impact of neurofibromatosis type 1 on school performance. *Journal of Child Neurology, 23,* 1002–1010.

Chapter 9: Visual Processing Speed

1. Montgomery, J. W., & Windsor, J. (2007). Examining the language performances of children with and without specific language impairment: Contributions of phonological short-term memory and speed of processing. *Journal of Speech, Language, and Hearing Research, 50,* 778–797.

2. Sattler, J. M. (2001). *Assessment of children: Cognitive applications* (4th ed.). San Diego, CA: Author.

3. Willcutt, E., Pennington, B., Olson, R., Chhabildas, N., & Hulslander, J. (2005). Neuropsychological analyses of comorbidity between reading disability and attention deficit hyperactivity disorder: In search of the common deficit. *Developmental Neuropsychology, 27,* 35–78.

4. Fletcher, J. M., Lyon, G. R., Fuchs, L. S., & Barnes, M. A. (2007). *Learning disabilities: From identification to intervention.* New York: The Guilford Press.

5. Gregg, N., Coleman, C., Davis, M., & Chalk, J. C. (2007). Timed essay writing: Implications for high-stakes tests. *Journal of Learning Disabilities, 40,* 306–318.

6. Windsor, J., & Kohnert, K. (2009). Processing speed, attention, and perception in child language disorders. In R. G. Schwartz (Ed.), *Handbook of child language disorders* (pp. 424–444). New York: Psychology Press.

7. Prigatano, G. P., Gray, J. A., & Gale, S. D. (2008). Individual case analysis of processing speed difficulties in children with and without traumatic brain injury. *The Clinical Neuropsychologist, 22,* 603–619.

8. Babikian, T., & Asarnow, R. (2009). Neurocognitive outcomes and recovery after pediatric TBI: Meta-analytic review of the literature. *Neuropsychology, 23,* 283–296.

9. Taylor, H. G. (2009). Children with very low birthweight or very preterm birth. In K. O. Yeates, M. D. Ris, H. G. Taylor, & B. F. Pennington (Eds.), *Pediatric neuropsychology: Research, theory, and practice* (pp. 26–70). New York: The Guilford Press.

10. Calhoun, S. L., & Mayes, S. D. (2005). Processing speed in children with clinical disorders. *Psychology in the Schools, 42,* 333–343.

11. Mayes, S. D., & Calhoun, S. L. (2007). Learning, attention, writing, and processing speed in typical children and children with ADHD, autism, anxiety, depression, and oppositional-defiant disorder. *Child Neuropsychology, 13,* 469–493.

12. Willcutt, E. G. (2010). Attention-deficit/hyperactivity disorder. In K. O. Yeates, M. D. Ris, H. G. Taylor, & B. F. Pennington (Eds.), *Pediatric neuropsychology: Research, theory, and practice* (pp. 393–417). New York: The Guilford Press.

13. Prifitera, A., Weiss, L. G., & Saklofske, D. H. (1998). The WISC-III in context. In A. Prifitera & D. H. Saklofske (Eds.), *WISC-III: Clinical use and interpretation* (pp. 1–38). San Diego, CA: Academic Press.

14. Taymans, J. M., Swanson, H. L., Schwarz, R. L., Gregg, N., Hock, M., & Gerber, P. J. (2009, June). *Learning to achieve: A review of the research literature on serving adults with learning disabilities.* Washington, DC: National Institute for Literacy.

Chapter 10: Achievement

1. Snyder, L., & Caccamise, D. (2010). Comprehension processes for expository text: Building meaning and making sense. In M. A. Nipplod & C. M. Scott (Eds.), *Expository discourse in children, adolescents, and adults* (pp. 13–39). New York: Psychology Press.

2. Lyon, G. R., Shaywitz, S. E., & Shaywitz, B. A. (2003). Defining dyslexia, comorbidity, teachers' knowledge of language and reading: A definition of dyslexia. *Annals of Dyslexia, 53,* 1–14.

3. Shaywitz, S. E. (1998). Current concepts: Dyslexia. *New England Journal of Medicine, 338,* 307–312.

4. Shaywitz, S. E. (2003). *Overcoming dyslexia: A new and complete science-based program for overcoming reading problems at any level.* New York: Knopf.

5. Shaywitz, S. E., Morris, R., & Shaywitz, B. A. (2008). The education of dyslexic children from childhood to young adulthood. *Annual Review of Psychology, 59,* 451–475.

6. Fletcher, J. M., Shaywitz, S. E., Shankweiler, D. P., Katz, L., Liberman, I. Y., Stuebing, K. K., et al. (1994). Cognitive profiles of reading disability: Comparisons of discrepancy and low achievement definitions. *Journal of Educational Psychology, 86,* 6–23.

7. National Council on Disability. (2003, September). *People with disabilities and post-secondary education.* Position Paper. Retrieved March 14, 2007, from http://www.ncd.gov/newsroom/publications/2003/education.htm

8. Silver, C. H., Ruff, R. M., Iverson, G. L., Barth, J. T., Broshek, D. K., Bush, S. S., et al. (2008). Learning disabilities: The need for neuropsychological evaluation. *Archives of Clinical Neuropsychology, 23,* 217–219.

9. Gregg, N. (2009). *Adolescents and adults with learning disabilities and ADHD: Assessment and accommodation.* New York: The Guilford Press.

10. Lindstrom, J. H. (2007). Determining appropriate accommodations for postsecondary students with reading and written expression disorders. *Learning Disabilities Research & Practice, 22,* 229–236.

11. National Institute for Literacy. (2009, June). *Learning to achieve: A review of the research literature on serving adults with learning disabilities.* Washington, DC: Author. Retrieved February 28, 2010, from http://www.nifl.gov/publications/pdf/L2ALiteratureReview09.pdf

12. Sireci, S. G., Li, S., & Scarpati, S. (2003). *The effects of test accommodations on test performance: A review of the literature* (Research Report No. 485). Amherst, MA: Center for Educational Assessment.

13. Cohen, A. S., Gregg, N., & Deng, M. (2005). The role of extended time and item content on a high stakes mathematics test. *Learning Disabilities Research & Practice, 20,* 225–233.

14. Ofiesh, N. S., & Hughes, C. A. (2002). How much time? A review of the literature on extended test time for postsecondary students with learning disabilities. *Journal on Postsecondary Education and Disability, 16,* 2–16.

15. Swanson, H., Hoskyn, M., & Lee, C. (1999). *Interventions for students with learning disabilities: A meta-analysis of treatment outcomes.* New York: The Guilford Press.

16. Hook, P. E., & Haynes, C. W. (2009). Reading and writing in child language disorders. In R. G. Schwartz (Ed.), *Handbook of child language disorders* (pp. 424–444). New York: Psychology Press.

17. Persky, H. R., Daane, M. C., & Jin, Y. (2003). *The nation's report card: Writing 2002* (NCES 2003–529). Washington DC: National Center for Education Statistics, Institute of Education Services, U.S. Department of Education.

18. Stackhouse, J., & Wells, B. (1997). How do speech and language problems affect literacy development? In C. Hulme & M. Snowling (Eds.), *Dyslexia: Biology, cognition, and intervention* (pp. 182–211). London: Whurr.

19. Berninger, V. W., Rutberg, J. E., Abbott, R. D., Garcia, N., Anderson-Youngstrom, M., Brooks, A., et al. (2006). Tier 1 and tier 2 early intervention for handwriting and composing. *Journal of School Psychology, 44*, 3–30.

20. Gregg, N. (2007). Underserved and underprepared: Postsecondary learning disabilities. *Learning Disabilities Research & Practice, 22*, 219–228.

21. Gregg, N., Coleman, C., Davis, M., & Chalk, J. C. (2007). Timed essay writing: Implications for high-stakes tests. *Journal of Learning Disabilities, 40*, 306–318.

22. Geary, D. C. (2003). Learning disabilities in arithmetic: Problem-solving differences and cognitive deficits. In H. L. Swanson, K. R. Harris, & S. Graham (Eds.), *Handbook of learning disabilities* (pp. 199–212). New York: The Guilford Press.

23. National Mathematics Advisory Panel. (2008). *Foundations for success: The final report of the National Mathematics Advisory Panel*. Washington, DC: U.S. Department of Education. Retrieved February 10, 2010, from http://www2.ed.gov/about/bdscomm/list/mathpanel/report/final-report.pdf

24. U.S. Department of Education. (1990–2007). *National assessment of educational progress*. National Center for Educational Statistics. Retrieved April 8, 2010, from http://nces.ed.gov/nationsreportcard/

25. Horn, L., & Nuñez, A. (2000). *Mapping the road to college: First-generation students' math track, planning strategies, and context of support* (NCES 2000–153). Washington, DC: U.S. Department of Education.

26. Horowitz, J. E. (2005). *Inside high school reform: Making the changes that matter*. San Francisco, CA: WestEd.

27. Geary, D. C. (1993). Mathematical disabilities: Cognitive, neuropsychological, and genetic components. *Psychological Bulletin, 114*, 345–362.

28. Geary, D. C., Hamson, C. O., & Hoard, M. K. (2000). Numerical and arithmetical cognition: A longitudinal study of process and concept deficits in children with learning disability. *Journal of Experimental Child Psychology, 77*, 236–263.

29. Badin, N. A. (1983). Dyscalculia and nonverbal disorders of learning. In H. R. Myklebust (Ed.), *Progress in learning disabilities* (vol. 5, pp. 235–264). New York: Grune & Stratton.

30. Ostad, S. A. (1998). Comorbidity between mathematics and spelling difficulties. *Logopedics Phoniatrics Vocology, 23*, 145–154.

31. Gross-Tur, V., Manor, O., & Shalev, R. S. (1996). Developmental dyscalculia: Prevalence and demographic features. *Developmental Medicine and Child Neurology, 38*, 25–33.

32. Fuchs, L. S., Fuchs, D., Hamlett, C. L., Lambert, W., Stuebing, K., & Fletcher, J. M. (2008). Problem solving and computational skill: Are they shared or distinct aspects of mathematical cognition? *Journal of Educational Psychology, 100*, 30–47.

Chapter 11: Emotional Functioning

1. Albano, A. M., Chorpita, B. F., & Barlow, D. H. (1996). Childhood anxiety disorders. In E. J. Mash & R. A. Barkley (Eds.), *Child psychopathology* (pp. 196–241). New York: The Guilford Press.

2. Roblek, T., & Piacentini, J. (2005). Cognitive-behavior therapy for childhood anxiety disorders. *Child and Adolescent Psychiatric Clinics of North America, 14*, 863–876.

3. David-Ferdon, C., & Kaslow, N. J. (2008). Evidence-based psychosocial treatments for child and adolescent depression. *Journal of Clinical Child & Adolescent Psychology, 37*, 62–104.

4. Huberty, T. J. (2009). Interventions for internalizing disorders. In A. Akin-Little, S. G. Little, M. A. Bray, & T. J. Kehle (Eds.), *Behavioral interventions in schools: Evidence-based positive strategies* (pp. 281–296). Washington, DC: American Psychological Association.

5. American Academy of Pediatrics Council on School Health. (2009). Policy statement—guidance for the administration of medication in school. *Pediatrics, 124*, 1244–1251.

6. Pavuluri, M. (2008). *What works for bipolar kids: Help and hope for parents.* New York: The Guilford Press.

7. Jenson, W. R., Clark, E., & Burrow-Sanchez, J. (2009). Practical strategies in working with difficult students. In A. Akin-Little, S. G. Little, M. A. Bray & T. J. Kehle (Eds.), *Behavioral interventions in schools: Evidence-based positive strategies* (pp. 247–264). Washington, DC: American Psychological Association.

8. Lencz, T., Smith, C., McLaughlin, D., Auther, A., Nakayama, E., Hovey, L., et al. (2006). Generalized and specific neurocognitive deficits in prodromal schizophrenia. *Biological Psychiatry, 59,* 863–871.

9. Niendam, T. A., Bearden, C. E., Johnson, J. K., McKinley, M., Loewy, R., O'Brien, M., et al. (2006). Neurocognitive performance and functional disability in the psychosis prodrome. *Schizophrenia Research, 84,* 100–111.

10. Niendam, T. A., Bearden, C. E., Zinberg, J., Johnson, J. K., O'Brien, M., & Cannon, T. D. (2007). The course of neurocognition and social functioning in individuals at ultra high risk for psychosis. *Schizophrenia Bulletin, 33,* 772–781.

Chapter 12: Social Skills

1. Hay, D. F., Payne, A., & Chadwick, A. (2004). Peer relations in childhood. *Journal of Child Psychology and Psychiatry, 45,* 84–108.

2. Tremblay, R. E., Nagin, D. S., Séguin, J. R., Zoccolillo, M., Zelazo, P. D., Boivin, M., et al. (2004). Physical aggression during early childhood: Trajectories and predictors. *Pediatrics, 114,* e43–e50.

3. Frankel, F. (1996). *Good friends are hard to find: Help your child find, make, and keep friends.* Los Angeles: Perspective Publishing.

4. Witvliet, M., van Lier, P. A. C., Cuijpers, P., & Koot, H. M. (2010). Change and stability in childhood clique membership, isolation from cliques, and associated child characteristics. *Journal of Clinical Child & Adolescent Psychology, 39,* 12–24.

5. Mikami, A. Y. (2010). The importance of friendship for youth with attention-deficit/hyperactivity disorder. *Clinical Child and Family Psychology Review, 13,* 181–198.

6. Rich, E. C. (2011). Rejected children. In S. Goldstein & J. A. Naglieri (Eds.), *Encyclopedia of child behavior and development.* New York: Springer.

7. Frankel, F., Myatt, R., Sugar, C., Whitham, C., Gorospe, C. M., & Laugeson, E. (2010). A randomized controlled study of parent-assisted children's friendship training with children having autism spectrum disorders. *Journal of Autism and Developmental Disorders, 40,* 827–842.

8. Bagwell, C. L., Newcomb, A. F., & Bukowski, W. M. (1998). Preadolescent friendship and peer rejection as predictors of adult adjustment. *Child Development, 69,* 140–153.

9. Barkley, R. A. (2010). Deficient emotional self-regulation: A core component of attention-deficit/hyperactivity disorder. *Journal of ADHD & Related Disorders, 2,* 5–37.

10. Kasari, C., Locke, J., Gulsrud, A., & Rotheram-Fuller, E. (2010, July 30). Social networks and friendships at school: Comparing children with and without ASD. *Journal of Autism and Developmental Disorders.* DOI 10.1007/s10803–010-1076-x.

11. Calkins, S. D., & Keane, S. P. (2009). Developmental origins of early antisocial behavior. *Development and Psychopathology, 21,* 1095–1109.

12. Hinduja, S., & Patchin, J. W. (2010). Bullying, cyberbullying, and suicide. *Archives of Suicide Research, 14,* 206–221.

13. Pollastri, A. R., Cardemil, E. V., & O'Donnell, E. H. (2010). Self-esteem in pure bullies and bully/victims: A longitudinal analysis. *Journal of Interpersonal Violence, 25,* 1489–1502.

14. Burns, S., Cross, D., & Maycock, B. (2010). "That could be me squishing chips on someone's car." How friends can positively influence bullying behaviors. *Journal of Primary Prevention, 31,* 209–222.

15. Peeters, M., Cillessen, A. H. N., & Scholte, R. H. J. (2010). Clueless or powerful? Identifying subtypes of bullies in adolescence. *Journal of Youth in Adolescence, 39,* 1041–1052.

16. Newman, R. S., & Murray, B. J. (2005). How students and teachers view the seriousness of peer harassment: When is it appropriate to seek help? *Journal of Educational Psychology, 97*, 347–365.

17. Hay, C., & Meldrum, R. (2010). Bullying victimization and adolescent self-harm: Testing hypotheses from general strain theory. *Journal of Youth and Adolescence, 39*, 447–459.

18. Rivers, I., & Noret, N. (2010). Participant roles in bullying behavior and their association with thoughts of ending one's life. *Crisis, 31*, 143–148.

19. Wang, J., Iannotti, R. J., & Nansel, T. R. (2009). School bullying among adolescents in the United States: Physical, verbal, relational, and cyber. *Journal of Adolescent Health, 45*, 368–375.

20. Peckham, C. (2010). Cyberbullies and cybervictims—What's the clinican's role? An expert interview with Gwenn Schurgin O'Keeffe, M.D. Retrieved October 25, 2010, from Medscape Pediatrics.

21. Pornari, C., & Wood, J. (2010). Peer and cyber aggression in secondary school students: The role of moral disengagement, hostile attribution bias, and outcome expectancies. *Aggressive Behavior, 36*, 81–94.

22. Agatston, P. W., Kowalski, R., & Limber, S. (2007). Students' perspectives on cyberbullying. *Journal of Adolescent Health, 41*, S59–S60.

23. Frankel, F., Myatt, R., Cantwell, D. P., & Feinberg, D. T. (1997). Parent-assisted children's social skills training: Effects on children with and without attention-deficit hyperactivity disorder. *Journal of the Academy of Child and Adolescent Psychiatry, 36*, 1056–1064.

24. O'Connor, M. J., Frankel, F., Paley, B., Schonfeld, A. M., Carpenter, E., Laugeson, E. A., et al. (2006). A controlled social skills training for children with fetal alcohol spectrum disorders. *Journal of Consulting and Clinical Psychology, 74*, 639–648.

25. Laugeson, E. A., Frankel, F., Mogil, C., & Dillon, A. R. (2009). Parent-assisted social skills training to improve friendships in teens with autism spectrum disorders. *Journal of Autism and Developmental Disorders, 39*, 596–606.

26. Mikami, A. Y., Lerner, M. D., Griggs, M. S., McGrath, A., & Calhoun, C. D. (2010). Parental influence on children with attention-deficit/hyperactivity disorder: II. Results of a pilot intervention training parents as friendship coaches for children. *Journal of Abnormal Child Psychology, 38*, 737–749.

27. Williams White, S., Keonig, K., & Scahill, L. (2007). Social skills development in children with autism spectrum disorders: A review of the intervention research. *Journal of Autism and Developmental Disorders, 37*, 1858–1868.

28. Durlak, J. A., Weissberg, R. P., & Pachan, M. (2010). A meta-analysis of after-school programs that seek to promote personal and social skills in children and adolescents. *American Journal of Community Psychology, 45*, 294–309.

29. Frankel, F., & Myatt, R. (2003). *Children's friendship training*. New York: Brunner-Routledge.

30. Laugeson, E. A., & Frankel, F. (2010). *Social skills for teenagers with developmental and autism spectrum disorders: The PEERS treatment manual*. New York: Routledge.

INDEX

ABOUT THE AUTHORS

Karen L. Schiltz, PhD, is an Associate Clinical Professor (volunteer) at the Semel Institute for Neuroscience and Behavior at the University of California, Los Angeles. She has 25 years of experience assessing children with attention, memory, learning, and behavioral difficulties. She maintains a private practice in pediatric neuropsychology in Calabasas, California.

Amy M. Schonfeld, PhD, is a clinical psychologist with a specialty in pediatric neuropsychology. Her research interests and publications have involved neuropsychological functioning and the effects of prenatal alcohol exposure.

Tara A. Niendam, PhD, is an Assistant Professor at the UC Davis Department of Psychiatry. She has published multiple articles on cognition and functional outcomes in psychiatric illness.